Justice for
victims and offenders

R\

st,

v

Justice for victims and offenders

a restorative response to crime

MARTIN WRIGHT

Open University Press
Milton Keynes • Philadelphia

Open University Press
Celtic Court
22 Ballmoor
Buckingham
MK18 1XW

and

1900 Frost Road, Suite 101
Bristol, PA 19007, USA

First published 1991

British Library Cataloguing-in-Publication Data

Wright, Martin
    Justice for victims and offenders: A restorative
    response to crime.
    I. Title
    346.6

    ISBN 0–335–09697–2
    ISBN 0–335–09696–4 pbk

Library of Congress Cataloging-in-Publication Data

Wright, Martin.
    Justice for victims and offenders : a restorative response to
crime / Martin Wright.
        p.   cm.
    Includes bibliographical references.
    ISBN 0–335–09697–2 (hardback) ISBN 0–335–09696–4 (pbk.)
    1. Victims of crimes. 2. Reparation. 3. Criminal procedure.
4. Corrections–Philosophy. 5. Criminals–Rehabilitation.
I. Title.
HV6250.25W75   1991
364.6–dc20
                                                        90-26086
                                                            CIP

Typeset by Stanford Desktop Publishing Services, Milton Keynes
Printed in Great Britain by St Edmundsbury Press, Bury St Edmunds, Suffolk

Contents

Foreword

This timely and thought-provoking book comes just as the public debate on the future shape of our criminal justice system is gathering momentum. Politicians as well as lawyers and magistrates will find much to stimulate, and I hope it will also be widely read by the general public.

Practically everyone is agreed on the need to reduce the numbers of those sent to prison. This is not simply to avoid overcrowding and the resulting explosive situation, but because we can do better by those who offend. Martin Wright's 'restorative and participatory approach' offers a constructive alternative and begins to spell out some of the practical alternatives. His suggestion of a Department of Crime Prevention would be a structural innovation. I think this proposal needs a good deal more thought.

Martin's deep involvement in penal reform positions him strategically to explore the necessary link between concepts of punishment and current schemes of reparation and mediation. Drawing on experience from abroad is particularly helpful. We can learn much from the experiments (and mistakes!) of others.

Above all I value the emphasis on the people in the system. Offenders, victims, the public and court officials all have a role to play. This speaks to me of New Testament principles: respect for individuals, especially those most vulnerable, and the price that has to be paid for true justice.

I have known the writer for many years and I respect greatly his commitment to a humane welfare system and a safer society. I hope that this valuable contribution to a continuing debate will receive the attention it deserves.

Stanley Booth-Clibborn
Bishop of Manchester

Acknowledgements

I am grateful to the Barrow and Geraldine S. Cadbury Trust, the Hilden Charitable Fund, and the Central Research Fund of the University of London for financial support, which in particular made it possible for me to visit the United States and Canada in 1983; and to the Max Planck Institute for Foreign and International Criminal Law, Freiburg im Breisgau, Federal Republic of Germany, for a fellowship in 1984, which enabled me to use its comprehensive library and to make comparisons with the German system of official mediators. In all three countries those involved in reparation and mediation were generous with their time and hospitality, all of which I greatly appreciate; their help towards formulating my ideas was indispensable.

I am grateful to all the respondents who gave thoughtful answers to a long questionnaire (summarized in Chapter 5), especially the one who said that she found it interesting.

A fuller version of the comparative review of state compensation for victims of violence appeared in *Justice of the Peace* (1 August 1987). Part of the survey on principles of victim/offender reconciliation was presented at the Third International Institute of Victimology, Lisbon, Portugal (1984) and subsequently published in *Victimology* (1985: 10, 631–44). Several people kindly took the trouble to read these and offer constructive comments before publication, in particular Elizabeth Burney, Burt Galaway, David Miers, Helen Reeves and Howard Zehr. Paul Wahrhaftig gave me a full account of the early development of mediation in the United States. Particularly generous with their time and ideas have been Burt Galaway, Tony Marshall and Howard Zehr, and members of the Executive of the Forum for Initiatives in Reparation and Mediation (FIRM). I should like to thank all of them.

I am also grateful to my supervisors, Professors Paul Rock and Terence Morris at the London School of Economics, for their painstaking guidance.

Finally I should like to thank my family for their forbearance, and both them and friends and colleagues for their support and will-power which helped me to complete this project.

Note

This book has grown above all from my association with the *Howard League for Penal Reform* and the *Forum for Initiatives in Reparation and Mediation*. If you want to help the development of these ideas, so that they can be put into practice as part of a more constructive response to crime, please join either or both of these independent organizations. They welcome both active members, and those who only want to support the work through their subscriptions. Members are kept informed through regular publications.

Howard League for Penal Reform, 708 Holloway Road, N19 3NL, England. Tel. (071) 281 7722.
Forum for Initiatives in Reparation and Mediation, 19 London End, Beaconsfield, Bucks. HP9 2HN, England. Tel. (04946) 71177.

Views expressed are personal, and not necessarily those of Victim Support or the above mentioned organisations.

Definitions

It may be useful at the outset to define terms which are sometimes used in differing senses.

Conciliation Here used as synonymous with mediation, although some writers use it to mean 'shuttle diplomacy' (see Mediation).

Counter-deterrence Undesirable consequences sometimes produced as side-effects of deterrent measures, for example when heavy penalties lead offenders to go to extreme lengths to avoid punishment.

Deterrence by enforcement A policy of attempting to deter crime based primarily on the probability of detection.

Deterrence by punishment A policy of deterring crime based primarily on the severity of the punishment.

General incentive A policy of maintaining social order based on enabling people, as far as possible, to lead fulfilling and rewarding lives without breaking the law.

Mediation Negotiation between persons or groups in conflict, including victims and offenders, with the assistance of mediators who facilitate the process but do not impose a solution. The aim may be to express feelings, resolve a dispute, or agree on reparation. The term usually refers to face-to-face negotiation, but the mediators may act as go-betweens for those unwilling to meet. This method is often called 'shuttle diplomacy', conciliation or indirect mediation.

Punishment A measure imposed on a law-breaker, of which the primary characteristic is that it causes pain or unpleasantness, or is intended to do so (see Chapter 2).

Reparation Actions to repair the damage caused by the crime, either materially (at least in part) or symbolically. Usually performed by the offender, in the form of payment or service to the victim, if there is one and the victim wishes it, or to the community, but can include the offender's co-operation in training, counselling or therapy. Reparative actions can also be undertaken by the community.

Restitution Here used in the English sense of restoring goods or money (except in American quotations, where it is synonymous with reparation).

Restorative justice A form of criminal justice based on reparation, in the senses given above.

Restrictions A general term for restriction of liberty, including controlling supervision, withdrawal of permission to engage in certain activities, etc. According to context it may include detention.

Sanction A measure imposed on offenders after a criminal act. Here used primarily for non-punitive measures such as reparation.

Shuttle diplomacy See Mediation.

For abbreviations, see index.

1

Crime as conflict: criminal law and the restorative principle

Crime and punishment are traditionally associated. Even definitions of crime generally include punishment: it is an act prohibited by law for which a duly convicted offender can be punished. But that has not always been the case. In other periods and cultures the response has been a restorative one: offenders make up for what they have done. This also means that offenders make reparation to the people they have wronged, not to the State – except for crimes such as treason which are committed against the State rather than an individual. Many crimes arise from a conflict between individuals, for example when a dispute leads to an assault or criminal damage, or when, after partners have separated, one of them breaks in to take property which he or she claims to own. Crimes between strangers can also be regarded as conflicts, since one person has deprived the other of his or her rights, imposing his will by force or deception.[1]

In more recent times victims have not been treated well. Until the eighteenth century they had to prosecute at their own expense; gradually the State took over this burden, but the result was to leave the victim on the margin. Until the last two or three decades they received little or no compensation, and have often not even been told if a suspect has been apprehended or a trial has taken place, unless they are required as witnesses, in which case they are subjected to inconvenience and even distress.

This state of affairs is beginning to be recognized and improved; meanwhile offenders have seldom had the opportunity – which could be regarded as a right – to make amends. Even when they do, they are robbed of the credit for doing so when it is regarded primarily as punishment, something unpleasant inflicted on them, rather than as reparation, a positive action they have performed to make up for the harm caused by their offence.

Historical perspective

According to some writers, victims fared better in the Middle Ages; they received compensation from offenders and were directly involved in the process.

A Howard Association pamphlet asserted (without quoting sources) that the rights of the injured party were gradually appropriated by the 'violent greed of the feudal Barons and Ecclesiastical powers' who took away the offenders' property and punished them, but practically ignored the victims (Tallack 1900: 11–12).

In Anglo-Saxon times crimes of violence were held in check largely by the fear of private vengeance (Stephen 1883 I: 60); like many deterrents, when it had to be used it had disastrous effects – private war, blood feuds and anarchy. Kings saw the need to check this destructive feuding. King Ine of Wessex (688–726) imposed a penalty if revenge were taken before justice had been demanded, and King Alfred (871–901) ordained 'that the man who knows his foe to be homesitting fight not before he demand justice of him' (Holdsworth 1956 II: 43–4). Trial by combat was introduced as a modified form of private war, according to Stephen (1883 I: 61) (although Pollock and Maitland do not accept this view – 1898 I: 33n). 'The object of the lawmaker', Stephen continues, 'was rather to reconcile antagonists upon established terms than to put down crimes by the establishment of a system of criminal law as we understand the term' (Stephen 1883 I: 61).

In order to regulate the enforcement of justice it was necessary to ensure the presence of the alleged culprit. After the Norman conquest the system of *frank-pledge* (free security) was developed in much of England. It has been described as a kind of collective bail, not after the individual's arrest, but as a safeguard in anticipation of it. People had to be enrolled in a tithing of ten or more: if one member committed an offence the others had to produce him for trial, on pain of a fine. The balance between freedom and responsibility is encapsulated in a law of William I: 'Every man who wishes to be accounted as free shall be in pledge' (Holdsworth 1956 I: 14–15).

It became possible to appease the feud by the acceptance of payment of composition (in Scotland, *assythment* – Mackay 1989): originally some kind of arbitration was probably used to fix the amount, and later a detailed scale of compensation emerged (Pollock and Maitland 1898 I: 46, 53). In so far as there was a golden age of the victim, this was it: 'in Anglo-Saxon and other Germanic laws the idea of wrong to a person or his kindred was still primary, and that of offence against the common weal secondary, even in the gravest cases' (Pollock and Maitland 1898 I: 46). But class justice seems to have been practised: compensation for injury was confined largely to the nobility and the warrior class. 'The noble could murder and be quit for a fine to the Church and the dead man's family and the King . . . the poor man would be killed or mutilated for the most trivial of offences' (Pike 1873 I).[2] As for the poor man, with no kin, who became a victim, the historians do not say how he could enforce his claim. It appears that composition worked among equals, for example among the warrior class (and perhaps among serfs, although no evidence appears to have survived), but the majority of poor thieves, murderers and rapists were hanged, burned, drowned or mutilated, while from those who had the wherewithal as much money as possible was extracted by the victim or the lord, whoever had the most power. There was no question of equality before the law. Such a system, even if reparation was a key element, hardly deserves a halo (Geis 1975: 150).

The practice of *infangthief* gave the thief's captor (the victim) a choice between summarily executing him or allowing him to be redeemed in return for his *wer*, the price set upon every free man according to his rank. *Infangthief* is not known to have been practised after the time of Edward III, except in Halifax (Stephen 1883 I: 61–2, 64). The Anglo-Saxons adopted the principle, also found among Germanic tribes, that offenders should make two payments of composition for injuries other than homicide, *bót* to the injured party and *wite* to the lord or king (Pollock and Maitland 1898 I: 451; Holdsworth 1956 II: 47). The word *bót* carries the sense of advantage or making better, being related to the word 'booty'; it is also linked to the German *Busse*, making amends or penance. *Wite* connotes blameworthiness, and also punishment, ranging from a fine (the usual meaning) to the torments of hell. There were detailed scales of payment, based on the *wer* of the victim or the nature of the injury (Pollock and Maitland 1898 I: 53). These rules appear to have faded out by the time of Glanvill, whose *Treatise* written at the end of Henry II's reign (about 1187–9) does not mention them (Pollock and Maitland 1898 I: 166). Later, under Edward I (1272–1307), in one of many instances of the blurred distinction between criminal and civil law, legislators gave double or treble damages to 'the party grieved' (Pollock and Maitland 1898 II: 522).

The victim's claim to compensation or *bót* was circumscribed, however. The owner of stolen goods lost his claim unless the thief or robber had been convicted on an 'appeal' (private prosecution) (Holdsworth 1956 II: 361). Already under the law of Ethelred (866–71), only a first offender was required to pay *bót*; a person who was unlucky enough to be the victim of someone who had offended before could obtain 'no other *bót* than the head' (Stephen 1883 I: 58). A number of offences were in any case *bótless* or unemendable, i.e. the penalty could not be commuted to a payment; these were broadly speaking the 'traditional' felonies such as housebreaking, arson and treason against a lord (Stephen 1883 I: 58; Pollock and Maitland 1898 I: 456). Homicide was atonable, except for *morð* (killing by poison or witchcraft) but if a stranger were killed, two-thirds of the *wer* payment went to the king (Pollock and Maitland 1898 I: 52). The victim of a theft had to use the proper procedures to recover his goods. If he took them back by breaking into the thief's house, he risked being treated as a thief himself, in the thirteenth century (Holdsworth 1956 III: 279); if they had been taken feloniously, the crown had a prior claim to them (p. 280) and if he received back stolen property upon an agreement not to prosecute the thief, he committed the offence of *theft bote* (Stephen 1883 I: 502).

Another theme that makes an early appearance, after a distinct criminal law had begun to take shape, is the availability to the victim of two options, civil and criminal. It is variously reported that 'angry litigants preferred to settle purely civil causes of action by criminal proceedings', to gratify their desire for revenge

(Holdsworth 1956 II: 197); and that about the middle of the thirteenth century, the injured party would sometimes say nothing of the felony, but would sue for damages (Pollock and Maitland 1898 II: 489). This was in effect a return from vengeance to *bót*, except that the amount was not fixed by law.

Thus there was a time when victims could obtain compensation under certain circumstances (although evidence about the enforceability of these laws does not appear to be available); what of the claim that the grasping feudal lords, prelates and kings appropriated it? It is true that the administration of justice was profitable (Pollock and Maitland 1898 I: 106, 145, 153), and the reason for the victims' choice of civil action, referred to above, was that if the felon was convicted his property escheated to the crown (Holdsworth 1956 II: 358); indeed 'the loser of stolen goods might thank his stars if he was able to get them back again, so keen was the king in pursuit of "the chattels of the felons"' (Pollock and Maitland 1898 II: 495). In 1255 Henry III was in need of funds and ordered his justices to impose monetary penalties. Of the seventy-seven people presented for murder seventy-two were outlawed, which meant that all the accused's property was forfeit (Jeudwine 1917: 155–6). During the thirteenth century, money collected from fines was equal to one-sixth of the king's revenue (Ziegenhagen 1977).

This does suggest that the monarch recognized a source of revenue other than ever-unpopular taxation. At an earlier stage, however, it was the lords and bishops who replaced the kinship group as the recipients of *wer* and *wite*, as feudalism developed in England in the Anglo-Saxon period between 700 and 1066, according to Jeffery (1957/1969: 21). Under the land tenure system of *sake* and *soke*, the recipient of a grant of land could hold private court for his subjects and pocket the profits of jurisdiction. By the time of Cnut (1016–35), most of the moots of the hundreds had passed into the hands of private lords. Maine, however, interprets the process differently (1930: 417): the church, he says, was concerned to mitigate the sanguinary ferocity of punishment, and therefore ordained that (except in case of treason) secular lords might take the *bót*, in money, instead of inflicting harsher punishment. Either way, the effect on the ordinary victim and offender was the same: 'The man who had land judged the man who had not', in the words of the constitutional historian Stubbs (quoted by Jeffery 1957/1969: 23; Pollock and Maitland 1898 I: 43, 106–7).

Kings were concerned to centralize this prerogative: not only was it for the sake of the revenue, but also there were power-political, administrative and philosophical reasons. Politically, the king could win support by giving these rights to thegns and prelates, such as the Abbot of Battle, who had all the royal forfeitures in his domain, and the Bishop of Winchester, who had breach of the peace and *hámfare* (attack on a man's house) (Pollock and Maitland 1898 II: 453–4). Later, when they became powerful enough, kings asserted the right to impose their jurisdiction: private settlements of crimes which could be regarded as public wrongs undermined the power of the Crown and could not be allowed. 'To kill a man . . . has become an offence against the king, representing, as it were, the injured community' (Diamond 1951: 151).

Administratively the system of reparation and fines needed overhaul, because by the time of the *Leges Regis Henrici Primi* (shortly before 1118) the tariff had become very complex, and was breaking down under its own weight (Pollock and Maitland 1898 I: 105–6). The sums demanded bore no relation to the offender's wealth. Many could not pay and were enslaved or outlawed, according to Pollock and Maitland (1898 II: 458, 462); these authors do not say whether it was the victims' *bót*, the lords' *wite*, or both, that were excessive. So in the twelfth century the fixed *wite* was replaced by discretionary money penalties, amercements, which varied with the gravity of the offence and the means of the offender; the fixed *bót*, by damages assessed by a tribunal (Pollock and Maitland 1898 II: 458, 514–15, 522–3). At this stage it may have been the centralization and codification that made individually negotiated composition no longer necessary, rather than the king's desire to grab moneys that would otherwise have been paid to victims.

King Henry II (1154–89) was concerned with judicial and administrative reforms, following his defeat of the baronage; among other things he created the system of judicial circuits for the exaction of the king's dues and the rendering of the king's justice (Green 1888: 111) and in 1178 a permanent central court of professional judges (Pollock and Maitland 1898 I: 138, 154–5). He claimed jurisdiction over the main crimes ('pleas of the crown') such as homicide, robbery and rape. The right to *wer* was transferred from the kinsfolk to the king (Pollock and Maitland 1898 II: 458). There was, however, great scope for judicial corruption, and for a time after the Assize of Northampton in 1176 Henry had to restrict the number of justices to five, and reserve appeals from their court to himself in council (Green 1888: 111; Pollock and Maitland 1898 I: 145). By the thirteenth century the itinerant justices were undertaking their *eyres* (journeys) and inflicting fines and amercements, but there is no longer any mention of *bót* (Pollock and Maitland 1898 I: 201). By the time of Richard I, at the end of the twelfth century, the majority of towns had obtained exemption from the murder fine to the king (Pike 1873 I: 171). If, earlier, compensation to the victim had been superseded by fines to the Crown, the latter now gave way to deterrence and retribution in the form of physical punishments, commonly hanging or beheading (Hibbert, 1966: 22). As the monarchy grew more powerful, the king no longer had to content himself with mediating between citizens: he took over the judicial role, and enforced his judgments.

The philosophical justification for the changes is that 'the wrong done to an individual extends beyond his own family; it is a wrong done to the community of which he is a member; and thus the wrong-doer may be regarded as a public enemy' (Pollock and Maitland 1898 I: 47; cf. Holdsworth 1956 II: 50). This reflects changes in the organization of society. In a pastoral community the overlord took no notice of civil wrongs as between individuals, except to assist, for a fee, in enforcing the payment of the customary compensation. The conception of killing as a crime, that is an offence against the community, did not exist until the State had the power and the will to enforce penalties for such offences

(Jeudwine 1917: 88–9). Society came to be personified by the Crown: 'the king, in whom centers the majesty of the whole community, is supposed by the law to be the person injured by every infraction of the public rights belonging to that community': the magistrates' power to punish derives from the social contract to which citizens notionally subscribe (Blackstone 1778/1973: 187, 192). It was coming to be felt more and more strongly that the suppression of crime was not the affair only of injured individuals or their kin (Holdsworth 1956 II: 257); evidently the belief, which is still widespread, that the courts could suppress crime was already taking hold. The king has become 'the source of justice, the lord and patron of his people, the owner of the public lands', as Stubbs put it (quoted by Stephen 1883 I: 67). But the advantage was not necessarily financial: from the time of Edward I grew the action for trespass, a speedy quasi-criminal proceeding which led to compensation to the plaintiff as well as punishment of the defendant. As time went on, however, the infliction of punishment changed from being a source of revenue to the heavy expense that it is today (Pollock and Maitland 1898 II: 516).

Linked to the philosophical aspect was a religious one, according to Mackey (1981). Instead of focusing on the offence, Christianity stressed the idea of personal morality. The effect was 'to shift attention from righting the offense to concern for the spiritual and moral being of the offender'. As 'the problems of the individual offender became divorced from their economic, physical and social contexts [concern] for salvation and achievement of eternal life tended to overpower concern for the righting of earthly wrongs' (Mackey 1981: 18–19).

Besides their limited entitlements victims also had a prerogative, or duty: to prosecute the case. In the days of *infangthief* the victim could be everything from police officer to executioner. From an early period individuals have had the right to prosecute, which they still retain (Stephen 1883 I: 445), although at one period this would involve them in a trial by battle (Stephen 1890: 20).[3] From the beginning of Edward III's reign (1327–77), anyone might arrest an offender (Stephen 1883 I: 189). 'The first . . . principle of the law of England on this subject is that everyone, without exception, has the right to use the Queen's name for the purpose of prosecuting any person for any crime' (Stephen, 1890: 156); the involvement of the Crown means that it is no longer a trial between two private litigants (Maitland 1885: 140), and the matter is taken out of the original prosecutor's hands (Stephen 1883 I: 496).[4] The king relied partly on private prosecutions in the cause of law and order (Holdsworth 1956 II: 197), but in Edward III's reign they were falling into disuse, and the prospect of obtaining heavy damages was used as an inducement to the injured man to fulfil his role (Holdsworth 1956 II: 453). Moreover, restitution of stolen property could not be had unless the thief or robber had been convicted by private prosecution; from 1529 it was also obtainable where the criminal had been convicted upon an indictment, provided that the owner had helped secure the conviction (Holdsworth 1956 II: 361). Other inducements to prosecute were offered. A reward of 40 shillings was offered to anyone arresting and successfully

convicting a felon (Highwaymen Act 1692) with exemption from parish duties
as well under the Tyburn Ticket Acts of 1699 and 1706. For victims of violence
the reward was 60 shillings under the Criminal Justice Act of 1826.[5] But corruption crept in: Jonathan Wild, in the early eighteenth century, ordered thieves to
steal from named people, and then advertised his services as 'thieftaker general'
and 'mediated' between victims and thieves (Rumbelow 1971). As late as 1822
it is reported that the medieval offence of *theft bote* was still big business: when
robbers, for instance, had been apprehended, the prosecution would be stopped if
the money was returned (Birnie 1828).

In the seventeenth century examples of mediation are recorded, where the
offender was known: this saved the victim the trouble and considerable expense
of prosecuting. So frequently did such disputes need settlement that a local
figure, a parson possibly, would come to be seen as an appropriate mediator.
One woman, asked why she had not reported a theft more promptly, replied that
'she was in hopes by fayer means to have persuaded [the accused] to make her
satisfaction, and did try the mediation of her friends to attayne the same' (Sharpe
1980). But less 'fair means' such as dismissal, physical chastisement, humilia-
tion, ostracism and the poor law were also used by victims and the community
against suspected offenders (Sharpe 1980).

By the eighteenth century the victim again had a prominent role in the administration of justice, through bringing prosecutions and deciding on the charges.
But the victim/prosecutor could suffer loss of time, worry and sometimes intimidation by the offender's friends (Ramsay 1980: 63) and also had to bear all the
expense (Stephen 1883 I: 498). This put law and the legal system at that time
very much in the hands of the ruling class; it was overtly based on the protection
of property (Ramsay 1980: 20, 45–6). But, according to Ramsay, to prosecute
was almost regarded as a failure: people of substance relied mainly on the *threat*
of prosecution, which would be withdrawn in return for confession, restitution
and apology – sometimes in the form of a letter in the county newspaper
(Ramsey 1980: 59, 64; Hay 1975). This procedure is an interesting precursor of
the present-day practice of the Inland Revenue and Customs and Excise, who
also have recognized the advantages of using the threat of prosecution to secure
reparation, rather than going to the trouble and expense of actually prosecuting,
which merely secures punishment. The Commissioners of Customs and Excise
have power to 'stay, sist or compound any proceedings for an offence' as they
see fit (Customs and Excise Management Act 1979, sec. 152), and the
Committee on Enforcement Powers of the Revenue Departments (1983) considered that 'in appropriate cases, compounding is an effective and streamlined
alternative way of ensuring justice through financial restitution and the payment
of a penalty' (p. 412; cited by Fennell 1989).

Composition, of course, can work only when offenders are identified, and
especially if they are known to, or in the employment of, the victim. But as 'huge
conglomerations of poor labourers' were cramped into slums, with no personal
relationship between them and their employers, the 'delicate balance of

paternalistic responsibility and subtle threat' was absent. They were seen by the well-to-do as the 'dangerous classes'. Associations for the prosecution of felons were formed to share the cost of criminal proceedings, and more formal methods of peacekeeping were developed (Shubert 1981). Eventually the first form of legal aid was introduced: the cost of prosecution of felonies began to be borne by the county in 1752, and by the Crown in 1778 (Maitland 1885: 141; Stephen 1883 I: 498). Characteristically the authorities did not pay enough to cover all the costs and the fee of a good lawyer. But as the police took over more and more of the work and expense of bringing prosecutions, the number of crimes, especially larcenies, brought to trial increased considerably (Philips 1977: ch. 4).

In the nineteenth century the pendulum began to swing further in the victim's favour. The Malicious Damage Act 1861 allowed the owner of damaged property to obtain some recompense. Forfeiture of felons' property to the Crown, which by now yielded little revenue, was abolished by the Forfeiture Act 1870. This allowed the (criminal) court to order the payment by the offender of compensation up to £100 for loss of property, on application by the victim (sec. 4). Still in force is the Riot Damages Act 1886 which, like its forerunner the Riot Act 1715, asserted the principle that the local community should compensate victims of riots (Bailey and Tucker 1984). Apart from this, the State does not today compensate for loss of property through crime, except to a limited extent in Northern Ireland; the distribution of risk is effected by individual citizens through insurance, provided they can afford it. Recently much greater emphasis has been placed on compensation by the State and the offender (see Chapter 3); it is now possible for courts to make a compensation order as the sole sanction.

Summary

An action is criminal only because the ruler or government says it is and imposes sanctions on those who commit it. Even the most serious crimes have been dealt with by civil procedures in some societies, and perpetrators required to pay damages rather than undergo punishment. Where sanctions are imposed by the governing authority, it is commonly assumed that they will consist of punishment, but early history as well as recent legislation show that this is not inevitable; the sanction may consist of reparation, which need not be punitive in intent, even though it may be felt to be so. Here, 'punishment' will mean penalties that are intended to be unpleasant, painful and usually retributive; 'sanction' will be a more general term including rehabilitative or reparative measures, which may be demanding but do not depend on unpleasantness for their effects.

Criminal justice need not always employ coercion, and procedures based on consent may have advantages. There is also scope for a process in which more concern is shown for the victim, as has been shown in the United Kingdom, North America and elsewhere.

Historical and anthropological reviews show that many simple societies function with little or no distinction between civil and criminal wrongs; indeed some do not have a system of law as understood in the complex societies of today, but rather a procedure for restoring the balance through reparation in individual cases where one citizen has harmed another. Only later is this concept superseded by the notion that a crime harms the State, which should react by punishing the offender.

Chapter 2 will look at criticisms of the outcome of conventional western criminal proceedings (sentencing), and of criminal procedure, in order to show some of the reasons for the demand for an alternative. Chapter 3 will review recent developments in compensation, community service and other moves in the direction of restorative justice. Examples will be given in Chapter 4 from anthropologists' accounts of mediation processes, showing similarities and differences by comparison with present-day western practice. One way in which the use of mediation differs from conventional western ideas is the recognition that the process is not just a formal means of arriving at a decision consistent with a complex, ever-growing body of law and precedent, but has a reconciling function. It has been said that until we get something better than criminal justice, we need better criminal justice. The question at the outset of a new century is: could restorative justice prove to be 'something better'?

The ideas of reparation and mediation have been brought together in victim/ offender reconciliation programmes, whose development is described in Chapter 5. Finally Chapter 6 outlines the possible shape of a restorative and participatory system of justice.

Notes

1 For convenience, either pronoun will be used to refer to both sexes, where appropriate.
2 I am grateful to Dave Burnham for drawing these points and quotations to my attention.
3 It appears that trial by combat remains on the statute book in Scotland, although it was abolished in England in 1819. Two Scottish brothers, John and Paul Burnside, charged with armed robbery, applied to have their cases dealt with by means of a duel with the Lord Advocate or his representative. But their application was refused – possibly because they neglected the rule under which they must, in the presence of their accusers, throw down a white glove (*Guardian*, 20 April 1985).
4 A private prosecutor is no longer entitled to conduct a prosecution unless authorized by the Director of Public Prosecutions, under the Police and Criminal Evidence Act 1984 and the Prosecution of Offences Act 1985 (*R.* v. *Ealing Justices*, ex parte Dixon, *Guardian*, 18 May 1989: 39).
5 The idea of encouraging victims to do their public duty is still current, although it is now subordinate to the compensation of the victim: the Criminal Injuries Compensation Board may refuse or reduce compensation if the victim did not report the crime promptly to the police.

__ 2 __

Criminal procedure: the means overshadowed by the end

Criminal procedure is not traditionally regarded as having an inherent value but as merely a means to an end. One objective is to ascertain facts. Did the accused commit the offence? If so, are there any exculpating or aggravating circumstances? The second is to make decisions. Should the case be proceeded with? If so, what sort of punishment or treatment should be decided upon, how much (for a fine or compensation order) and for how long (in the case of time-based orders such as probation, disqualification, community service orders or imprisonment)? There are, however, as we shall see, a few instances in which the value of the process itself for participants is recognized.

The existing system has many merits; otherwise it would not have lasted so long. The courts and the legal system are, as Tony Marshall comments, predicated on the centrality of justice – or due process, predictability, procedural rectitude, protection of the rights of the defendant, and strict adherence to established rules. 'Insofar as these are the major considerations the system is as perfect an instrument for carrying them out as has yet been imagined'(Marshall 1985: 156). But it is also, even on its own terms, open to a number of criticisms. These imply that it could be reformed; more radical critics, however, maintain that the problem is a structural one, inherent in the system itself. This chapter will suggest that the emphasis on the conviction and punishment of defendants actually distorts the process. Justice has one foot on the brake, applying safeguards such as 'due process' to make sure the innocent are not punished, and the other on the accelerator, pushing against those safeguards so that they do not enable the guilty to escape. But the process can have its own value, of which examples are given.

Critique of adversarial procedure

The criminal justice process is much criticized. The delays in bringing cases before the courts are followed by the speed and 'routinization' with which the 'people-processing machine' then operates (Blumberg 1967: xx, quoted by

Bottomley 1979: 106–7). Both problems are aggravated by the volume of work confronting the courts. Court proceedings are 'busy and mechanical', 'technocratic events that did not touch the lives of defendants', according to John Calhoun, president of the Justice Resource Institute in Boston (Felstiner and Williams 1980: 3). Yet the system sometimes seems not to want to be relieved of its burden: one German observer of US mediation projects found some of them 'struggling for a caseload large enough to justify the existence of the program', and others getting 'only the pettiest of petty offenses' referred (Weigend 1981); he attributes this to

> the strange phenomenon of system jealousy: in spite of frequent claims of unmanageable caseloads and impending breakdown, agents of the criminal justice system in many jurisdictions appear to cling to each single case as though it were absolutely vital for the survival of the system.
>
> (Weigend 1981: 45)

A fundamental objection is that criminal justice cannot be achieved in the absence of social justice (American Friends 1971: 16, quoted by Bottomley 1979: 112); Von Hirsch (1976) ended his book on the reform of justice with the same thought. Since we have to start from where we are now, perhaps we should not be inhibited by that, but look for processes that may themselves contribute a little to healing some of the conflicts in contemporary society.

The present system, however, perpetuates criticized practices, as many studies have shown. Disparities in the treatment of offenders are widespread, whether it be due to the social class of the offenders (e.g. Sanders 1985) or to the attitudes of law enforcement officers as they exercise their discretion (Bottomley 1979: ch. 3). Indeed the excessive use of discretion is frequently criticized, although it is clearly impossible to eliminate it entirely. Not only is the system biased in the way it concentrates its law enforcement on the crimes of the underdog rather than those of the 'white-collar criminal', but also having caught low-status offenders and taken them to court, its procedures put them at a further disadvantage – so much so that they are often referred to as 'victims' of the system. One example is the continued use of the dock for some defendants. The Law Society has condemned this as placing the accused in 'a singularly invidious position' and impeding free and uninterrupted access between defendants and their legal advisers. It leads to inequality, since not all defendants are placed in the dock. Both the Law Society and the Howard League (1976) have recommended its abolition.[1] Another example is that a defendant remanded in custody is more likely to be convicted and to receive a custodial sentence (Bottoms and McClean 1976: 214–16).

Defendants are offered a number of choices (summary or jury trial, not guilty plea, guilty of a lesser offence, and so on). Over two-thirds of defendants in one study, for example, who changed their plea from 'not guilty' to 'guilty' after being committed to the Crown Court for trial by jury, appeared to have been involved in negotiation (Baldwin and McConville 1977: 27, quoted by

Bottomley 1979: 109). The choices are, it is true, somewhat forced ones, in which the defendant often feels peripheral and powerless (McConville and Baldwin 1981: 13), but sufficient to introduce an element of negotiation into the proceedings. Thus there is some precedent for the negotiation which will be proposed in Chapter 6.

The faults of the process are sometimes blamed on its adversarial nature; but only a small minority of ordinary criminal cases are contested; partly as a result of plea negotiations, the adversarial model is not much in evidence (McConville and Baldwin, 1981: 28). The inquisitorial system used in other European countries is less adversarial, but still open to criticism of the way victims are treated (Rössner and Wulf 1984).

The system's faults can to a limited extent be eliminated in the light of experience, and the procedure has been improved over the years. But reform is possible only up to a point, because the aim of the system is to secure convictions and then, generally, to impose punishment.[2]

It has become a commonplace to observe that court proceedings are based essentially on win/lose, guilty/not guilty principles. Only at the margin are background details such as provocation or contributory negligence allowed to introduce shades of grey into the black-and-white decision. Thus both defendants and victims are liable to be cut short if they try to mention background information which they regard as relevant (Shapland *et al.* 1985: 64; King 1981: 87; McBarnet 1976). As the objective is to secure convictions, questions are asked if there are too many acquittals,[3] and the system becomes unworkable if too many defendants contest their cases. It could be this structure, rather than the presence of 'bad apples in the barrel' (over-zealous or unscrupulous police officers or lawyers), that puts pressure on those within the system to use inhumane interrogation methods or to negotiate guilty pleas in return for the prospect of reduced punishment. This is a pair of mirror-images: the law enforcement agent's temptation to bend the rules to secure conviction, and the accused's temptation to suppress or falsify facts, for example by intimidation or bribery, in order to escape it. Similarly punishment is the mirror-image of crime; a coercive act is met by a coercive response. But as practitioners of non-violence have shown, this is not the only, or even the most effective, way.

The exclusion of the victim

Offenders are usually passive spectators at their trial, and victims are left out of it altogether, except sometimes as witnesses. In the last twenty or thirty years attention has been drawn to this neglect (see e.g. Wright 1977; Harding 1982; Victim Support 1988, 1990). There are further reasons for criticizing criminal law and procedure from the victim's point of view. One of these is the adversarial nature of the proceedings. The procedure is based on the assumption that conflict is abnormal and should be suppressed. Advocates of mediation, however, regard conflict as normal: its expression within the community tends to inform and educate, according to Shonholtz (1983), whereas the standards and behaviour modelled and projected by criminal justice are minimal. A high standard of individual and personal behaviour is modelled and projected by neighbourhood entities such as schools, churches and libraries, Shonholtz says; mediation maintains this tradition.

Researchers, practitioners and politicians have begun to give attention to the way victims are treated within the system (e.g. Maguire 1980; Shapland *et al.* 1985), particularly in the USA (e.g. Knudten *et al.* 1977) but also in other countries, such as the Federal Republic of Germany (Rössner and Wulf 1984). A basic criticism is that victims are not kept informed of the progress of their case, or lack of it. The failure to respect their feelings can begin while the case is still being investigated. Shapland *et al.* (1985: 28–31) give examples of police being, as one victim put it, 'helpful towards themselves and not very helpful towards me'; for example they may take a statement while the victim is still in a dazed condition. One victim was left to walk forty minutes home without shoes because he had no money for a taxi. Even families of murder victims have hitherto been neglected by the system, although a report by Victim Support (1990) may mark the beginning of a change. An aspect which has attracted much public attention is the questioning of women who report that they have been raped; in a television programme on 18 January 1982, a *cinéma vérité* camera team filmed the remarkably insensitive police interrogation of a woman. There have been considerable improvements, such as the creation of special examination suites, but some time after the programme it was still suggested by Ian Blair, himself a police officer, that some police 'readily give the impression of believing that a large number of rape allegations are false', and that these cases, together with those considered unsuitable for prosecution on grounds of insufficient evidence, are often classified as 'no crime'. This has the effect of reducing the number of cases appearing in the police statistics as not cleared up (though it is not suggested that it is done for that purpose), while denying to the victim the recognition that she has been a victim (Blair 1985: 59–62). Conversely police may decide to go ahead with a prosecution against the wishes of the victim, which may also cause distress (Shapland *et al.* 1985: 46–8).

When the victim is required to attend court to testify, there is a tendency to treat him or her as an 'item of evidence' (Rössner and Wulf 1984: 8), a 'nonperson' (Shapland 1983: 20). There are repeated reports of victims routinely incurring expenses and loss of earnings (with inadequate reimbursement), uncomfortable waiting-rooms or corridors, sometimes in the presence of the defendant's family or friends, deprivation of property held as court 'exhibits', lack of child-care arrangements, and the inconvenience of repeatedly adjourned hearings (Victim Support 1988). The police, whose priorities include not only bringing suspects to court but also being seen to do so, provide information to the press, sometimes giving details about victims without their consent (Shapland *et al.* 1985: 41–2; Rössner and Wulf 1984: 44–5; Geis 1981: 67–8).

Once a case reaches the courtroom, those victims who are required as witnesses often find that the traditional procedures are not 'victim-friendly'. A repeated complaint is that they are not allowed to tell their story in their own words, but are required to give precise answers to questions based on the advocate's definition of what really happened; if they do not, they may be publicly denigrated, or even inculpated. The adversary system can be traced back to the medieval concept of justice by ordeal, or to the Hobbesian war of all against all (McBarnet 1976: 4, 9–10, 12, 15–17; Rössner and Wulf 1984: 69; Griffiths 1970: 414). A leading British lawyer, Sir David Napley, advises advocates that they 'may, and indeed should, cross-examine the prosecution witnesses in order to demonstrate their unreliability or incredibility'; he does not mention that one of them may be the victim, who should be spared distress, although he does make the general point that the advocate should not put insulting questions to a witness, or put questions as to character or credibility unless the advocate believes them to be well founded (Napley 1983: 64, 77–8). An American author even asserts that defence counsel should be prepared to cross-examine for the purpose of discrediting an adverse witness whom the counsel knows to be telling the truth (Freedman 1966, quoted by Griffiths 1970: 404). Such extreme views may not be widespread, but their existence makes it unsurprising that crimes are not reported at all by 'victims who, despite intensified efforts to provide protection in the criminal process, fear the psychological or social pressures of cross-examination' (Rössner and Wulf 1984: 14). Their fear is not without reason, particularly in the case of victims of rape. Their evidence is treated with scepticism, judges do not always protect them from improper questioning, they are questioned in intimate and embarrassing detail even when this is not necessary because the point at issue is consent, and it is still possible to find a judge who thinks that a woman says no when she means yes (Lees 1989a, 1989b; *Guardian, Independent*, 11 April 1990).

A repeated charge is basic lack of courtesy and consideration: this is mentioned by three separate contributors to Galaway and Hudson's *Perspectives on Crime Victims* (1981: 70, 303, 405) and examples from Britain are given by McBarnet (1976). This particular complaint was not raised by victims in Shapland's sample, though some found both the defence and the prosecution difficult to handle. The general inference is that the victim's treatment in court is a result not of the inconsiderateness of individual advocates but of the adversarial process – the court 'battle' – in which victims remain 'shadowy and indistinct' and are not accorded a status other than that of a witness (Shapland *et al.* 1985: 63–7).

The traditional criminal process is suited neither to determining the amount of compensation nor to reconciling the parties. Hitherto it has been no one's job to compile information on the victim's losses; Shapland found that the police did not have the time, and the prosecution and the court each tended to think it is the other's job; most clerks even thought that the victim had no right to apply for compensation in open court (Shapland *et al.*, 1985: 141–3). Yet without evidence of loss, courts can refuse to order compensation.[4] They are advised to make an order only in straightforward cases, although since the Criminal Justice Act 1988 they have to give reasons for not doing so. It has been held that if there is any dispute as to the loss a compensation order should not be made and victims of theft should be left to seek compensation in the civil courts (*R.* v. *Kneeshaw* [1974] *2 WLR 432; R.* v. *Vivian* [1979] *1 WLR 291*). In Germany, according to Rössner and Wulf (1984: 54), many courts are unaware of a provision of the Penal Code that if the offender voluntarily makes adequate reparation, the court should 'as a rule' not make an order (para. 56b(3) of the Penal Code (StGB)).

Pros and cons of punishment

The traditional association of crime and punishment is not as clear as it seems. The real point about crimes is not that they are punishable but that they are harmful (to people, the State or community, animals, or the environment); many harmful acts are not defined as criminal, while some not-very-harmful ones are. The list of crimes varies at different times and places; requiring reparation can be a response at least as valid as inflicting punishment.

It is also necessary to consider punishment itself more closely: what it is and what it does. It means the deliberate infliction of pain, or at least inconvenience, on a convicted person; thus if it is not unpleasant (if for example prison is a respite from even worse conditions outside) it has failed in its primary object. Confusion is caused by those who use 'punishment' to include rehabilitative and reparative measures which, by this definition, are not punishments, because their primary purpose is constructive. They may be demanding, and deprive a person of time or money, but that is not their primary intention. In this book the generic words sanction, measure and sentence will be used to include both punitive and non-punitive orders of courts.

Punishment is generally assumed to be a deterrent. This word comes from the same root as 'terror', and implies frightening people into good behaviour through fear of painful consequences. Thus rehabilitative and reparative sanctions are not primarily deterrents; they may none the less have a secondary effect as disincentives. The rightness of punishment – the deliberate infliction of pain on the State by its citizens – should not be accepted without question. Some say that it is simply wrong (Six Quakers 1979), just as torture is wrong. Certainly there are grave objections to exemplary punishment: inflicting extra pain on the minority who are caught in the hope of deterring other persons unknown. Some accept it provided that it is not cruel, inhuman, degrading or excessive; or that it is effective – and indeed more effective than other measures. This is too complex a subject to discuss here, but it is generally accepted that the effect of deterrence is at best limited, and that probability of detection is more significant than severity of punishment. Punishment may be regarded as effective in denouncing crime, but that too can be achieved by other methods (as we shall see).

The other consideration, often neglected, is that punishment has 'counter-deterrent' side-effects which must be weighed against, and may outweigh, any success in the primary aim of deterrence or denunciation. The most important of these is that the more severe the punishment, the greater the lengths to which the offender is tempted to go in order to escape it – from procedural devices to bribing or intimidating witnesses and even murder. Severe punishment and stigma can make offenders an object of pity, and make it harder for them after-wards to obtain accommodation and employment. After-care resources, statutory or voluntary, are required to overcome these effects, which are the result of the State's own action. Punishment makes people think of themselves rather than their victims; it often hurts innocent members of the offender's family. It also affects the process of criminal justice.

The traditional answer to the objections to punishment has been to propose that the aim should be the rehabilitation of the offenders – shorthand for requir-ing them to take part in whatever counselling, training or therapy they may need to help them to live without resorting to crime. This involves many assumptions which cannot be explored here; for example it implies that the 'problem' lies in individuals, whereas their social circumstances may have contributed to their behaviour. Another difficulty with rehabilitation is that it is related to the offender's needs, rather than the seriousness of the offence, and therefore does not perform the function of denunciation. But if this is tackled by combining rehabilitation and punishment, as has been common practice since the Gladstone Committee of 1895, they counteract each other: the punishment is made less deterrent, but undermines the rehabilitation which depends on winning the offender's trust and co-operation.

General incentive

In comparing rehabilitation with deterrence, there is a fundamental lack of sym-metry which is generally overlooked: we have individual deterrence and general deterrence, individual rehabilitation and – what? If punitive measures are assumed to broadcast a message to other citizens, saying 'If you are caught break-ing the law, this could happen to you', why should not rehabilitative, or re-educative, ones also contain a lesson? Advocates of punishment have caricatured the re-educative message as something like: 'Criminal justice is being taken over by social workers, who feel sorry for criminals and ignore victims; and criminals despise such weakness.' In the 1970s, for example, Lord Justice Lawton spoke of 'the age of the compassionate fools' in which idealism had overcome common sense (e.g. *Daily Mirror*, *Daily Mail*, 2 September 1978). A decade later a leading member of the Conservative government spoke of 'the advocates of a society in which social conduct has no rules, no morals, no sense of right and wrong, no inhibitions'; 'Where there is no punishment worthy of the name, crime prolife-rates. . . . Sentencing should not go to the point of becoming inhumane or disproportionate to the offence; equally, it must not fail to deter crime' (Rt Hon. Norman Tebbit MP, press release of a speech on 9 April 1986). The 'rehabilitators' have not been very successful at countering this with their own more civilized message, which might be to the effect that they do not condone offending, and society should certainly take action when crimes are committed, but they believe in social justice and the best way to persuade potential offenders to have respect for other people is to demonstrate that other people have concern for them, as well as for their victims; the use of retribution does the opposite. The rehabilitators have compounded their failure by going up two blind alleys: the 'medical model', which treated offenders as if they suffered from a psychological defect which could be 'treated', and the social deterministic one, which went so far towards blaming social conditions for delinquency that it seemed to deny offenders' accountability for their own actions. What is more, they have failed to point out that the advocates of 'just deserts' (a euphemism for punishment) are themselves in a more unpleasant dead-end: at least the rehabilitators, despite some excesses, were in the main trying to help people, not to hurt them. Punishment, as Nils Christie (1982) has reminded us, is about the infliction of pain.

Another approach is now being proposed. The negative message of general deterrence would be replaced by one which does not condone the crime or excuse the criminal, but reaffirms accepted values. The aim would be, not to create a society in which people in general were afraid to break the law, but one in which they could live sufficiently rewarding lives without doing so. Individual deterrence meanwhile would be replaced by a message to the offender saying in effect: You have harmed someone else, so you must make up for it by doing something constructive for the victim or for the community; but if you need help, other members of society will try to provide it. We will show concern for the victim, not by taking it out on you, but by offering support to him or her, by requiring you to make reparation, directly or indirectly (and if necessary enabling you to do so), and trying to reduce crime in future.

The effects of punishment on criminal procedure

If the process is distorted by being aimed at conviction, rather than being valued for its own sake, this effect is intensified by the fact that conviction usually leads to punishment. Participants in the system easily come to feel that it is not too serious if the punishment begins a little early. The public degradation ceremony need not wait until the conviction, but can begin during the trial (Schur 1973: 122), for example by penning the accused in the dock (Howard League 1976) and still, in some US states, in chains. There is often a presumption of guilt – otherwise, it is assumed, the prosecution would not have been brought – and hence it is seen as 'permissible to regard the courtroom experience itself as an exercise in deterrence, and to attempt to make it as unpleasant as possible for defendants' (King 1981: 19).

Thus the procedure, far from healing, can be damaging: the process 'cannot be separated from its actual, practical, concrete substantive effects' (Griffiths 1970: 409). Many defendants do not feel fairly treated, or even understand what is going on; one described it as 'mumble-jumble' (Schur 1973: 161, 162). The spectre of punishment may also drive the defence lawyer to use all possible methods, including some which may be painful to the victim:

> the consequences of a conviction are so pointless, so calculated to do nothing but harm to the convicted man and so little apparent good for anyone else, that the most socially-conscious and ethical lawyer can whole-heartedly believe it his duty to secure an acquittal in any permissible way.
>
> (Griffiths 1970: 408)

Juries' verdicts may be affected by their expectation that if they convict, the defendant will be sent to prison, or at least by sympathy with a defendant who is probably guilty but whom they do not wish to see punished, according to McCabe and Purves (1972: 35–8), but in their study they classified only 9 per cent of acquittals as 'wayward'. One senior police officer has alleged that some jurors have said they refused to convict, despite damning evidence, because they do not believe in jail (*Daily Mail* 26 March 1986). Since research on actual jurors in this country is not permitted, it is hard to confirm or refute this; it is consistent with the public opinion surveys which have found that most members of the public (who are mostly potential jurors) would often be satisfied with restorative sanctions (Wright 1989). That does not of course prove that they would go to the length of refusing to convict, but the possibility remains. Heavier prison sentences for rape make it harder to secure convictions, in the view of one researcher (Lees, 1989a: 10; 1989b: 15).

To be wrongly punished is even more serious than to be wrongly convicted. The more severe the punishment, the more necessary it is to safeguard the accused, even at the expense of letting the victim see the wrongdoer walk free; as Sir James Stephen remarked, the saying that it is better that ten guilty men should escape than that one innocent man should suffer is probably 'due to a considerable extent to the extreme severity of the old criminal law, and even more to the capriciousness of its severity' (1883 I: 438–9). This is accepted as having influenced juries, and also witnesses like one Mary Rowell who, questioned as to her identification of a highway robber, said: 'Yesterday, I thought I could swear to him, but to-day it touches so near death, I think I could not swear to him' (quoted by Ramsay 1980: 24). Even the courts acted in the same spirit, seizing upon trivial errors in indictments to save offenders from the gallows (Philips 1977: 107–8; Cornish *et al.* 1978: 59). Courts in some countries refuse to extradite offenders to countries where offenders run the risk of being tortured or executed. Similar scruples affected not only individual participants but also the procedural rules themselves: hence the introduction of safeguards such as the defendant's right not to be questioned, the exclusion of hearsay evidence and the right to peremptory challenge of jurors. By degrees further safeguards were added: defendants' rights to have counsel to represent them (1640 – Stephen 1890: 39),[5] and make a final speech to the jury (1836), to give evidence in their own defence (1898), and to appeal against conviction (1907 – Hampton 1982: 1–3). Similarly in the United States it was the severity of imprisonment which led the Supreme Court to require that everyone accused of a felony, or at risk of a substantial prison sentence, should be represented (*Gideon* v. *Wainwright, 1963; Argersinger* v. *Hamlin, 1972*).

As the defendant tries to escape conviction and punishment, with the help of the safeguards provided, some people in the law enforcement agencies form the impression that the safeguards are over-scrupulous. The safeguards are unofficially eroded, for example during interrogation, or even withdrawn by law, as in the extension of police powers of arrest, search and other functions in the Police and Criminal Evidence Act 1984; the right of peremptory challenge of jurors has been withdrawn by the Criminal Justice Act 1988.

Effects of punishment on the victim

The fear of punishment may spur the offender to blame the victim, for example by alleging provocation (Shapland *et al.* 1985: 66), and may increase the victim's reluctance to report an offence, if he or she is conscious of having 'dirty hands' (Hall 1975/1981: 320–1). Other victims do not report crimes because of fear of retaliation, and of those who did report, 14 per cent of victims of violence did in fact experience retaliation in Shapland's study (Shapland *et al.* 1985: 109). Fear of retaliation is presumably strongest when victim and offender are known or related to each other; just as deterrents work most effectively when the offender is most likely to be discovered (for example in an army barracks or an oil rig – Duff 1985), so the threat of reprisals has most impact where offenders are likely to discover who reported them. Fear of reprisals by the offender was given as a reason for not reporting crime by 1 per cent of those replying to the British Crime Survey, and 4 per cent in the Islington Crime Survey (quoted by Young 1988: 167). A US survey of those who did not report family offences such as desertion and non-support found that 7 per cent of them gave fear of reprisal as their reason, as did 7 per cent of victims of simple assault and 13 per cent of victims of aggravated assault. One of the most common reasons for not reporting aggravated and simple assaults, family crimes and consumer fraud was 'that the offense was a private matter or that the victim did not want to harm the offender', given by 50 per cent or more (US President's Commission, 1967a: 22; 1967b: 18). This does not specify what proportion gave not harming the offender as a reason, nor does it identify punishment as opposed to other aspects of criminal justice such as the stigma of a court appearance; but evidently reluctance to be responsible for the offender's punishment was a factor in at least some cases. It is possible, therefore, that more such offenders would be reported and (subject to safeguards which will be discussed in Chapter 5) mediation offered to them and their victims – a justifiable piece of 'net-widening'.

Conversely the existence of punishment may lead a few victims to press false charges, or genuine ones that would otherwise have been ignored, as a means of retaliation in the course of a row; indeed it was because of the risk of malicious prosecutions that the preliminary hearing by magistrates was originally introduced (Cornish *et al*. 1978: 61; Ramsay 1980: 45–6, 62).

Safeguards and improvements for victims

The position has improved in relation to keeping victims informed about the progress of their case: in April 1988 chief police officers were asked to undertake this, provide information leaflets about compensation, and collect information about losses or injuries to pass to the Crown Prosecution Service (Home Office Circular 20/1988, quoted in *Victim Support* September 1988). This has recently been confirmed in the *Victims' Charter* published by the Home Office (1990b).

The picture is changing in other respects also. Schemes for State compensation of victims of crimes of violence have been set up in several countries (see Chapter 3). In the United States reparation (restitution) has been promoted by a considerable body of legislation and numerous specialized programmes (reviewed e.g. by Harland 1980). Most of these programmes, however, are incorporated into the traditional criminal justice system, which remains unsuited for reconciliation. Victims want not only reparation but also answers to questions such as 'Why me? How did this person know I was away?', according to Zehr and Umbreit (1982) and other reports. As the prosecution takes its course, the victims

all but disappear from the case-file, leaving only the few characteristics which justify the criminal law action and are relevant to furnishing evidence: they are entirely infused with a legal logic indifferent to the expectations harboured by members of society in real-life social interactions.

(Zauberman 1984: 26)

But 'criminal justice alternatives do not make sense and cannot be successful politically or otherwise unless victims are part of the equation' (Zehr and Umbreit 1982: 65).

The many complaints about the court process have led to attempts to remove some of its worst features, particularly where sexual offences are involved. In England and Wales, for example, the victim of rape remains anonymous (Sexual Offences (Amendment) Act 1976 sec. 2, amended by Criminal Justice Act 1988), and should not be cross-examined about her sexual experiences with persons other than the defendant, except with the judge's permission. This is still not firmly enforced, however, and it does not extend to victims of other sexual assaults. In the Federal Republic of Germany witnesses under 16 years of age can be heard by the judge alone (Eser 1983: 239); the new Victim Protection Law also extends the court's power to restrict unnecessary personal questions to the victim, to exclude the public during such questioning, and to exclude the defendant if questioning a witness in his presence would occasion serious danger to the witness's health (Jung 1987). Under the Israeli Law of Evidence Revision (Protection of Children) 5715–1955 youth interrogators are appointed and children under 14 may be interrogated only by them. Evidence which they record is admissible in court, and the interrogator's permission is required before a child may be heard as a witness in court. However, a person may not be convicted on the evidence of the youth interrogator alone, unless it is corroborated by other evidence (Reifen 1966). Judge Reifen claimed that in the ten years since the law came into force, more people had reported such offences. In Britain, live television links are now permitted in the Crown Court at centres which have the facilities, so that children can give evidence from outside the courtroom in cases involving offences of sex, violence or cruelty (Criminal Justice Act 1988). The use of recorded video evidence is proposed in the Criminal Juctice Bill 1990.

One suggestion sometimes made to counter these difficulties is that victims should be entitled to representation in court to protect them, for example by advising on their right not to reply, speaking for those whose ability to testify is in some way limited, claiming the right to exclude the accused or the public from the court, and challenging the need for compromising questions and unsubstantiated derogatory statements made by the defence in mitigation. In the Federal Republic of Germany the Federal Constitutional Court held (8 October 1974) that every witness, including therefore victim-witnesses, is entitled to make use of legal support. Under the Code of Criminal Procedure (StPO, para. 170) victims must be told if prosecutors have used their discretion to stop the case, for example 'for lack of sufficient cause', so that victims can if they wish force a prosecution (para. 172–6) (Rössner and Wulf 1984: 55). Victims are allowed to be 'co-prosecutors' (*Nebenkläger*) and to be represented at public expense in certain cases; this applies principally to victims of crimes such as libel, slander and assault who would have had the right to bring a private prosecution if the public prosecutor had not done so, and to close relatives of victims who have been killed (Eser 1983: 206; Schädler, 1989). Given the adversarial tradition, however, this is said by some German observers to lead to a more antagonistic court atmosphere, provoking the accused to counter-attack against the victim. It is thus neither an aid to reconciliation nor a protection for the victim; a victim's advocate should be both (Rössner and Wulf 1984: 73–8). The Victim Protection Law 1986 gives victims in this category the right to legal representation, with financial assistance if necessary (Jung 1987), and to be informed, on request, of the outcome of the case (new para 406d, Code of Criminal Procedure, quoted by Jung 1987). It also gives victims the right, through a lawyer, to see documents.

Hitherto, neither victims nor their representatives had the right to be present or to put questions.

In Britain there seems to be no likelihood of legal aid for this purpose, but there is a move to entrust the responsibility to the Crown Prosecution Service, for example by urging prosecutors 'to intervene when necessary to correct any misleading speech in mitigation' (Home Office 1990b: 18).

Another reason for trying to ensure greater consideration for the victim and to check the tendency for the defence to give victims a hard time, in its efforts to avoid or minimize punishment, is that many victims and other witnesses fail to co-operate because they experienced so much discomfort and waste of time: they often do not come to court to give evidence, or do not report the crime at all. During the 1970s the Law Enforcement Assistance Administration therefore made grants to Victim/Witness Assistance projects. State compensation to victims of crimes of violence spread through the United States, although in the absence of a national health service its awards are largely absorbed by medical expenses, and most do not include compensation for pain and suffering (Harland, 1981: 414–15). In many places projects were established to encourage courts to order offenders to pay compensation ('restitution' in US terminology), as described for example by Harding (1982).

One aspect which has been given greater prominence in the United States is the involvement of victims in the existing criminal justice system. In the 1970s proposals were beginning to be made that the victim should be entitled to influence the law enforcement process, by requiring the police to make an arrest pursuant to a complaint by a victim, and by making his or her views known at the time of sentencing or parole decisions, for example by agreeing to accept reparation (Hall 1975/1981). But *how* should they be involved? The victim in every criminal prosecution should have a constitutional right 'to be present and to be heard at all critical stages of judicial proceedings', according to the US President's Task Force on Victims of Crime (1982: 114), under the chairmanship of Ms Lois Herrington, a lawyer with an interest in domestic violence, later Assistant Attorney General of the United States. After graphic descriptions of experiences of being a victim (focused primarily on violent crimes), and of victims' experiences of the criminal justice system, the report makes recommendations for legislation and other action, such as

1 that 'victim impact statements' should be supplied to courts before sentencing
2 that restitution (reparation) be required in all cases, unless the court gives specific reasons for not doing so
3 that parole should be abolished, and that in the meantime parole hearings should be open to the public
4 that the Sixth Amendment to the United States Constitution should be amended so as to guarantee not only the rights of the accused but the right of the victim 'to be present and to be heard at all critical stages of judicial proceedings'.

The United Nations Crime Congress in Milan in 1985 modified this to say that the victim's views should be 'presented and considered' (United Nations 1986: Annex para. 6(b)). Action is being taken on some of these. Victim impact statements are required by the federal Victim and Witness Protection Act 1982, and by a number of states. Several states require or at least encourage the court to order the offender to pay restitution to the victim, except for stated reasons (American Bar Association 1983: 19, 23). Hitherto the victim has not normally been a party to negotiations and decisions such as plea bargaining and sentencing, but in the United States to a limited extent victims can already influence some stages of the process (Hall, 1975/1981; Heinz and Kerstetter 1981). In thirty US states victims of violent crime (or their survivors) have a right to describe their feelings at sentencing and parole hearings, but the American Bar Association has found that only 10 per cent do so nation-wide; a California study found 3 per cent do so. A senior judge commented, 'A sentence should not vary depending on whether a victim makes a statement or not' (*New York Times* 29 September 1989: B5).

If the court paid attention to the victim's views when deciding the *sentence*, sentences might be more severe or more lenient, but they would certainly be more inconsistent. The proposals of the Herrington Committee (US President's Task Force on Victims of Crime, 1982), and the legislation based on them, may be seen as in some ways arguing for the rights of the victim at the expense of those of the offender. Thus the United States Supreme Court has held victim impact statements to be inadmissible in capital cases, on the grounds that the jury's decision could be swayed by 'irrelevant factors such as the degree to which the victim's family is willing and able to articulate its grief', rather than the blameworthiness of a particular defendant. But the court noted that a number of states permit victim impact statements in some contexts, and expressed no opinion on their use in non-capital cases (*Booth* v. *Maryland*, cited in *NOVA Newsletter*, July 1987: 5).

In Britain there has been general agreement that victims should not be asked to make such decisions: 'There is no evidence . . . that most victims would like the responsibility of deciding an offender's future' (Victim Support 1984a: 3). As Helen Reeves of Victim Support has pointed out (personal communication), the defendant should, in fairness, have the right to challenge such statements by appealing, which would expose the victim to a further court appearance and cross-examination. If the court ignored them little would be gained, and victims would feel frustrated.

There is a case for presenting the victim's request for *compensation* by the offender, with supporting evidence; but in many cases this could be dealt with by mediation outside court. A major concern has been providing information to the victim about the progress or otherwise of the case. This was found in the research of Shapland and colleagues (1985) and reiterated by a Victim Support working party, which also opposed the idea of victim impact statements (Victim Support 1988).

Potential value of the process

In one or two cases the value of the process itself, not merely as a means to an end, has been recognized. The distinguished Israeli Judge David Reifen saw a potentially therapeutic role for the juvenile court in establishing human contact between the judge and the delinquent (Reifen 1967/68: 773–4). Unlike the magistrates described by Parker (1974: 170), he considered

> that it is not enough to impress young delinquents with the solemnity of the procedure, it is equally necessary that the judge should penetrate the way of thinking and the feelings of those who appear before him. In certain cases the tension created by the court hearing has great value if it can be used for therapeutic ends. It awakens the desire for reparation which actually exists in many delinquents.
>
> (Reifen 1967/68: 779).

He also tried to involve the parents in the process in court, having

> observed that if the court shows itself understanding towards the actions of the delinquents in the parents' presence, the parents in turn can adopt this attitude towards their children and thus sometimes improve their relationships with them. It is an evolution which begins in the court room and continues afterwards.
>
> (Reifen 1967/68: 780–1)

The importance of the process is recognized also in the system introduced in Scotland by Part III of the Social Work (Scotland) Act 1968 (implemented on 15 April 1971). This was based on the recommendations of the Kilbrandon Committee, which stressed that wherever possible at least one parent should attend the proceedings, to try to enlist his or her co-operation 'in an atmosphere of full, free and unhurried discussion', with the aim of adopting appropriate orders informally and by agreement in many cases' (SHHD 1964: 49–50). The procedure is in two stages. First, the case is referred (usually by the police) to an official known as a Reporter, who may, and often does, decide to 'take no official action' – a somewhat misleading expression, because it could mean writing a letter to the parents with advice or a warning, or deferring a decision to see what child and parents can do over three months; some Reporters meet the child and parents, and emphasize the possibility of putting right what the child has done, especially with regard to vandalism and thefts (Finlayson 1976).

Second, the Reporter may refer cases to the Social Work department: the Act's intention was to enable voluntary arrangements to be made where possible, for suitable measures of care. Only where the Reporter feels that compulsory measures are necessary are cases referred to the children's hearing. This can be done only in those cases (some 95 per cent) which are not disputed. Parents have a duty to attend the hearing where possible, and the panel in turn has a duty to try to elicit the views of the child and the parent; the chairman should ensure that child and parent really are involved in a fair and frank discussion (Children's

Hearing (Scotland) Rules 17(2)(c)–(d) 1971), without feeling intimidated or overawed by their surroundings. At most hearings panel members made a conscious effort to evoke participation by using an encouraging and non-directive style; the majority of subjects had a positive sense of being listened to and fairly treated, according to Martin and colleagues (1981: 93, 128, 216, 233). In some cases the hearing probably provides the first occasion on which parents and children sit down and talk through their situation. Only when it comes to deciding the outcome do the panels face the dilemmas (described in Chapter 1) as to whether the measures imposed should be based on punitive or rehabilitative criteria, 'deeds' or 'needs'.

Advocates of mediation believe that the process can enable concern to be shown for both victim and offender. Zehr (1982), who led one of the first victim/offender reconciliation programmes, not only shares the concern that 'Victims often feel left out because of their inability to get answers about the progress of their case', but also feels that they often grow angry and frustrated because they cannot 'find ways to deal with fears, phobias and stereotypes' (Zehr 1982: 14). On the other hand, offenders' 'further rejection through imprisonment and labeling as "ex-cons" only increases the problem. Rarely is the opportunity afforded an offender to be reconciled to society' (1982: 15). Zehr, however, has mainly in mind a different (and commoner) type of crime, such as burglary; also, he criticizes the system because it seldom requires offenders to 'face and thus understand the real human costs of their actions, finding out what it means in a burglary, for instance, to have one's privacy invaded' (1982: 4). His objection, in other words, is not that the present method is too hard on offenders but that it fails to make appropriate demands on them. (The application of these principles to victims and offenders will be described in Chapter 5.)

Notes

1 An exception is made by the Howard League in the case of top security prisoners, although this undermines the argument against disparity, and it could be said that for them, as for anyone else, the most effective security would be to place the defendant in a heavy courtroom chair at a large table, next to his or her advocate.

2 And, of course, to acquit the innocent; but they are assumed, probably correctly, to be a very small proportion of those brought to trial.

3 For example by the then Chief Constable of Leicester, Mr Robert Mark, whose allegations led to the study of acquittal rates by McCabe and Purves (1972).

4 'Although the court was entitled to make appropriate assessments of compensation where the evidence as to loss suffered was scanty or incomplete, where there were real issues as to whether any loss was suffered or as to its amount, justice required the prosecution to place evidence before the court.' One magistrate mentioned that the victims would have had difficulty in pursuing civil claims (*R.* v. *Horsham Justices*, ex parte Richards (D.C.), [1985] 1 WLR 986–993).

5 It has been suggested, however, that one motive for denying counsel to defendants was to ensure their participation in their own trial (Cornish *et al.* 1978: 58).

3

Compensation and reparation: an ideal reborn

In the first half of the twentieth century, reformers' attention was given to the offender rather than to the victim. In Britain, for example, legal aid, borstals, open prisons, the abolition of corporal punishment and numerous other innovations for offenders took up most of the attention of reformers. The index to the *Howard Journal* from 1921 to 1976 contains no reference to compensation, reparation or victims, and only one to restitution. Similarly in the United States there was only one reference to restitution in the Task Force Report on Corrections of the US President's Commission on Law Enforcement and Administration of Justice (1967c: 35) and none in the main report (Hudson *et al*. 1980: 13). The Commission did, however, carry out the first national survey of crime victimization, and recommended further regular research (US President's Commission 1967a: x, 20–2).

In Britain, some thought had been given to the victim from about the turn of the century. Courts were given power to return property to its apparent owners, if they claimed it (Police (Property) Act 1897). Courts could order the offender to pay compensation for property loss or damages for injury, up to £10 (since increased), but only where the offence was a relatively minor one leading to a probation order or a discharge (Probation of Offenders Act 1907); the power was seldom used. Compensation was payable when cruelty to an animal led to damage to the animal or to any person or property (Protection of Animals Act 1911, sec. 4) and for damage to property (Criminal Justice Administration Act 1914). Some of these provisions were updated and extended (Criminal Justice Act 1948, sec.11(2); Magistrates' Courts Act 1952, sec. 34; Malicious Damage Act 1964, sec.1; Criminal Damage Act 1971, sec. 8) but for half a century there were no significant innovations. Earlier statutes were repealed by the Criminal Justice Act 1972 (sec. 1(1)), which allowed compensation to be ordered, in addition to dealing with a person in any other way, for any loss, injury or damage resulting from an offence, without requiring the victim to apply. (More recent developments are discussed on pp. 32–8.)

Victims and 'victimology' began to be written about in the 1930s and 1940s, but at first only with regard to victims' interaction with offenders (Mendelsohn,

1963; von Hentig 1948). It was Margery Fry, for thirty years a leading figure in the Howard League for Penal Reform, who revived the concept of reparation by the offender (1951: 124–6), but she then turned her attention to the campaign for State compensation for victims of violent crime. This was taken up by the lawyers' campaigning group Justice (1962), and introduced shortly after her death.

This chapter will briefly review the concept that the State or the community should restore victims as far as possible to their former condition, through compensation and neighbourly support. Turning to reparation by the offender, it will describe the development of the concepts of direct and indirect reparation, and practice in the United Kingdom and United States, before the concept of mediation was introduced. Finally some of the issues raised for criminal justice will be considered: the symbolic and utilitarian functions of reparation, the legal and constitutional position, whether reparation would mean more, or less, unfairness than the existing system, and the practical question of setting the amount.

State compensation to victims of violence

The first schemes for State compensation to victims of crimes of violence were introduced in New Zealand and Britain in 1963 and 1964 respectively. By 1978 Miers found nineteen jurisdictions in English-speaking countries alone which had introduced it; by 1981 two-thirds of the United States had victim compensation statutes (Harland 1981). Other countries operating schemes include Austria, Denmark, France, Federal Republic of Germany, Ireland, The Netherlands, Norway and Sweden (Dünkel 1984).

It has been accepted in many western countries that the State should compensate victims of violence. This is an important step forward, but the principle on which it is done has not been made clear. This has led to inconsistencies, often for the sake of limiting the total expenditure. In Britain, after over twenty years, the Criminal Justice Act 1988 provides for victims of violence to be entitled by right to State compensation, subject to some restrictions, but its implementation has been delayed.

One basis for compensation is welfare. In France victims can receive an award only if they are in a serious material situation and cannot obtain sufficient reparation from elsewhere (France 1977). Some US states take the victim's financial hardship into account, but others (e.g. Massachusetts) consider that 'compensation is not a handout: it is restitution' (quoted by Edelhertz and Geis 1974: 84). In Britain there is no means test, but by an odd anomaly, people dependent on State benefits may lose them if they become victims and receive substantial compensation, because the award is regarded as 'capital', which disqualifies them from receiving benefits. People in employment suffer no such deduction.

Another basis for compensation could be that, since the State has taken over from citizens the right to use force to use force to defend themselves, and the duty of preserving the peace, it should compensate them if it fails to protect them. This was rejected by the Interdepartmental Committee on criminal injuries compensation, because 'The state is not liable for injuries caused by the acts of others' (Home Office and SHHD 1986: para. 4.2).

The basis stated by the Committee is 'to reflect the strong public sympathy for the innocent victims of violent crime' (Home Office and SHHD 1986: para. 4.2) – a mainly symbolic function. In practice, however, the British scheme has done more: it has compensated victims for loss of earnings, expenditure incurred because of disablement, and pain and suffering. Often this has a therapeutic value, as when it enables the victim to recover by having a holiday or moving house. In addition, medical care is provided by the National Health Service, unlike other countries, where much of the compensation can be consumed by medical costs; in the Federal Republic of Germany, for example, the relevant statute has been decribed as a 'Health Insurance Companies' Compensation Law' (Kirchhoff 1984: 163, 169).

But there have been restrictions. Victims' compensation may be refused or reduced if they have criminal convictions, even if these are unrelated to the current incident; the CICB, like the Committee, appears to consider that some victims are 'undeserving' (as the word 'innocent' in the above quotation implies – see Miers 1978: 37–42). But a 'social contract' of this kind should surely include all citizens unless they are implicated in the crime that caused the injuries. The scheme has also been restricted by the imposition of a lower limit (currently £750) below which victims receive no compensation. This is not based on principle, but saves money. A case could be made for excluding awards amounting to less than their administrative costs, but no such limit restricts the prosecution of offenders, so there is no logical reason why it should be applied to victims. It is true that most other countries set minima; some US states had a threshold of $100 or two weeks' loss of earnings, so that only 8 per cent of injured victims would be eligible (McGillis and Smith, 1983: Table III; Harland 1978); several, unlike Britain, have maxima (more details are given by Wright 1987).

These restrictions are unprincipled. One principled basis would be that all victims of violence should be eligible for compensation as part of society's response to crime. As far as possible their condition should be restored, and they should be compensated for what cannot be restored and for pain and suffering, to show concern and possibly help recovery. Another would be that their medical and material needs should be met through the National Health Service and the social security system, as should be done for any citizen in misfortune through accident, medical negligence or other causes; this is done in New Zealand's Accident Compensation Act (Ison 1980). The CICB would then compensate for the extra pain and suffering which arise because the injuries were caused by a crime.

For property crimes, the principle that the State should compensate for its failure to maintain order has been accepted only in the specific circumstances of a riot (Riot Damages Act 1886). Otherwise State assistance is available only to those dependent on social security benefits, through the ordinary welfare system. In Britain at present this is mainly limited to loans, which may not be granted if the individual already has a loan and cannot afford more repayments, or if the local welfare budget is exhausted (Peggs 1990). Thus the criteria applied to victims of violent crime are not used in the case of property crime. For those who can afford it, the risk can be distributed through insurance, but premiums often put this protection out of the reach of those with low incomes, living in high-risk areas. One mutual (non-profit) insurance company offers block insurance, which enables the risk to be shared among tenants anywhere in a local authority's housing, and allows them to pay weekly or fortnightly with the rent; however the premiums are still substantial for those on low incomes, and only a hundred or so local authorities operate the scheme.

In fairness, the risk should be shared by all citizens, through national insurance or general taxation, as has been repeatedly proposed, though not worked out in detail (Wasik 1978; Justice 1989: 27). There could be provision for those privately insured to opt out (Mawby and Gill 1987: 231) and the scheme could be limited to a 'safety net' (Labour Party 1990: 12). Compensation of individuals who have suffered, for material harm and for pain and suffering, should be an integral part of a restorative system of justice. More should be known about the *effect* of compensation on victims (Reeves, personal communication): is it enough, is it affected by the method of administration, do payments for pain and suffering, or bereavement, make them feel better?

The community makes amends: support for victims

Criminal injuries compensation programmes are a way for society, through the State, to show concern for victims of violence, expressed in the form, at once tangible and symbolic, of money. There is another way in which society, as the local community, can show its concern and offer practical help. The general concept has become known as victim support; specialist groups have been established for victims of particular crimes, such as rape crisis centres, women's refuges, and telephone helplines for children, and for survivors of incest and of homosexual assault.

The prototype victim support group was established in Bristol in 1974; its pattern has been followed in over three hundred local groups which have grown since then. Their concern is with all victims of crime. Unlike some organizations for victims in other countries, Victim Support has a policy of not expressing a view on sentencing, except in relation to compensation. The basic principle is that volunteers, recruited from the neighbourhood, contact the victim to show concern about what has happened and to offer reassurance and practical help.

Although volunteers receive some training, the service was conceived as first aid rather than specialist help: victims with special needs were to be referred to other agencies as appropriate. It was found, however, that for some aspects of victimization there is no agency with specialist expertise; Victim Support has therefore set up working parties and action research projects, with the help of relevant professionals and of victims themselves, to understand how best to meet the needs of, for example, children as victims, and families of murder victims.

In principle victim support groups offer their service to victims of any kind of crime, but hitherto they have generally excluded offences which do not usually make a serious emotional impact such as theft of or from motor vehicles, as well as non-criminal events such as accidents, because in most areas volunteers' time is a scarce resource. At the other end of the scale more and more local groups are handling the most serious offences of violence, as the National Association has developed training, and volunteers have acquired confidence and expertise. A further restriction on the number of victims to whom support is offered arises from the referral process. In some countries which have attempted to initiate victim support, the projects have relied on self-referral, which greatly limits the numbers; in Britain the great majority of referrals are made by the police. (In the case of serious crimes the victim's consent is asked first.) This means that the potential number of referrals approaches 100 per cent of victims of recorded crimes against individuals (and perhaps because the benefits of this are recognized, the policy has led to few complaints about the passing of information, in confidence, to Victim Support groups). Initially there was a tendency for police to select according to such factors as their perception of the victim's need or the victim support group's capability, but they are increasingly moving towards referral of virtually all individual victims (Maguire and Corbett 1987). This simple way of obtaining referrals, however, has meant that few groups have done much to invite other victims to come and seek help, but this is changing: some groups are opening shop-front offices, and the National Association has run a project to encourage victims of racial harassment to come forward.

What victims are offered is primarily an expression of concern on behalf of the community, and emotional support if needed. Practical help in repairing the damage caused by the crime is also offered where required, for example with getting doors, windows or spectacles repaired; filling in forms to replace welfare allowance books or to claim insurance or criminal injuries compensation, meeting other needs which come to light through the volunteer's visit; and conducting negotiations in case of difficulty. Where hardship comes to light, groups often assist with applications to the Department of Social Security or to charitable sources. They are taking on more serious cases involving violence, in which victims are more likely to be required to give evidence at the trial of the alleged offender; as a result increasing numbers of volunteers are becoming aware of the ordeal imposed on victims by the wait for the trial, the uncertainties of the courts' timetable, and the experience of giving evidence and undergoing cross-examination (Victim Support 1988). This is leading Victim Support to urge improvements in the administration of the system, and changes in the system itself; it has set up an action research project on victims and witnesses in court.

Thus the victim support model originally addressed needs, but emphasis is moving towards rights, such as the right to be kept informed, and to compensation which will be statutory in the United Kingdom for crimes of violence when the relevant sections of the Criminal Justice Act 1988 are implemented. The *Victims' Charter* sets out a number of guidelines, although in the absence of an enforcement mechanism they cannot be called rights (Home Office 1990b). In some jurisdictions, notably in North America, there are moves to declare victims' rights, without necessarily knowing what victims want or being able to ensure that they receive it. This raises the question as to the effects on victims of the schemes offering support; how far these features of the existing criminal process can be alleviated by means of reforms, and how far they are inherent in the system itself; and the effects on victims of being invited to involve themselves in such decisions. So far there seems to have been little research into the first of these (but see Maguire and Corbett 1987), and even less into the other two. When this is done it will provide baselines against which projects for reparation and victim/offender mediation can be measured.

Victim support on the British model has not developed much in the United States, although a similar project in Minnesota is described by Chesney and Schneider (1981). The emphasis has been more on victim/witness assistance programmes, which seek to secure the co-operation of victim/witnesses by treating them better in the criminal justice process, and on specialist services for victims of crimes such as rape and other violence against women and children.

The first refuge for battered women was set up in Chiswick, London, in 1972. During the early 1970s others were established in Britain and the United States. Meanwhile rape crisis centres were developed in the United States, with almost twenty-five founded by 1973, the first in Britain being in London in 1976. They have different styles of working, partly reflecting the nature of the crimes they deal with, and partly their origins in the women's movement. Some, especially in the United States, have come to resemble mainstream social service programmes, with public funding; others, particularly the rape crisis centres in Britain, have remained strongly independent of, and on occasion hostile to, the authorities. There is no national association of rape crisis centres, and hence no moves towards uniform standards such as Victim Support has constantly worked for. For these and other reasons, the funding of rape crisis centres remains insecure (*Guardian*, 29 March 1990). For the present purpose it is sufficient to note these as a substantial contribution to the community's response to victims of crime (further accounts are given by Oberg and Pence 1981; Rich 1981; Mawby and Gill 1987; T. 1988; Walklate 1989).

The State and the community can offer symbolic and tangible compensation and support for victims; at an individual level, reparation by the offender is of particular significance.

Reparation by the offender

The concept and the practice of requiring the individual offender to make amends lay largely dormant in the first half of the twentieth century. In Britain the few provisions were little used. The story is complicated by the fact that it was unfolding in different countries, especially Britain and the United States, at different rates; also there were two strands – reparation to the victim and to the community – which in Britain grew independently, but in the United States were treated as aspects of the same idea and often combined in one project. This short account will try to trace these developments more or less chronologically; then the concepts that have not yet been put into practice will be reviewed, followed by some of the issues which then have to be faced.

The developing concept of reparation

The idea of reparation was revived by Margery Fry in *Arms of the Law* (1951: 124–6). In countries where courts can impose unorthodox sanctions, such as the USA and Federal Republic of Germany, some judges became interested in it; one of these (in the FRG in the 1950s) was Karl Holzschuh, who earned the nickname of *der Schokoladenrichter* (the chocolate judge) for ordering juveniles to make reparation by such methods as buying sweets for children in hospital. His approach attracted publicity in Britain and the United States. The theoretical basis was developed, for example by Eglash (1958: 620), who suggested payments or service to the victim or the community. He also had in mind possible rehabilitative effects for the offender, pointing out that in punishment, the offender stands alone (or, he might have added, shares a cell and exchanges criminal know-how), but several offenders can join with other offenders or with other members of the public in indirect restitution through community service, which provides them with a shared experience and topic of conversation other than crimes and institutions. He called this 'creative restitution', whose aim is 'that a situation be left better than before an offense was committed'. (Victim Support volunteers sometimes achieve this, too.) In Britain a White Paper of the then Home Secretary R.A. Butler, *Penal Practice in a Changing Society*, raised the possibility of a re-examination of fundamental concepts, examining not only the obligations of society and the offender to one another, but also the obligation of both to the victim, including 'reparation by the offender to the victim, a concept of which modern criminal law has almost completely lost sight' (Home Office 1959: 7). This policy statement was not immediately followed by government action, but it announced the research project by Stephen Schafer, published in 1960 as *Restitution to Victims of Crime*.

Schafer, who had emigrated from Hungary, brought a knowledge of the German and other continental writing on the subject. He spelt out the distinction between compensation to the victim by society, and reparation to the victim by the offender, and traced their history. Reparation has veered back and forth

across the boundary between civil and criminal law, and has been associated
with various other responses to the commission of a harmful act: atonement,
damages, appeasement of victims (sometimes by working for them), the prevention of blood feuds, and punishment. Gradually punishment, imposed by the
State, took over. Schafer followed this by a survey of the compensation and reparation provisions of twenty-nine jurisdictions (updated in the second edition –
Schafer 1970). Many parts of the world are covered, although the inclusion of
more African cultures, and eastern ones such as Japan and China, would have
been valuable. His survey, moreover, sets out the legal position only, and gives
little indication of the proportion of victims who actually benefit; the German
joining of civil compensation to criminal proceedings (*Adhäsionsprozess*), for
example, is described at length, with only a passing mention of the fact that in
practice it is almost a dead letter (Schafer 1970: 39; see Eser 1983: 210–13). The
FRG's Victim Protection Law 1986 attempts to remove obstacles to its use, but
it is not yet clear whether this will succeed (Jung 1987).

When Schafer wrote, the provision for victims (in the countries studied) to
obtain compensation was almost entirely based in civil law, although some, such
as France, enabled the civil claim to be linked to the criminal trial. In some of
the United States, reparation could take the place of punishment. Schafer points
to the conflict between reparation and punishment. He takes the view that the
main virtue of reparation is as a form of punishment, giving more satisfaction to
the victim than mere revenge (1960: 120–5). In the FRG, too, there has been a
tradition of regarding punishment as affording 'satisfaction' to the victim; the
word '*Schuld*' means both 'debt' and 'guilt', and reparation came to be regarded
as a punitive sanction (Sessar 1982: 2, 7–8).

No country, Schafer found, allowed prisoners to earn enough to pay any significant amount (1960: 106–7), but even non-prisoners are seldom able to pay
much. In so far as they can pay, Schafer suggests a form of day-fine to overcome
inequalities of income (1960: 127). A British former assistant prison governor
proposed a 'self-determinate' sentence (K. Smith, 1964): prisoners would stay in
prison, earning market wages, until they had paid compensation and other liabili-
ties. The suggestion appears to aim at least as much at punishing the offender as
at compensating the victim, and the combination of a punitive philosophy with
the reluctance of many governments to pay prisoners a fair wage makes it
unlikely to be adopted widely if at all.

More detailed official attention was given to reparation in Britain by the
Advisory Council on the Penal System (ACPS), which produced a report on
Reparation by the Offender (1970b). This, while envisaging the use of reparation
in addition to other sanctions, did not ascribe a single aim to it but saw it, rather
unclearly, as both deterrent and 'redemptive'. The ACPS recommended that
courts should be able to order compensation more readily, but recognized the fre-
quent conflict between the seriousness of damage or injury and the offender's
means, especially when fines or costs are involved as well: 'for many young
offenders who turn to delinquency through boredom or frustration a long period

of enforcement . . . would mean an accumulation . . . of fines, costs and further compensation which it would be hopeless to expect would ever be paid' (1970b: 10), so the offender's means must be borne in mind. Increased powers to order compensation for both violent and property offences were given to courts in the Criminal Justice Act 1972, with no requirement that the victim has to apply for it.

Administratively, however, compensation has been regarded as an extension of the fine; it is collected by the same office. Courts were given the power, and broadly speaking left to get on with using it: some did, some didn't, or not very much. Four years after the new Act, the Lord Chancellor was receiving complaints that magistrates were not exercising their power as much as they should, and there were suggestions that some Benches were still unaware of the change in the law and did not contemplate making compensation orders unless constantly reminded by their clerks (Purchase 1976: 150, 149). Several years later, despite a growth in the number of compensation orders, a chief constable (*Guardian* 13 November 1982) and the Council of the Magistrates' Association (*The Times* 16 March 1984) have also felt it necessary to exhort magistrates to use their powers; the latter draws attention to the appropriateness of an award in cases of violence, to demonstrate 'that the interests of the victim are recognized', and a table of suggested amounts is given. It has been found that the main variable factor affecting the courts' decision whether to make a compensation order is whether the prosecution suggests it (Shapland *et al.* 1985: 137–8). The Criminal Justice Act 1988 exerts further pressure towards by making it obligatory for courts to give reasons if they do *not* order compensation.

The ACPS had also proposed (1970b: 43ff) that prisoners should be paid more, so as to enable them to pay compensation as well as to support their families, but it recognized that the victim's compensation would then depend on whether the offender had a large family to support. In the event, of course, there was no significant increase in prisoners' earnings; after research showing that ex-prisoners rarely pay full compensation (Softley and Tarling 1977), courts have seldom combined compensation orders with custodial sentences. This presents sentencers with a choice of priorities as between the presumed interests of society and of the victim; in cases of conflict, they appear to prefer the former.

The ACPS was in favour of preserving the victim's option of obtaining redress (where possible) in the civil courts, and recommended that this should be made possible at no expense to the victim. Either there should be 'nil contribution civil legal aid', or the State should undertake proceedings on the victim's behalf. The ACPS also proposed the introduction of criminal bankruptcy (1970b: 34ff), mainly as a means of recovering, for victims and other creditors, the assets of large-scale white-collar criminals; this has not, in the event, been widely used (Howard League 1984) and was abolished in the Criminal Justice Act 1988. Finally, the ACPS recommended that orders for compensation should receive priority over fines and costs (1970b: 51). This was implemented in the Criminal Justice Act 1982 (sec. 67).

The same section introduced for the first time the principle that compensation orders could stand alone, without being accompanied by another sanction. This was recognized as opening the door to a principle new to British sentencing: that a compensation order alone can be a sufficient sanction, contrary to what courts had previously held (*R*. v. *Lovett*, 11 Cox 602; *R*. v. *Inwood* (1974) 60 Cr. App. R. 70). It is not clear where the initiative for this provision came from; there had been little if any public debate about it, and so far the courts, whether through indifference or disapproval towards the principle of compensation as a sole sanction, have made little use of it. Once again, the principle of punishment is in conflict with the interests of the victim. Many courts feel that compensation alone is not enough, and impose a fine in addition; where the offender's means are limited, this tends to mean that a smaller amount of compensation is ordered (Newburn 1988: 11–12, 30).

The use of compensation orders in England and. Wales, after a peak of 129,400 in 1981, has tended to decline; in 1988 it was 108,000. This may be due to the courts' awareness of the unemployment rate among offenders, as the pattern for fines is very similar. About 4,500 compensation orders standing alone were made in 1988, some 4.2 per cent of the total number (Home Office 1989: 143). In the Federal Republic of Germany the Victim Protection Law follows recent British legislation in giving compensation priority over fines and costs, but it has not adopted proposals to build victim/offender mediation more firmly into the preliminary hearing, nor the British model of compensation orders standing alone (although this can be done when the prosecutor discontinues the case).

Relatively little has been published in Britain on the principles, as opposed to the practical details, of reparation. Neither Walker, in *Sentencing in a Rational Society* (1972), nor Cross, in *The English Sentencing System* (1975), mention compensation in their respective chapters on the aims of the penal system, as Wasik (1978) points out. Reparation is not one of the aims of sentencing listed by Ashworth in his detailed study (1983). It is given a short section in Walker's more recent textbook (1985: 115–17), but he considers it from a retributive point of view: his concern is for the amount of punishment imposed on the offender, rather than the amount of reparation the offender is required and enabled to make for the harm caused.

The Howard League (1977) noted that there was no provision for personal, as opposed to monetary, amends by the offender to the victim, and suggested that there should be. It also proposed a way of bringing rehabilitative measures, for those mentally, educationally or socially disadvantaged offenders who need them, into the conceptual framework of a system based on reparation: compensatory education, training or therapy would be offered to them, and they could make amends through self-rehabilitation, by accepting the offer and trying to put their new skills to good use (Wright 1982: 255). A recurring theme has also been that making reparation itself contributes to the rehabilitative process: a US judge, for example, who in his own court has followed Holzschuh's tradition of court-ordered reparation, asserts that 'Good sentences . . . should require offenders to make efforts toward self-improvement, thus removing them from their roles as losers and helping them to address their personal problems and character defects that alienate them from the mainstream of society' (Challeen 1980). He includes, among examples of making amends, not only direct reparation and community service, but also attending an alcohol treatment programme, undergoing plastic surgery, and taking speech therapy to overcome self-image problems. Both the Howard League and Challeen also see the provision of these various forms of support as a way in which the community can make reparation to those offenders who have started life under handicaps. These proposals, however, were not worked out in any detail. At about the same time it was suggested in the *Howard Journal* that the most effective way to demonstrate society's concern is to do things *for* victims and relieve their suffering, rather than for or against offenders (Wright 1977).

Some of the problems of compensation were recognized even before the new law was enacted. Mr William Deedes MP (as he then was) saw that there would be 'valuation problems' and that custodial sentences would reduce the prospect of reparation (*Hansard* [HC] 22 November 1971 col. 1012). From the other side of the house Mr Stanley Clinton-Davis MP also wondered how courts could form a competent view of the amount of compensation to be awarded; he suggested that once the court order had been made, a referee should be appointed, such as the county court registrar, to assess the amount. But he pointed to a further complication – the means of the offender. 'Causing hardship to the family of the accused could be counterproductive and easily lead to further crime' (*Hansard* [HC] 22 November 1971 col. 1024–5).

The place of compensation in the penal system was reviewed by Wasik (1978), who raised important unresolved questions, in particular whether the aim of punishment of the offender should take priority over the compensation of the victim (1978: 601). The ACPS report, he pointed out, put the victim firmly in last place: reparation should not be imposed where it would conflict with the sentence, nor where there are 'difficult issues of liability or quantum'. Wasik's proposed solution is to give priority to victims by means of a State compensation scheme enlarged to cover property damage. Offenders would be required to pay to the State scheme, not to the victim, an amount related to their intentions (and their ability to pay), not to the actual harm done. Such a compensation order should be considered in every case, and would take priority over fines and short or suspended custodial sentences. Wasik's formulation would determine the amount on a retributive, not a reparative, basis. In practice, however, there is a way of overcoming the problem of small and irregular payments made by offenders over a period, which can be a nuisance, or worse, keeping alive the memory of the offence long after victims would have preferred to forget it, yet not providing them with payments large enough to be of real use. After Home Office research confirming victims' dislike of payment by instalments, and lapses in payment (Newburn 1988: 37–8), the Green Paper *Punishment, Custody and the Community* (Home Office 1988b: 9) proposes that the courts should be able to pay the sum the offender has been ordered to pay (which might be less than the full loss suffered by the victim); the offender would then repay to the court in instalments. This has been endorsed by Victim Support (1989). Both of these would enable the victim to receive the money sooner, but they would reduce any sense that the offender was paying to the victim, although the wording of court orders could do something to stress that the offender was 'making it right'.

A variant of this principle is already operating in programmes for debt composition such as the 'resocialization funds' in the FRG. The 'reso-funds', as they are known, consist of a capital sum subscribed by commercial donors and charitable trusts. When people are in trouble with the criminal law as a result of debt, they are asked to tell their complete financial position to a probation officer, who then contacts the creditors and asks them to accept a sum within the offenders' means – the alternative being that offenders will probably pay little (or, if they go to prison, nothing). Creditors are asked to settle for a proportion of the amount owed. The fund then pays the agreed amounts to all the creditors, and offenders repay the fund in instalments. It is reported that the system has worked well so far (Wright 1988). Individual victims, as opposed to large commercial organizations, should ideally be paid as 'preferential creditors'; or the State could pay their cash loss, while offenders could pay 'symbolic' amounts for pain and suffering, related to their ability to pay.

The question of the 'quantum' has continued to give trouble. It has been held that compensation orders should not be oppressive, and even if paid by instalments, the period should not be a long one (*R. v. Miller* [1976] CLR 694). The Court of Appeal decided in 1979 that 'no order for compensation should be made unless the sum claimed by way of compensation is either agreed or has been proved' (*R. v. Vivian* [1979] 1 AIIER 48). Many magistrates have allegedly felt, since this judgment, that once a solicitor stands up and says 'My client disputes that amount', they may not make a compensation order, according to the journal *Justice of the Peace* (1980). It is nobody's job to inform the victim that evidence of value will be required, nor to draw such evidence to the court's attention, although, *Justice of the Peace* continues, the police

> largely acknowledge a moral responsibility to inform the loser and will usually undertake to draw to the court's attention his desire for compensation. Since, however, the matter is not central to the interests of the prosecution, the way in which such an application is made is all too often less than satisfactory.
>
> (*Justice of the Peace* 1980: 416)

An attempt was made in the Criminal Justice Act 1982 to allow courts more latitude in assessing the amount of compensation: sec. 67(a) hints that the prosecutor could represent the victim's interests, by providing that compensation orders shall be 'of such amount as the court considers appropriate, having regard to any evidence and to any representations that are made by or on behalf of the accused or the prosecutor'. This was not to the liking of the courts, however, and the previous

position (as in *Vivian*) appears to have been largely restored by the decision in *R.*
v. *Horsham Justices* which (as mentioned in Chapter 2) requires the prosecutor to
place evidence before the court if there is any substantial dispute about the amount
lost. Victim Support has pointed out that many victims are not present in court
when sentence is passed and have no routine opportunity to apply for compensation; it suggested that the responsibility for applying for compensation orders
should be statutorily placed on one of the relevant agencies (*NAVSS Newsletter*
February 1987). The Home Office has now asked the police to collect information
about compensation and pass it to the Crown Prosecution Service to present to the
court (Home Office Circular 20/88), and the courts (as we have seen) are required
to give reasons if they do not make a compensation order. The *Victims' Charter*
recommends that the CPS should routinely ensure that case papers include information on the victim's injury or loss (Home Office 1990b: 24).

Reparation in the United States

Meanwhile reparation was becoming popular in the United States. Its spread,
unlike that in Britain, was not initiated by legislation; it was often linked with
community service, which in Britain developed separately (see pp. 40–41). The
American picture is of individual projects, of which the first was a residential
centre in Minneapolis YMCA for selected men paroled from Stillwater
maximum security prison, and later from the reformatory at St Cloud, both in
Minnesota. Arrangements for the offender to meet the victim, to negotiate reparation and make payments, were envisaged from the start; it is reported that when
meetings took place they were cordial, but many victims did not want to take
part. One account gives the impression that the emphasis was more on benefiting
the offender than the victim: the director is quoted as wanting to persuade
victims to think differently about criminals, and they were asked to travel some
miles to the prison for the meeting (Serrill 1975).

The development of programmes was encouraged by the Office of Juvenile
Justice and Delinquency Prevention, which in 1978 launched a $30 million
National Juvenile Justice Restitution Initiative, awarding grants to a total of
eighty-five projects in twenty-six states, Puerto Rico and the District of
Columbia. Some 60 per cent of these found funding with which to continue after
the initial three-year period (Armstrong *et al.* 1983: 11). Although the courts
already had wide powers to attach conditions to probation orders, or specifically
to order reparation, the initiative was followed by legislation encouraging or
even requiring courts to order monetary 'restitution' wherever practicable in
nearly all states by the end of 1979, and community service in about one-third of
the jurisdictions (Harland 1982: 57–8; Hudson *et al.* 1980: 14–15).

A survey in 1978–9 by the National Assessment of Adult Restitution
Programs found eighty-eight restitution projects for adults operating, fourteen
planned, and six which had ceased operation (Hudson *et al.* 1980: 16). Only six
(all based on community service) had been in existence for more than five years

(Hudson *et al.* 1980: 75). The survey included projects using reparation, community service, or a combination, in at least 75 per cent of their cases. Only twenty-nine of the projects arranged direct victim/offender contacts, and those were not routine; similarly 21 per cent made occasional use of personal reparation through service offered by the offender to the victim (Hudson *et al.* 1980: 73). Projects varied in the seriousness of the offences which they would accept: some took only felons, others a proportion or none at all. Numbers were relatively low: the median annual number of admissions for community service projects was 418, while for those using monetary reparation or a mixture the figure was between 85 and 45 (Hudson *et al.* 1980: 71). There are apparently no estimates of the total number of eligible cases per year in each catchment area, from which the actual referrals as a proportion of the possible could be calculated. The twenty projects selected for closer study gave various replies to the question asking what was the original problem to be addressed; most said it was to reduce the use of prisons, or fines, or courts; only five mentioned victims or reparation. Although the sample was not a random one, this probably approximates to the relative priorities in other projects, both in the USA and in Britain (Hudson *et al.* 1980: 49; Marshall 1985: 4). A common pattern was for a project to evolve from the informal use of community service as a sanction for petty offenders with low incomes (Hudson *et al.* 1980: 92). There are some in which reparation or community service can be imposed as the sole sanction; in others, these measures are combined with rehabilitative or punitive ones (probation or custody).

Repeatedly Hudson and his colleagues were forced to the conclusion that the aims of these programmes need to be clarified. According to different writers and programme descriptions, community service or reparation can be combined with punitive or rehabilitative measures, or they can themselves be punitive or rehabilitative, or they can aim at easing pressures on the system (courts and prisons); all of these can be assimilated within conventional thinking about the aims of criminal justice. Or they can set themselves a different aim, reparation, as an end in itself or to restore some of the harm done to the victim or the community (Hudson *et al.* 1980: 17–20). Alternatively they can persuade themselves and others that all these aims can be achieved at once. 'When an overriding rationale is not established, conflicts are bound to occur' (Hudson *et al.* 1980: 30); for example

> Should a program subordinate offender rehabilitation interests by requiring an offender to accept low-paying work in order to make restitution rather than pursuing educational or vocational opportunities? Resolution of issues such as this will occur on an operational or case-by-case basis unless multiple program purposes are prioritized.
>
> (Hudson *et al.* 1980: 20)

Adapting the report's conclusions (1980: 135, 174–5), criteria may be suggested for evaluating the success of reparation programmes; these will be outlined at the end of this chapter.

Community service as indirect reparation

The original community service project was for female traffic offenders in Alameda County, California, in 1966 (Hudson *et al.* 1980: 14). Local initiatives followed in various parts of the United States, often combined with reparation programmes. In Britain community service orders were introduced by a different route. First a government advisory committee chaired by Baroness Wootton suggested the idea (ACPS 1970a); Parliament accepted it, and legislation gave the courts specific powers to make orders (not merely to add community service as a condition of probation). Five experimental areas were designated, and a senior probation officer in each was given responsibility for making them work. This they did, not only by finding tasks and persuading courts to make orders, but also by obtaining largely sympathetic media publicity. Other probation areas queued up to be allowed to introduce schemes; within a few years all had done so. In most cases individual probation officers were given the organization of community service as their sole task: forty-five of the fifty-six probation areas had officers working full time, and forty required field probation officers to obtain agreement from community service staff before recommending an offender to the court for community service (Fletcher 1981; 1983). Thus in most areas there were people whose sole job it was to make community service succeed, and this probably helped to increase the use of the new measure. In the Criminal Justice Act 1982 the minimum age for community service orders was reduced from 17 to 16. However, it cannot be said with certainty that the method of introduction was the key to success; day training centres, introduced on a similar basis at the same time, have taken much longer to 'catch on'. Perhaps it was the reparative element that helped community service orders to attract the interest of the probation service and the support of the public (Shaw 1982). The number of orders increased steadily, reaching 37,240 in 1984, but declining slightly to 35,300 in 1988; and the number reconvicted while subject to an order has remained low (about 10 per cent). A consumer survey found that offenders themselves generally accepted the idea of community service; any criticisms were more of the way it was put into practice than of the concept. There can be no doubt that when it works, it works very well; every area has success stories of offenders whose work enhanced their beneficiaries' lives and their own (Wright 1984).

The aims of community service orders, however, have always been ambiguous. This stems from the original ACPS report itself, which said that they could be regarded, according to taste, as more constructive and less expensive than imprisonment, retributive, educative (because they can bring offenders into contact with people who need help), rehabilitative or reparative. Already in the first five experimental areas there was a divergence of view (Pease *et al.* 1975: 8; Pease 1981: 23). Probation officers put reduction of the prison population first, followed by 'penalty', 'reparation to the community' and 'help to offender'; supervisors exactly reversed this order of priorities (Pease 1981: 35). Thus offenders, having committed an offence which in no way merits imprisonment, may be sentenced to community service by one court for 'rehabilitative' reasons; if they re-offend and are brought before a different court which believes that community service should be used only as an alternative to prison, they may be regarded as having 'had their last chance' and be sent to prison (Pease 1981: 23–4).

This is bad news for the offender and also for anyone trying to use the measure consistently or evaluate its 'success'. Neither can be done unless there is a consensus as to the order of priority of the principal aims and objectives. If the primary aim is to reduce the prison population, community service orders have not succeeded, although it is possible that without them even more people would have been sent to prison. In the period 1973–84 the proportion of offenders sentenced to community service rose from nil to 7.5 per cent, but the proportion imprisoned (excluding fully suspended sentences) also rose, from 7.9 to 9.7 per cent, and for borstal or youth custody it more than doubled, from 2.0 to 4.4 per cent. It was the fine that dropped, from 51.3 to 41.4 per cent (Home Office 1984; 1985b: table 7.4).

Theory overtakes practice

Much of the practice of both reparation and community service appeared to accommodate both aspects of the reparative concept within traditional thought-patterns on criminal justice. Some of the theory, however, began to go further: the term 'restorative justice' began to be used, meaning not a new form of punishment, rehabilitation, or reducing pressure on the system, but a different principle, repairing (as far as possible) or making up for the damage and hurt caused by the crime. This can be done for the victim, if there is one, and if the victim wishes it; otherwise it can be done for the community. Three North American authors who helped to spread the idea are Gilbert Cantor, Randy Barnett and Ab Thorvaldson.

The criminal justice system is unfair and ineffective, according to Cantor (1976), in a frequently quoted article in the journal of the Philadelphia Bar Association. It is unfair because (Cantor says, oversimplifying somewhat) the essence of crime is poverty rather than wickedness; this is compounded by the fact that, having no money, the indigent offender is unable to pay reparation and is therefore made to pay with his body.

As for ineffectiveness, the amount of crime and the proportion committed by people previously convicted are evidence of failure to eradicate it; even as retribution it is a failure, because such a small proportion of offenders are punished. What is more, the availability of punishment provides people with an excuse not to seek more effective prevention strategies:

As long as we can 'buy' the remedies of two cops in a car, higher sentences for rape, and the death penalty, we are spared the pain of considering the eradication of slums, equality of opportunity, and radical alteration of the political-economic system wherein 'the mass of men lead lives of quiet desperation' (Cantor 1976: 108).

Quoting the view that anti-social behaviour is best dealt with by non-violence and by education based on self-government, Cantor proposes 'civilization' of the treatment of offenders, through money damages, including punitive damages, but payable in manageable instalments, adjusted to earning power. To arrive at the amount there should be facilities for composition between the parties (1976: 111). For the vast majority, Cantor believes, 'our refusal to imprison will diminish the likelihood of future violence so that the net result of the entire decriminalization program will be a safer and less violent society' (1976: 112). The civil standard of proof could then be adopted: 'preponderance of evidence' rather than 'beyond reasonable doubt' (1976: 109). For the 'savage few' (Cantor's quotation marks) who apparently cannot be 'civilized' – 'those who are not treated within the mental health system but who appear to lack the will or the power to avoid violent behavior – [there must be] sufficient restriction and supervision to result in apprehension for any occasion or threat of violence' (1976: 111–12) and if necessary treatment and confinement (1976: 108) and the new principle should be introduced in two stages, with murder and rape left for a few years. Altogether such a programme, Cantor claims, would help victims (although only a small proportion of them) and would hold the offender responsible by calling upon him 'to clean up his mess' and 'put himself right with his human family' (1976: 113).

The case for replacing punishment by reparation is taken a step further by Randy Barnett (1977), an academic at Harvard Law School, who subsequently worked in the state's Attorney's Office, Cook County, Chicago. Punishment, he argues, is open to serious objections, and the new paradigm should be based on its 'complete overthrow'. He quotes the criminologist Del Vecchio: 'The alleged absolute justice of repaying evil for evil . . . is really an empty sophism. If we go back to the Christian moralists, we find that an evil is to be put right only by doing good' (Barnett 1977: 283). The infliction of punishment may generate sympathy for the offender, and does not provide him with skills (1977: 284–5). If it is used on deterrent grounds, there is no guidance as to how much can justifiably be imposed, and to treat criminals as means to the ends of others raises serious moral problems. If the main justification is to affect others, 'The judicial process becomes, not a truth-seeking device, but solely a means to legitimate the use of force' (1977: 282).

Proposing a paradigm based on 'pure' restitution (i.e. without punitive intent), Barnett recognizes that this would involve major shifts of perspective in favour of the victim. For one thing, the offence would be seen as primarily against the individual victim, not the State (1977: 287); for another, in answer to critics who find the paradigm insufficiently retributive or deterrent, he states that '*Our goal is not the suppression of crime; it is doing justice to victims*' (Barnett 1977: 296; his emphasis). The distinction between crime and tort would collapse. As for victimless crimes, they would cease to be crimes. It is not clear whether Barnett would retain some form of sanction for administrative misdemeanours, or indeed for 'white-collar crimes', which may be very serious although no individual victim can be identified.

Another advocate of reparation is Ab Thorvaldson, until recently director of research of the Ministry of the Attorney-General, British Columbia. Reparation, he suggests, offers a way out of the punishment/rehabilitation argument (Thorvaldson 1980b: 17). He presents viewpoints of a 'reparativist' and a critic: when rehabilitators accept reparative measures, they concede that offenders should be held accountable; when denunciators do so, they concede that suffering is not the only currency for repayment (1980b: 23). Reparation should have an independent status as a sentencing aim. It cannot achieve all sentencing aims; for example it is not yet known whether it affects behaviour (1980b: 23–5). Like others, Thorvaldson argues in favour above all of clarification: 'The "multiple-aim" arguments for compensation are not so much in error as they are unsystematic and ultimately ineffective' (Thorvaldson 1983). This leads him to accept that, to meet the different aims of deterrence, rehabilitation, denunciation and reparation, there may have to be multiple sanctions for a single offence (1981: 128). Louis Blom-Cooper, then chairman of the Howard League for Penal Reform, speaking at the Canadian National Symposium on Reparative Sanctions, agreed: compensation is superior to punishment and should be 'a prime instrument of penal policy and practice', but in some cases it might not be 'sufficient' (to meet the other aims of sentencing, presumably) and might need to be 'reinforced by an additional fine or some other non-monetary sanction' (Blom-Cooper, in Thorvaldson 1985: 16). But if offenders receive the full punishment they will often refuse to pay compensation in addition; Sessar (1982), a German observer, makes this point, and opts for a model similar to Blom-Cooper's. For the general run of not very serious crimes, he says, reparation should 'fully or partially absorb public disapproval, so that *to this extent* further punishment becomes superfluous or even dysfunctional' (1982: 14, his emphasis). Sessar foresees some problems, however. The most serious crimes are those where 'the existing sentencing system with its symbolic attempt to defend . . . public order will probably remain a salient instrument', yet those are the very ones where there is the greatest need of reparation (and, some would add, reconciliation). Wealthy offenders might be able to buy their way out of the sanctioning system; wealthy and/or provocative victims might not be morally entitled to reparation; with reparation regarded as a form of punishment, it would be difficult to decide whether to base the amount on harm/damage or on the gravity of the offence.

Thorvaldson studied community service in England, and considered its place in sentencing theory; his arguments (1978) are relevant to reparation in general, and merit summarizing in some detail. He identifies a sentencing aim not previously included in standard textbooks on sentencing: to see that offenders 'give something back to society'. Writing before the idea of mediation had become so widespread, he advocated a view of reparation based on society rather than on the individual victim: the victim is not an island unto himself, and a hurt to the victim is in principle a hurt to all; so the job of the reparative sentence is 'not to assist the individual victim of crime, but rather to vindicate the principles of justice the crime violates. One could hardly design a sentence more suited to that task than community service' (Thorvaldson 1978: 77–8).

The *aims* of sentencing are distinguished by Thorvaldson from its *effects*, which may or may not follow the achievement of aims, but are not the factors determining success or failure; although he might have added that an otherwise justifiable aim may have to be abandoned if it entails unacceptable side-effects, such as a breach of human rights or a steep rise in recidivism. The effects of sentencing include requiring the offender to *suffer, receive* or *give* (1978: 125). Suffering may be symbolic (expressive) as in the case of retribution, or it may have a utilitarian (instrumental) aim, as with deterrence. In either case the suffering, or at least inconvenience, is an essential. It is based on fear and power, not reason and moral principle (1978: 136–7).

To receive rehabilitative efforts is in his view an essentially passive role, likely therefore to lower one's self-esteem; and since probation emphasises the consequences of behaviour on oneself, not on others, it too does not encourage one to think of moral principles (Thorvaldson 1978: 132–4). (Since he wrote, with growing involvement of probation officers in victim support and mediation, this is beginning to change.) It also has overtones of determinism (1978: 110), because of its reliance on changing offenders' environment as a means of influencing their behaviour.

To give, by making reparation, on the other hand, does not necessarily entail suffering *by* the offender, and thus it may fail to satisfy the denunciator if it does not, or the rehabilitator if it does (Thorvaldson 1978: 112, 113). Nor need it involve assistance *to* the offender. Reparation can be 'pure', limited in proportion to the harm done (1978: 42) on an analogy with the 'justice model', or it can aim to be utilitarian, educating offenders in the moral values of society; but its value is, according to Thorvaldson, in the principle it expresses (1978: 63). It stresses offenders' accountability for their actions. The emphasis of community service is not on offenders' needs but their strengths; not on their lack of insight but their capacity for responsibility; not on their vulnerability to social and psychological factors but on their capacity to choose. Thus there is little resemblance to traditional rehabilitative methods or aims – this is 'not only a change of methods but a change of goals' (1978: 59–60).

The reparative position is a moral one, closer to that of the denunciators, who have something in common with retributivists: it includes a desire to convey principles of justice to the public and the offender, and to influence attitudes. Thorvaldson sees the reparative philosophy as capable of making the aims of both denunciators and rehabilitators compatible, if both are prepared to make some concessions (although since he is thinking primarily of community service, his paradigm does not directly involve the victim, as Barnett's and others do). Denunciators normally expect to achieve their aims by means of punishment, but they may be willing to replace it by reparation, particularly since it requires effort by the offender. Rehabilitators, Thorvaldson argues, might not like the fact that in some cases reparation can be felt to be a form of punishment, since it involves deprivation of time or money, but they may accept community service (CS) so long as it includes potentially rehabilitative features such as contact with law-abiding citizens – volunteers and beneficiaries – and opportunities to increase skills and self-esteem. Thus reparation through payment of compensation, in Thorvaldson's view, would probably be acceptable to rehabilitators only if they could be persuaded that the effect on the offender was educative rather than punitive;

> CS represents a basic response to wrongdoing – the moral response – in a form which is palatable to deterministic and humanitarian approaches: justice can be done without necessarily requiring the intent that offenders suffer; requiring justice can have beneficial effects not only for society at large but for individual offenders.
>
> (Thorvaldson 1978: 117).

The conclusion is that by its nature the primary aim of community service must be counted as reparative, since any suffering or rehabilitative consequences are secondary effects. In a survey of offenders, Thorvaldson found that 84 per cent of those who favoured community service did so for reasons of principle, not because it was a 'soft option'; 46 per cent of those actually given community service recognized a reparative element. Not only that, but also on criteria such as leading offenders to show regret for their offences and promoting self-understanding, community service threatens to 'beat probation at its own game' (1978: 289).[1]

Evaluation

The present criminal justice system does not lend itself to evaluation, because of the ambiguities about what it is trying to achieve. First, it is divided into those who make decisions (sentencers) and those who carry them out. The quality of sentencing is more or less unmeasurable. Second, those who administer the sanctions may have different aims from the courts and from each other. The court sends people to prison as a punishment (as the cliché has it) but the prison staff deny holding them there *for* punishment. The prison service claims to want to release them at least no worse than on arrival; but its annual reports give prominence to low escape rates at least as much as to low reconviction rates.

Would a reparative system be any clearer, let alone more successful? There would still be a division between deciders and enforcers. Several writers have suggested that there should be a single primary aim, which is an advantage for clarity (e.g. Hudson *et al.* 1980, p. 39 *supra*; Thorvaldson 1983, p. 43 *supra*; Marshall 1985, p. 75 *infra*); it would be the restoration of the victims, and hence the community, as nearly as possible to their previous condition. The effects traditionally associated with sentencing would still be present, but would be secondary. Thus the first subsidiary criterion would be the proportion of cases in which the victim benefited. The next would be the execution of the orders, assessed simply by the extent to which reparation was completed. Denunciation, in so far as it depends on the reaction of public opinion, could be determined only by conducting surveys from time to time, and, as with present sentencing, by the occurrence or absence of public outcry – an unreliable indicator, made more so by the activities of the media. One component of denunciation, however, is the extent to which the victim is satisfied with the outcome and, given the greater involvement of victims in the process, it would not be impossible to collect routinely the views of those whose offenders were brought to court. Consistency would not be a criterion, since sentences would be individualized.

Adapting the conclusions of the survey of reparation projects by Hudson *et al.* (1980: 135, 174–5), it may be suggested that most programmes include some of the following criteria for evaluating their success:

Restorative criteria

1 The proportion of victims given the opportunity to meet their offender – without pressure to do so – whether or not they take advantage of it.
2 The proportion of offenders who make reparation, voluntarily or by order of the court (or the proportion of *serious* offenders who do so).
3 Of these, the proportion who complete their reparation, through payments, service, etc.
4 The extent to which the victims' loss (or at least their wish for reparation) is met; or the number of hours, and value, of service to the community.

Retributive or denunciatory criteria

5 Citizens' perception of reparation or community service as a fair sanction.
6 Victims' perception, likewise.
7 Offenders' perception, likewise.

Of the aims listed, nos (1) to (3) serve the symbolic function of justice, (4) to (6) are primarily of benefit to the community and the victim, and (7) to the offender.

Other possible criteria include reductions in (8) recidivism, (9) prison population (or number sent to prison), and (10) cost per order, but these should be regarded as limiting factors, in the sense that they should affect policy only if instead of a reduction there was an unacceptable increase; (9) and (10) are of benefit primarily to the system. Obviously there are other benefits: in some ways (2), (3) and (9) may benefit offenders, and (8) and (10) the community, for example.

As for the aim of reducing crime, it would be recognized that under the proposed model responsibility would belong not with the criminal justice process but with an agency devoted primarily to that objective; the level of crime in society would therefore be a criterion for evaluating the work of that agency, and indeed of other government departments concerned with social wellbeing, rather than of criminal justice. Crime reduction programmes could be evaluated by the usual methods such as before-and-after measurements, and comparisons of experimental and control areas. This would be regarded as independent of the success or failure of reparation. Other factors could be monitored, such as the offender's sense of fairness, the number of people imprisoned, the courts' backlog, the recidivism rate, and the cost; these would not be regarded as primary criteria but as limiting factors: if the first were too low, or any of the others too high, remedial action might be required, or, in the extreme case, if the malfunction could be shown to be specifically due to the use of reparation, the whole approach would be called into question, just as the existing system is called into question by its performance on all these criteria.

Note

1 The foregoing section is adapted from Wright (1984).

4

Justice without lawyers: enabling people to resolve their conflicts

As the concept of a reparative outcome was developing, new thinking also emerged about criminal and civil procedure, both of which had also been under criticism (see Chapter 2). Some of the inspiration for change came from anthropological studies of other cultures, in which the distinction, if any, is differently drawn. It became apparent that in western law, too, the dividing line was not as clear as had been assumed, for several reasons.

First, some civil disputes, if unresolved, lead to criminal acts. It is impossible to know in advance which of them will do so, but with hindsight it is often clear that a criminal act arose from a dispute. Conflict resolution can therefore have a place both in crime prevention programmes and in society's response to crime when it occurs. Home Office research found that six out of ten male murderers, and nine out of ten female ones, had killed someone known or related to them (Gibson and Klein 1961, cited by West 1965). Among crimes of violence, McClintock (1963: 36–9) found that nearly half the offenders were known or related to their victims; in New York, the figure was over half, and even for property crimes it was 35 per cent (Vera Institute 1977). In a sample of 989 cases of violent crime reported to the police in a medium-sized Swedish town, 55 per cent of assailants were known to their victims (Wikström, 1985: 82–3). In the British Crime Survey it was reported that one-third of crimes of violence, including some causing severe injury, were committed by an assailant who was known or related to the victim (in one-sixth of the cases, a husband, relative, lover or ex-lover) (Hough and Mayhew 1983: 20). Part of the explanation, it has been suggested, is that people use informal means to punish each other (Black 1983); this is, after all, what in many cases the law would do if they gained access to it. But of course only some of these are potential cases for mediation.

Second, recourse to the criminal justice system is by no means always the normal or preferred response to law-breaking. In the case of theft by employees, for example, one response is to put up with it so long as it remains within tolerable bounds; another is simply to dismiss the offender, which achieves some of the aims of criminal justice (preventing repetition, deterring others) without its drawbacks (delay, cost in time and sometimes money, unwelcome publicity, harm to relations with employees) (Ditton 1977). In violent domestic disputes, the victim often does not report the offence, or having reported it does not proceed with the charge; this may be because she wants the offender only to be checked but not to receive the punishment which a court would probably impose, or fears that by causing him to be punished she would incur retaliation. The Vera Institute found that a high proportion of dismissals of prosecution was due to 'complainant non-cooperation'. Tax-collectors do not use the criminal law unless they have to, because civil procedures work better in securing payment; trades union legislation often employs civil sanctions such as sequestration of assets rather than criminal ones, because the latter would be counterproductive.

At first theory and practice in mediation appear to have developed simultaneously and more or less independently. The most significant innovation, probably, was the practical one, the creation in 1971 of the Night Prosecutor Program in Columbus, Ohio; thereafter theory appears to have provided much of the impetus for practice, so perhaps it will be more convenient to consider a few of the leading theoretical contributions first: the ideas from other cultures, and the contrast between the western concept of law and the important place of the process in less complex societies. Then, after a review of the early development of mediation in the 1970s, partly inspired by anthropologists, it may be useful to suggest how various types of mediation schemes can be classified and evaluated, and to consider some criticisms.

Ideas from other cultures

In the 1960s and 1970s, as dissatisfaction with the conventional justice system grew, a number of legal theorists in the United States were becoming aware of descriptions of the traditional practices in other cultures. These, instead of trying to make the rambling edifice of the law more serviceable by demolishing parts of it and adding new extensions, seemed to offer a fundamentally new approach.

The Harvard jurist Lon L. Fuller, studying the principles of dispute resolution, found that some conflicts arising from relationships are too complex to be justiciable: a judge applies some principle to the decision of a case, and cannot adjudicate where there are no principles (Fuller 1963, quoted by McGillis and Mullen 1977: 24–5). In mediation Fuller discerned some features of a different kind. Law is a structure, in which a set of norms is defined; mediation is a process, 'commonly directed, not toward achieving conformity to norms, but toward the creation of the relevant norms themselves' (Fuller 1971: 308). Fuller shows how, since mediators claim no authority, they can empower people to regain control over their own relationships, rather than 'assume that all social order must be imposed by some kind of "authority"' (1971: 315); mediation's central quality is 'its capacity to reorient the parties toward each other, not by imposing rules on them, but by helping them to achieve a new and shared perception of their relationship, a perception that will redirect their attitudes and dispositions toward one another' (1971: 325). He warns, however, that mediation is not suitable where questions of fact have to be decided, such as whether *A* drove through a red light, nor where the underlying relationship is such that 'it is best organized by impersonal act-oriented rules' (1971: 328, 330).

One of the articles most often cited in literature on mediation is James Gibbs's on the traditional moot of the Kpelle people of Liberia. Despite cultural differences, this example shows aspects which are and are not incorporated into some present-day western theory and practice.

The first parallel is that among the Kpelle the moots exist alongside courts which are used for cases of assault and theft 'where the litigants are not linked in a relationship after the trial'. According to Gibbs (1963/1967: 278–9) the courts' authoritarian style restricts the opportunity to air grievances surrounding the case: the 'harsh tone tends to drive the spouses farther apart rather than reconcile them. The moot, in contrast, is more effective in handling such cases.' The moot is thus comparable to projects that offer an alternative to courts, but not to those, like the Victim/Offender Reconciliation Programs (see Chapter 5), operating after conviction. The mediator is chosen by the complainant, which is unlike the western method: in the Institute for Mediation and Conflict Resolution, New York, for example, any mediator with links to either participant is disqualified (Wahrhaftig 1982: 82). The proceedings begin with statements by the two parties, the complainant speaking first, which seems to be almost universal in mediation. In the Kpelle moot, however, spectators may attend and take part, a practice not found in most US schemes; the Community Boards of San Francisco, with their emphasis on community involvement, are an exception. The Kpelle tradition, unlike many western models, does not adopt the principle that the two opening statements shall be uninterrupted. Proceedings are orderly, but informal and even convivial: the mediator requires anyone who speaks out of turn to bring rum for all present (Gibbs 1963/1967: p. 281). Gibbs does not say whether this always contributes to the orderliness of the proceedings.

The airing of grievances is more complete than in court, and the range of relevance is extremely broad. The hearing in the moot takes place promptly, unlike that of the court, and in informal surroundings. All of these features are commonly found in US mediation projects. Gibbs considers that the moot's procedure is not only conciliatory but also therapeutic (1963/1967: 277, 284). He states that the Kpelle also make no unilateral ascription of blame, although elsewhere he speaks of the 'winning' and 'losing' parties (1963/1967: 282) and of mediation foundering because no one will be the first to admit fault – whereas US projects often make a virtue of not requiring such an admission. The aim is to reach an acceptable consensus. The 'losing' party apologizes and brings token gifts, and rum or beer for those who heard the case (rather as, in some circles in British society, an offender against the norms can atone and secure reacceptance by buying a round of drinks). But in addition, the 'winning' party gives a smaller token in return, to show good will; this is analogous to mediated agreements described in western literature as incorporating concessions or undertakings by both sides. In the Kpelle procedure, a group of those present may take either party on one side for discussion; if this happens in an US project, it is done by the mediators, and they generally see both parties.

Finally, both methods work on the basis of rewarding socially approved behaviour, or in psychological terms 'positive reinforcement'. Gibbs speaks of praise, concern and affection; in one US project, when juveniles have made reparation by completing community service, they are invited to receive certificates at a ceremony. The longest applause is given to those who have worked the most hours – who are those whose original offence was the most serious (Swann, personal communication).

A common technique is to allow participants to talk about anything they consider relevant, and to vent their spleen and aim for the 'minimax' goal – give a little, get a little, as in the Mexican Zapotec court, which has some features of a moot. The judge combines the roles of mediator, adjudicator and therapist (Nader 1969: 85–8; Nader and Todd 1978).

How are mediated agreements enforced? In the moot in Tanzania, where cases from petty offences to homicide were resolved by mediation, 'although compensation of twelve shillings was agreed to, only six shillings and twenty cents were actually handed over. People did not expect the rest to be paid' (Gulliver, 1969: 48). Once injuries had healed satisfactorily 'the matter was now ended: it should not be raised again, or the whole dispute might be renewed.' Thus what mattered was first the amount agreed publicly, which symbolized the seriousness of the offence, and second the closure of the incident; the amount actually handed over was less important. (This may be compared to the western practice of imposing prison sentences intended to express the seriousness of the crime, then releasing some classes of prisoners earlier.) In these small, cohesive societies, the participatory process of justice helps people, and particularly the victim, to clarify and affirm the norms of behaviour (Christie 1977). Gulliver criticizes the 'fruitless concern with what "law" is, instead of concentrating on what "law" does' (in Nader 1969: 17).

Other authors turned to eastern countries. In China, for example, litigation was (as in the United States) time-consuming, degrading and costly, though partly for different reasons (cruel and lazy magistrates, not legally trained, who left the work to corrupt clerks); however, there was an ancient tradition of mediation to fall back on (Lubman 1967). Social order depended largely on *li* (moral and customary principles for polite behaviour) and *yang* (yielding), which was regarded as virtuous because it prevented friction. These were combined with the *pao-chia* system, in which each ten-household unit was required to report crimes and the whereabouts of criminals – a remarkable parallel to the Anglo-Saxon *frank-pledge*. Mediation was seen as superior to adjudication, which is 'coercive', and to *fa* (law) 'a clumsy system of punishments directed only at strengthening the state and lacking proper regard for "an ordered world of peace, harmony and simple contentment," and the cultivation of the individual' (Lubman 1967:

1,290). But from the adoption of Confucianism after the harsh Ch'in rule was dissolved in 210 BC to the establishment of the republic in 1911, *li* proved insufficient to govern the empire, and much of it yielded to law.

A comparable approach is found in a very small eastern society, the Friendly Islands, where expressed anger gains no sympathy (and even results in sanction), but the expression of being pained at the hurt does so. It is then appropriate for offenders to make a public act of apology and reconciliation, by which they do not lose face, but win approval (Marcus 1979: 76–7), rather as Members of Parliament in Britain are treated with forbearance when they make a personal statement in the House of Commons admitting that they have been at fault.

Law and process

One basic comparison between traditional and 'new wave' mediation is that in simple societies the underlying principle of resolving conflict is often not the *law* as the basis for a decision imposed by a learned judge, but a *process* to enable the parties themselves or their supporters to reach an agreement, which is expressed by an experienced conciliator. Importance is not attached to precedent (Nader 1969: 84); 'law' is a western concept (Gulliver 1969: 12). The Koreans believe that 'to tell the truth and nothing but the truth' is meaningless because no one can tell objective truth (Nader 1969: 84); as an American jurist and judge remarked, 'facts are guesses' (Frank 1949: ch. 3). Village tribunals are 'less anxious to find "truth" and give "justice" than to abate conflict and promote harmony' (Rudolph and Rudolph 1967: 258). In a significant article Abel (1973: 222) quotes the anthropologist Evans-Pritchard as saying that 'In a strict sense the Nuer [of the Sudan] have no law. There are conventional compensations for damage, adultery, loss of limb and so forth, but there is no authority with power to adjudicate on such matters or to enforce a verdict.' Later, however, Evans-Pritchard appears to have conceded that the definition of law could be extended to cover this process, and Malinowski criticized the 'error' of defining the forces of law in terms of central authority, courts and constables (Abel 1973: 223). In one approach disputes are seen as deviations from a trouble-free norm, with an authority that decides individual cases according to an established body of rules and precedents, while in the other, disputes are regarded as a normal feature of the human condition, requiring a process in which the parties themselves are helped to reach an agreement acceptable to them, with a procedure that is not merely a means to an end but an essential part of attaining reconciliation.

Other anthropologists, like Gluckman and Bohannan, in their studies of the Barotse and the Tiv respectively, concentrated on the judicial *processes*, rather than the institutions or rules: it is a question of compromise, bargaining, not a zero-sum, win-or-lose decision (Roberts 1979: 199–201). Gluckman (1968) makes the comparison: 'In developed systems of law, written pleadings by the parties, usually presented by their counsels, have to be stated according to particular formulas which strip away what is believed to be irrelevant'; by contrast, in tribal societies 'Litigants are allowed to state their respective claims in apparently full, and often seemingly irrelevant, detail'. Indeed were they to be confined to directly relevant issues, 'they would be robbed of their main method of arriving at the truth' (Gluckman 1955: 95). Here Gluckman seems to suggest that 'truth' is the goal, rather than the other goals identified by Nader and Christie such as norm-setting, having everything 'out in the open' and thus reducing tensions. Elsewhere, however, Gluckman sees the judges in tribal courts as 'attempting to reconcile the parties and enable them to resume living and working together'; he notes that 'The Lozi disapprove of any irremediable breaking of relationships. . . . Therefore the court tends to be conciliating, it strives to effect a compromise acceptable to, and accepted by, all the parties' (Gluckman 1955: 20–1). Another example is the Kuta (council or court) of the Barotse; it may quote precedents, but 'More often, the judges cite not past court decisions, but actual instances of upright behaviour, to show how people ought to behave. . . . Law in this sense is constantly exhibited in the conformity of upright people to norms' (Gluckman 1955: 93).

Towards a western model of mediation

The interest in other models was born of disillusion with current western justice and the desire to do something about it, although there may also have been some attraction to the ideal of the simple community. One strand in the development of mediation was a meeting of minds between community activists and anthropologists. Among the former was Paul Wahrhaftig, a civil rights lawyer, who in 1969 was leading a bail reform project of the American Friends' Service Committee. Being interested in the spread of ideas, he produced a newsletter, the *Pre-Trial Justice Quarterly*, and organized conferences. On his project's advisory committee was a young anthropologist, Michael Lowy, who had written a thesis on the use of moots in villages in Ghana, and put forward the idea that bail reform and pre-trial diversion from the criminal justice system had the effect of extending the net of State control to people who otherwise would not have been convicted. Instead, he proposed that the concept of the moot should be transformed into urban neighbourhoods in the United States. This aroused the interest of activists like Wahrhaftig, who soon changed the title of his newsletter to *The Mooter*, and later to *Conflict Resolution Notes*. (This account is based on a personal communication from Wahrhaftig in 1988.)

Another strand in the development of mediation in the US, and its introduction into Britain, was the work of the Society of Friends (Quakers). In the 1960s they gave training in non-violent techniques to marshals of civil rights marches. Two Quakers who had been working with juvenile delinquents, Eileen Stief and Betsey Leonard, felt that court procedure was unsuited to many of their cases. They trained as mediators, and in 1976 the Friends' Suburban Project in

Philadelphia started the Community Dispute Settlement Program with Eileen Stief as director. In 1982 the first National Conference on Peacemaking and Conflict Resolution brought together mediators from different backgrounds, including four British representatives – two Quakers and two from the Newham (London) Conflict and Change Project.

Transatlantic contacts included a workshop on the technique of 'Conflict Mediation in the Community' at the Friends' International Centre, London, in 1984 led by Betsey Leonard. Conferences and courses were organized by Dr Chris Mitchell, then of the Conflict Management Research Group, City University, London, with North American speakers such as Dean Peachey of Community Justice Initiatives, Kitchener, Ontario, and David Forrest of the Institute for Mediation and Conflict Resolution, New York. A 'reparation forum' was formed in May 1984, and in December 1984 it was constituted as the Forum for Initiatives in Reparation and Mediation (FIRM) (see p. 83).

The case for reform based on decentralization, rather than for replication of existing institutions, was put forward by, among others, Richard Danzig, then a professor at Stanford Law School. At a conference in late 1972 he described the 'liberal's dilemma' in the reform of justice: we are excellent at diagnosing problems, such as discrimination against the poor and ethnic minorities, but we tend to come up with solutions that require those in power, such as judges, to agree with our analysis. Danzig legitimized these ideas, notably in an influential article in the *Stanford Law Review* (1973). Concerned with what he saw as the over-centralization of city government in New York, he advocated a package of measures to give self-determination and cohesion to local communities, such as the right to determine whether certain activities should be treated as crimes, and the organization at neighbourhood level of police units, analogous perhaps to Britain's special constables or traffic wardens, to deal with minor matters of order maintenance. Of Danzig's suggestions, the 'community moot' was the one which attracted support: for local disputes and minor delinquency, he proposed, we could 'stop thinking of courts as adjudicators, and view them instead as parts of a therapeutic process aimed at conciliation of disputants or reintegration of deviants into society' (Danzig 1973: 42). There would be no compulsion, no records suggesting guilt, and the complainant would have nothing to lose by turning first to the moot (1973: 47–8). He drew examples from, among others, some of the anthropological studies mentioned above (notably James Gibbs 1963 and Laura Nader 1969; Lowy, incidentally, had studied under Nader).

Few contributions have been as widely quoted in the literature on mediation as the Norwegian Professor Nils Christie's lecture in Sheffield in 1976, 'Conflicts as property' (Christie 1977). Starting with an anthropological example from Arusha, Tanzania (see also Gulliver 1969), he sees the law, its procedures and even its buildings as complex and remote from ordinary people's lives. Conflicts, civil or criminal, ought to belong to their participants, but have been stolen by lawyers and other professionals; in criminal ones, the State has deprived the victim of rights to full participation. Society is also the loser, however. It is widely assumed that the criminal law is necessary for the regulation of society, because it defines the limits of acceptable behaviour. In fact, however, the details of what society, through its laws, does or does not permit, are often difficult to decode; the degree of blameworthiness is often not expressed in the law at all, but in the sentence imposed by a particular judge on an individual offender. Christie argues that this theft of the conflict by the State, this procedure restricted to the narrow legal definition of what is relevant, deprives us all of *'opportunities for norm-clarification'* (his emphasis); the victim and the offender could explore the ramifications of the case and the degree of culpability. He proposes a court that would be victim-oriented, with appropriate reparation by the offender (and welfare help *to* the offender when needed); and lay-oriented, with 'lay judges' who would take part in conflict solutions only a few times each, so that other community members could share the experience. Experts, if unavoidable, would be kept to a minimum. He makes the assumption that victims would actually want to participate; this is not always the case, but when they do, surveys have found that the great majority are glad to have done so.

Different cultures have their own insights about handling disputes. The Social Conciliatory Commissions in Poland do not take cases which could be presented in a state court unless the prosecutor of the court has discontinued the case and referred it to them (Kurczewski and Friske 1978: 170); the Community Boards of San Francisco have a similar policy. In Northern Nigeria, among the Tiv, disputants simply tell their stories, with no information excluded as irrelevant; a resolution is sought which 'will facilitate their necessarily continuing interwoven relationships' and professional attorneys are not allowed to appear (Bush 1979: 269, 271, 280) Similar approaches are being used in western mediation. Also recognized, in Tanzania, is the problem of inequality between participants; the solution may lie in 'judicial [or mediators'] activism' to redress the balance (Bush 1979: 309–10). Professor Sander, however, a lawyer who has worked to spread mediation, thinks that mediators should not jeopardize their neutrality, and the balance should be restored by allowing a traditional lawyer to represent the underdog (Sander 1984: 103). A common feature is the recognition that conflict is not abnormal: it is 'part of the cosmic order', as the Cambridge (Mass.) Dispute Settlement Center (*c.* 1982) puts it. It cannot be stamped out, but can be used 'for the purpose of positive change'. Mediation is 'a discipline which permits conflict to happen as safely as possible'.

The implications of introducing such an approach into a system which has developed along very different lines would, of course, need to be thought out. It is possible, for example, as the National Institute for Dispute Resolution (in the USA) concedes, that a law intended to improve the lot of consumers would have little effect if many consumer disputes were being resolved through mediation or 'an informal adjudication body which based its decisions on what seems fair and just in the particular case without regard to statutory or decisional law' (Marks *et al.* 1984: 54). Again, a system that might be effective with teenage first offenders might have to be modified when dealing with, say, professional shoplifters. Christie may have had more individual disputes in mind; even so, it is not clear from his picture how the 'norm clarification' would be spread beyond the participants and the lay judges. Most of the western mediation projects influenced by Christie's ideas hold sessions in private. His article begins with a moot on a 'sunny hillside' in Tanzania; no reporters attended because nearly all the village was there. But few people in the west attend such events, and (in Norway and elsewhere) sunny hillsides are not always available when required.

The spread of mediation

Concurrently with the academic debate, the new concept of mediation was being put into practice, at first in the United States and later elsewhere. Wahrhaftig had found in the early 1970s that some mediation projects had started independently of his network: the Community Assistance Project in Chester, Pennsylvania, and the Columbus, Ohio, Night Prosecutor Program, as well as some based on arbitration: the '4A' projects (Arbitration As An Alternative) in Rochester, New York, and Philadelphia. By 1982 some 200 mediation schemes in the United States (and a few in Canada) were listed by the American Bar Association (Ray 1982). The pioneering projects have often been described (e.g. McGillis and Mullen 1977; Tomasic and Feeley 1982; Alper and Nichols 1981; Marshall 1985), so it is sufficient to summarize the work of only a selection of them. It will be seen that all of them take at least a proportion of criminal cases, where there is a relationship between the victim and the offender. The examples used are mainly American, because there are as yet few British projects, and even fewer evaluations.

Night Prosecutor's Program, Columbus, Ohio

The first major mediation programme was born not of academic theory but of a prosecutor's intuitive recognition that the court was not meeting the needs of litigants, combined with his wish to reduce the backlog of cases in his court. The City Attorney of Columbus, Ohio, James Hughes, together with Professor John Palmer of Capital University Law School, saw that people were acquiring a criminal record, with all that that entails, for offences such as assaults, menacing threats or larceny, as a result of disputes within a family, neighbourhood squabbles or disagreements between landlord and tenant. In addition, court hours suit the convenience of the court's staff rather than its customers. Palmer acknowledges his debt to Dr A.M. Roosenburg of the Van Der Hoeven Kliniek in the Netherlands, where 'in many cases of interpersonal disputes the most effective deterrent to future unacceptable behavior was to have the disputants confront each other in a controlled setting' (Palmer 1974: 14). If it could work among the highly disturbed patients of the clinic, could it not succeed in more ordinary cases?

Citizens who came to 'file a warrant' (lay an information) were diverted to the project: the complainant and the accused were told to appear for an administrative hearing, held in the evening in about a week's time. (Later it was found that many participants were on shift work, so day-time hearings were also held.) Even minor disputes were referred, because 'if a person is sufficiently agitated to want to file a criminal charge against someone', the case has potential for erupting into a major felony (Palmer 1974: 14). (This would presumably be Palmer's defence against the allegation that, by referring such cases to mediation rather than merely declining to prosecute, the programme was 'widening the net of social control'.) Graduate law students were used as 'hearing officers' (the word 'mediators' was at first not used as a title, but only descriptively). They built up experience on which the training of many later mediators has been based; for example, 'The most successful resolutions have proved to be those in which the parties themselves suggest a solution', and 'Emotional outbursts are common . . . , without the opportunity for the controlled display of emotionalism, shouting and other forms of confrontation, the basic issues often do not come to the surface' (Palmer 1974: 15).

In the first full year of Federal funding (to 1 September 1973), 3,992 cases were diverted from the criminal justice system to the Night Prosecutor Program (Palmer 1974: 17). During that year the programme decided to accept complaints from retail establishments regarding bad cheques, which was to lead to a massive increase in its workload. It was soon receiving some 7,800 referrals of disputes annually, and 10,200 bad cheque cases (but these are the numbers of cases initially referred; the number processed is considerably smaller). Hearings are scheduled at thirty-minute intervals, with longer for complex cases and up to thirty in half an hour for cheque cases (McGillis and Mullen 1977: 114). If the parties do not attend, or fail to reach agreement, prosecution remains a possibility.

The project has been criticized for being in effect a debt collection agency (McGillis 1982: 67) and for its 'very limited community participation' (Alper and Nichols 1981: 135–6). These authors also say that it is 'too concerned with the allocation of blame'. If true, this transgresses a tenet of mediation programmes that they should be non-judgemental; it may have to do with the project's use of law students as mediators and its location within the criminal justice system.

Institute for Mediation and Conflict Resolution

A dispute centre was established in New York in 1975 by the Institute for Mediation and Conflict Resolution (IMCR), itself created five years earlier by the Ford Foundation to train people in mediation techniques, in the wake of the civil disturbances of the 1960s. A large court-based project, it evolved a style of mediation and disseminated it through training programmes. Two women working for a pre-trial diversion programme in New York, Ann Weisbrod and

Sandi (Freinburg) Tamid, looking for new ideas, contacted Paul Wahrhaftig. He sent them information about the emerging concept of community mediation. They developed a proposal, interested George Nicolau, the president of IMCR, secured backing from the police and funding from the Law Enforcement Assistance Administration (LEAA), and started up on 1 March 1975 (Wahrhaftig, personal communication 1988; McGillis and Mullen 1977: 134–5).

In its first year it recruited and trained a panel of fifty-three volunteer mediators from various sections of the community, and began accepting referrals from two police precincts, followed by two more and the Housing Authority Police (McGillis and Mullen 1977: 136). It also took referrals from the Summons Part of the Criminal Court, and other sources. Cases referred include criminal offences 'between people who knew each other and thus would be amenable to mediation'. The original list included harassment, menacing, assault, and subsequently felonies such as burglary, robbery and rape have been accepted (McGillis and Mullen 1977: 138), but only where the attitude of the victim indicates 'that a felony sentence for the defendant would not be the adequate disposition of the case', for example when 'the real issue is the relationship between the parties, and not the conduct on a particular occasion' (Weigend 1981: 36).

In the first ten months there were 1,657 referrals; of these, some 800 were resolved prior to the hearing (and the dispute centre states that its very existence made this possible, by providing an alternative to court action); about 400 were resolved at hearings (McGillis and Mullen 1977: 137). By 1983 some 17,000–18,000 cases a year from Manhattan and the Bronx were screened, with a further 15,000 at the centres run by the Victim Services Agency (VSA) in Brooklyn and Queen's (interviews with David Forrest, director of the IMCR Center, and John Blackmore and Chris Whipple of the VSA in 1983). The Brooklyn programme is designed to deal with felony charges involving acquaintances.

Although independently managed, the large mediation centres in New York are closely integrated with the criminal justice process and have taken pressure off it: indeed they have replaced the former Summons Court for non-arrest summonses, most of which involved three to five court appearances (interview with Mark Smith, Brooklyn Mediation Center in 1983). The centre issues a Request To Appear (RTA), which is 'like a summons', to the complainant, who then serves it on the respondent in the presence of a police officer or adult third party (interview with David Forrest in 1983). Participation by the respondent is voluntary, but the alternative is a court appearance; respondents may regard this as a threat, but it could also be a promise, since there is a US tradition that citizens are entitled to their 'day in court'.

The IMCR has been criticized for taking on too large a volume of work, often relying on single volunteer mediators. Industrial bargaining techniques are not necessarily applicable to personal disputes because in the former, the mediator's aim is 'not so much to make disputants communicate with each other, but to bring forth "concessions" so that an agreement can be drafted', according to Thomas Weigend; he describes the parties sometimes sitting in embarrassed silence after a session, avoiding eye contact, while a mediation agreement was drawn up (1981: 49). Felstiner and Williams (1980) similarly say that its training focuses on the technique rather than on preserving relationships. Others would say, however, that although making people friends is desirable, mediators in a short session do not set themselves such an optimistic goal: their more realistic aim is to help the parties to find an acceptable basis for co-existence, and to communicate in future should the need arise. The Brooklyn Center was perceived more positively by disputants than the court process, although it was not suitable for all types of cases (R.C. Davis 1982).

The mediation techniques used and taught by the IMCR are worth describing in some detail, because they have been widely adopted, with variations, by other mediation projects. (This account is based mainly on McGillis and Mullen 1977: 141–3, and Felstiner and Williams 1980, with additions from the interviews cited above, and observation of mediation sessions.) At first the 'ground rules' are explained by the mediators (sometimes only one), and the participants are asked to accept them. These include agreeing to remain seated, not to interrupt the opening statement or use offensive language, and to try to work towards an agreement. The mediator explains that all proceedings are confidential: only a copy of the agreement is kept on file. A feature of the IMCR Center, which most others have not adopted, is that participants are asked to agree in advance to arbitration if mediation should be unsuccessful. (This is known as 'med-arb'.) The IMCR says that only about 5 per cent require arbitration, and it saves the unsuccessful cases from ending up in court, but the proportion is much higher elsewhere: 40 per cent in Rochester, NY, Community Dispute Services Project (McGillis 1982: 71). It is argued that the possibility of an imposed solution might deter some participants from being candid during the mediation hearing, and that arbitration either should not be used or should be carried out by a different person (Sander 1976, quoted by McGillis and Mullen 1977: 67–8). Other projects stress that mediators have no authority: the solution should come from the participants themselves. An exception is made for breaches of one party's basic rights, particularly through violence: mediators do not allow an agreement saying 'I will stop hitting her if ... '.

After the preliminaries, each party is invited to give his or her version of the dispute and its background, without interruption, followed by general, and sometimes heated, exchanges. Mediators are trained to use listening skills (such as eye contact, summarizing what is said to confirm that it has been understood, identifying points of agreement and encouraging further discussion). If necessary, mediators then talk with the parties separately, or discuss the case with each other or their supervisor, leaving the two parties separated or in the same room, depending on the progress made. This process, developed from IMCR's work on labour disputes, is described as 'caucusing' or 'shuttle diplomacy'. (A 'caucus' in American usage – from the Algonquin word for one who advises or encourages: SOED – simply means a private meeting, and need not have pejorative overtones.) A significant feature is that it is not necessary to secure agreement as to the precise facts, and mediators are trained not to allocate blame.

Finally the mediators invite the parties to draw up an agreement, in clear language, for their future conduct towards each other. Mediators should not make suggestions unless the negotiations are stuck. The agreement is written down, copies given to the participants and the Center's files, and rough notes torn up as a symbol of the confidentiality of the proceedings.

A case history may show how the process can work. It comes from the Southwark, London, Mediation Service (names and details have been disguised).

A wiry south Londoner objected to the black woman who had moved in next door. He kicked her gate, and she felt sure he had aimed the kick at her; she reported him for attempted assault. He complained that her dog had attacked his cat. He parked his car in front of her property; she moved it, and damaged it. The case had entered the criminal justice system before they heard about mediation, but the court deferred sentence until mediation had been attempted. Both agreed to take part. After the opening statements, they fought verbally for two hours, but ended with an agreement. He would repair the gate and move his car when required, and she would tell him when she was taking her dog into the garden so that he could make sure his cat was safe. They walked away arm in arm.

(Guardian 21 February 1990).

In some schemes, operating under less pressure than IMCR, there is an initial visit or telephone call, to explain mediation; this is counted as the first stage in the process, and sometimes it is sufficient to resolve the dispute. In some, there is a follow-up contact after two months or so, to check whether the agreement is holding. Others invite participants to come back if there are problems, and assume that no news is good news – which is not necessarily the case, since at least one evaluation found that the most common response to the breakdown of an agreement was to do nothing (Felstiner and Williams 1980: 112). They would claim, however, that even where an agreement is not reached, or not kept, the mediation process often takes some of the aggravation out of the dispute, and creates channels of communication so that if the dispute recurs, the parties will often feel able to reopen the discussion without the need to seek outside help.

Neighborhood Justice Centers

Danzig's (1973) proposal for community moots attracted considerable attention, particularly at the National Conference on the Causes of Popular Dissatisfaction with the Administration of Justice in 1976. A Task Force was set up, chaired by the Attorney-General, Griffin Bell, to consider reforms discussed at the Conference, and a central recommendation was for the development of Neighborhood Justice Centers (NJCs). This was taken up by the US Department of Justice (McGillis and Mullen 1977: 29–30). An adaptation proposed by Professor Frank Sander (1976) was used as a basis for three experimental Neighborhood Justice Centers set up in 1978 by the Department of Justice, in Venice/Mar Vista, Los Angeles; Kansas City, Missouri; and Atlanta, Georgia.

All three NJCs accepted a mixture of civil cases and criminal ones involving relationships, though the proportions varied; all of them recruited and trained community representatives as mediators. There were differences: Atlanta and Kansas City obtained referrals mainly from the criminal justice system, Venice/ Mar Vista mainly from the community through 'media outreach', although even this project was organized 'from the top down', in Wahrhaftig's view (1982). Atlanta received about three times as many referrals as each of the other two (2,351 in 1978/79). Kansas City, with 72 per cent of its caseload involving criminal matters, used arbitration as a last resort; this happened in about 8 per cent of its cases. Kansas City was unable to obtain local funds to continue when Federal funding from the Department of Justice ended (Roehl and Cook 1982). Venice/ Mar Vista makes a point of not coercing people into the project, so it does not take on cases where prosecution is pending, and there is no sanction of renewed prosecution if mediation yields no agreement; these policies have led to a relatively low rate of referrals and a high rate of complainants dropping out, but somewhat more cases are settled informally without a hearing. The typical procedure at an NJC hearing was based on the IMCR techniques and the broadly similar ones of the American Arbitration Association.

The evaluation of the NJCs was encouraging: '*mediation can work*' (Roehl and Cook 1982: 97; their emphasis). The three centres attracted nearly 4,000 cases in their first fifteen months; over one-third reached a mediation hearing, and of these 82 per cent resulted in a mutual agreement. But the cases referred from the criminal justice system were not enough to make a significant numerical impact: the largest centre, Atlanta, took about 2 per cent of the court's caseload (Roehl and Cook 1982: 106). Venice/Mar Vista succeeded in attracting about six cases a week, half its intake, from self-referrals. Most hearings were held within two weeks. The cost per case resolved varied from $142 to $589, and a larger caseload is needed to bring these figures down; but are there enough suitable cases, and can standards be maintained with a larger throughput? Follow-up interviews with 1,642 disputants after about six months showed overwhelming support for NJCs, and a high proportion of agreements were still holding; complainants in a small sample of comparable cases which went through the court system were less satisfied. Numerous other cities have set up similar programmes.

After the most important milestones in the early development of the mediation movement, there are several more projects which merit description in a general review, but selection is unavoidable. One noteworthy project is the Community Boards Program in San Francisco, which is distinguished by its philosophy and practice of independence from the justice system, and of grass-roots 'community empowerment'. It has extended not only a network of mediation centres but also understanding of mediation as a problem-solving technique. Its cases, however, are almost all non-criminal, and so are not central to the present study.

Other models

Another interesting model is the Boston, Massachusetts, Municipal Court Mediation Program. Its cases are mainly those where there is a relationship, but they include serious offences such as assault with a deadly weapon. Although independently managed (by the Crime and Justice Foundation, Boston), however, it is dependent on court personnel for most of its referrals, and the court retains the right to be informed of the outcome of mediation; most end in successful agreements, and the original court action is dropped or dismissed, but the remainder can be returned to court for trial. Mediators, though they act on a voluntary basis, are all lawyers (McGinness and Cinquegrana 1982). In seven years the project has received 1,406 referrals, almost all criminal cases. Just over 1,000 mediation sessions were held, for which a success rate of 88 per cent is claimed (figures from Crime and Justice Foundation 1988). In 1987, 65 per cent of cases referred involved assault and battery. Considerable energy has to be expended in securing referrals of cases from court personnel; this has also been the experience of British projects (G. Davis *et al.* 1987: 22).

Three main types of US mediation programmes are those run by the courts (Columbus, and Dorchester); those dependent on them for referrals and subject to their confirmation of dispositions (Boston Municipal Court programme, and IMCR), and those which are independent and non-coercive, hence receiving fewer referrals at a relatively high cost per case, with consequent difficulties in obtaining funding (Venice/Mar Vista, and San Francisco Community Boards). Courts are unwilling to refer relatively serious cases unless they retain control of the ultimate disposition.

For comparison it is worth looking to see how mediation has been transplanted into another country. The Community Justice Centres (CJCs) of New South Wales, Australia, are to some extent based on features selected from various US projects. They use volunteer mediators from a wide range of social and ethnic backgrounds (twenty-three languages besides English in 1984/85), with two mediators in each session; referrals are from a mixture of the justice system, other legal services, other agencies, and self-referrals; agreements are not court-enforceable, but if no agreement is reached, parties retain their right to go to court. Cases all involve relationships; in 1987/88 over a quarter involved violence or threats, and almost a further half, potentially serious incidents such as abuse, harassment, and property damage or theft (CJCs' annual reports). Thus the CJCs can claim that as well as dealing with some crimes, it is reasonably certain that they prevent others.

The CJCs not only have state funding but also are backed by law (Community Justice Centres Act 1983, replacing a provisional act of 1980), which among other things controls the use of the name 'Community Justice Centre', lays down that agreements cannot be imposed by arbitration nor enforced in courts, imposes a duty of confidentiality on mediators; and protects them from having to disclose information. The stated policy is that where the respective bargaining positions of the parties to a dispute are manifestly unequal, the session is terminated by the mediator or the director, and the parties left to pursue legal remedies (speech by the Hon. Francis Walker, Minister for Youth and Community Services, in Second Reading debate on the Act, reprinted in CJCs' Annual Report 1983/84). Police are authorized to refer disputing parties to a CJC rather than arrest them or lay charges. 'These provisions', the minister said, 'have been used extensively in cases of minor assault and other situations where a criminal sanction is unlikely to resolve a continuing dispute.' Where court proceedings are already pending, if the dispute is successfully resolved by mediation, they will normally be discontinued, except in cases of domestic violence. Landlord–tenant disputes are not accepted where the occupancy of the premises is at issue (Faulkes 1982: 42). Under a related Act, courts are given discretion to adjourn proceedings in order to refer cases to mediation. A later speaker in the debate said that Members of Parliament were among those who would welcome the availability of mediation to which they could refer cases.

The primary aims of the three centres, according to the statements given prominence at the beginning of their annual reports, are to be effective in resolving a substantial number of disputes (over a thousand a year); speedy (80 per cent of cases dealt with in less than thirty days), accessible (half the sessions held out of office hours, and one-third of the users were of non-English-speaking origin; the clientele includes some people from professional and managerial occupations), and reasonably inexpensive to the Treasury (just over $A 500 per case heard or conciliated in 1987/88). Importance is attached to the training not only of mediators (with debriefing after each session) but also of intake workers (NJCs Annual Report 1984/85)). The catchment area has been increased. A recent innovation is 'dispute counselling', an effort to provide advice to individuals and the general public about problem-solving 'do's and don'ts' (Annual Report 1987/88).

With their firm base of official support and funding, and several years' experience, they would seem to be capable of extending mediation services to victims and offenders with no prior relationship; but an attempt to start a Juvenile Mediation Reparation Scheme in 1987/88 had to be postponed for lack of funds (Annual Report 1987/88).

Organization

Even from this small selection of mediation programmes major variations are apparent, and for a clearer understanding of their similarities and differences it may be helpful to note their different organizational structures and methods of working. Among the most significant factors determining the nature of a project are its sponsorship and affiliation, its style of operation, and the types of case which it undertakes.

Sponsorship

The bases from which mediation projects operate can be placed on a scale from a western court to a grass-roots network: this, for some proponents, would be an ascending order of preference. Thus we have, among other permutations:

1 Night Prosecutor Program, Columbus, Ohio: sponsorship by the prosecutor's office, with the court, police and others (McGillis 1982: 69). Mediators are law students.
2 Brooklyn Mediation Center, New York: independent management, but operation closely integrated with justice system. Mediators, however, drawn from general public.
3 Boston Municipal Court Mediation Program: independent management, and has to persuade criminal justice system to refer cases. But mediators are lawyers, acting in a voluntary (*pro bono*) capacity.
4 Community Justice Centres, New South Wales, Australia: state funded under special legislation; but day-to-day management independent, with only a minority of cases referred from the justice system. Mediators are volunteers from the community, with emphasis on variety of languages and cultures. Agreements not court-enforceable.
5 Community Boards, San Francisco: independent management, referrals not accepted from justice system (unless it has relinquished jurisdiction). Mediators are volunteers from the community; policy of outreach and public education.
6 Community Association for Mediation, Pittsburgh: initiated and run on a personal basis by a community worker, with informal network of volunteers.

The community-based projects are labelled by Wahrhaftig (1982: 85ff.) as middle-class dominated (4), grass roots (5) and homespun (6).

Individual preferences apart, there are practical advantages and disadvantages in different forms of sponsorship, as McGillis and Mullen (1977: 47ff.) suggest. Private (voluntary sector) sponsorship helps a project to promote an image of neutrality, parties feel less stigmatized by bringing problems to it, there is likely to be more community involvement in management, but there may be difficulty in attracting cases unless good relationships can be developed with referral sources, including courts. Long-term funding may also be hard to secure. Sponsorship by a government agency, conversely, can help in securing referrals and funding; but there is a tendency to put pressure on people to attend, or even to compel them, and to see the goal as easing the load of the system rather than meeting the needs of individuals.

Style of operation

The basic principles of mediation do not vary much between projects, but there are differences in method. The method most widely described is face-to-face mediation, in private, between the parties, with one or two individual sessions if required; the Community Boards conduct sessions in public and do not use individual meetings, while at the other extreme the Newham Conflict and Change Project, in London, apparently places less emphasis on persuading disputants to meet, and relies largely on shuttle diplomacy.

Projects also vary in their degree of coerciveness, which is generally greater with projects more closely integrated with criminal justice. At one end of the spectrum, in the New York Dispute Resolution Center of the IMCR, complainants who report certain classes of criminal acts involving a dispute are referred from the criminal court for mediation. Not only are agreements legally binding and court-enforceable, but also if mediation fails an arbitrated solution can be imposed. Failure to appear or to keep the agreement results in the reactivation of criminal charges (Marshall 1985: 74). At the other extreme are the community-based projects which accept only self-referrals; agreements made there are generally not enforceable, though if the agreement is not kept the parties may be invited to meet and renegotiate it.

Types of cases

The categories of cases accepted by a mediation project depend on its links with the official system and on its philosophy. Community-based projects generally concentrate on neighbourhood disputes, which in legal terms would be classed as 'civil'. Some accept cases that could be treated as criminal, provided the two parties are in a relationship. Others, like Boston, take the latter type of case exclusively. Finally, there are projects which also accept criminal cases where there is no prior relationship (see Chapter 5).

Among the civil dispute resolution projects using mediation, there are also some specializing in particular types of disputes, such as divorce conciliation, small claims, housing, environmental disputes, and customers' complaints (the latter known in the USA as Better Business Bureaux) (McGillis 1982: 65–9). They may specialize, for example, in conflict management in schools; there is often a commitment to spreading understanding of ways of handling conflicts without confrontation. Mediation is of course extensively used in resolving labour disputes – in the United Kingdom by the Advisory, Conciliation, and Arbitration Service (ACAS). Some projects also *ex*clude specific types of disputes, for example those involving domestic violence or (like the Australian CJCs) those where tenants' entitlement to their home is at stake.

Critiques of mediation

The ideal of mediation has not won universal approval. Critics have argued that its advocates are trying to build too many ideals on a base that cannot sustain them, and that in certain circumstances it serves the interests of the powerful or the authorities rather than of those citizens who most need protection. There has also been criticism of some of its techniques, but that is a matter of practice rather than theory, and will not be dealt with in detail here.

Attempting the impossible?

The model of mediation used as an example by Danzig, Christie and others is that of small, relatively simple African societies. Can this nostalgia for the moot be a basis for dispute resolution schemes in complex western societies?

In looking to other cultures for inspiration, it is important not to idealize them: some primitive societies resolve disputes simply by fighting or retaliation. It is true that talking ('jaw-jaw') can reduce tension, but shouting can increase it; in one society, the Jale of the New Guinea Highlands, the language does not contain a word for settlement-directed talk, apart from one translated as 'shouting match' (Roberts 1979: 15, 116–20). Some simple communities, in addition to mediation, use coercive and even violent enforcement; the people's courts in socialist countries, which some have taken as a model, are often committed to implanting a new ideology, and some are empowered to impose penalties (Merry 1982: 173–4). (Or at least they were; the situation since the revolutions of 1989 is not yet clear.) It has also been suggested, for example by Felstiner (1974), that methods suitable for technologically simple, poor societies, with strong informal social control and little mobility, are not appropriate to technologically complex, rich societies where, among other things, it is much more feasible to deal with disputes by avoidance – 'lumping it'. But these reservations about mediation, expressed when the movement for neighbourhood dispute resolution had not been under way for very long, were questioned by Danzig and Lowy (1975); they conceded that mediation is not useful in all settings in a country like the United States, but considered that Felstiner underestimated both the demand for mediation and the personal costs of avoidance.

Others have criticized the over-optimistic reliance on 'community' initiatives, when all that can really be said of them is that they are local (Marshall 1986). If the legal system needs reform, we should not look for solutions to the 'mythical "community"' (Hofrichter 1977/1982: 246); 'community' can be an 'aerosol word' sprayed over deteriorating institutions (Basten 1982: 29). The concept of community is analysed by Wahrhaftig (1982: 95–7), who concludes that it should be seen as a network of relationships. This definition, however, tends to limit the size of the community, which in turn limits the potential caseload of community-based projects, and creates pressure to increase it either by obtaining referrals from the justice system or by extending the catchment area beyond the community. Without this, the project will, in order to remain solvent, have to obtain funding outside its municipality or rely on voluntary staffing.

One critic, Jerold Auerbach, considered that community dispute resolution worked where it was indigenous to an immigrant community – Jewish or Chinese for example – but became an instrument of extended social control when it was an adjunct of the traditional justice system, used mainly by the disadvantaged for whom the courts are often inaccessible (Auerbach 1983: 114, 120–5). This view assumes that traditional justice is the preferable method of resolving disputes, which is precisely what advocates of mediation were challenging. But some of them would agree with Auerbach, first, in being suspicious of 'top-down' introduction of what they wanted to be a grass-roots movement; Wahrhaftig, Shonholtz and others argued that the Neighborhood Justice Centers should be community based, and in the case of Venice/Mar Vista succeeded to some extent (Wahrhaftig, personal communication 1988). The Community Boards of San Francisco, initiated by Shonholtz in 1976, refused to take cases over which the official justice system still had any control. Second, many accepted that in some cases, for example where there was great disparity of power between the disputants and no genuine commitment to compromise on the part of the more powerful, for example a landlord, legal redress could be more appropriate.

But it is possible that mediation, besides resolving individual disputes, can contribute to the rehabilitation of communities. Sally Engle Merry, by no means an uncritical advocate of mediation, suggests that neighbourhood justice centres can limit the power of the State over the lives of individual citizens, and provide them with a greater ability to cope with their problems (Merry 1982: 188); but Tomasic, in the same volume, is not optimistic (1982: 230). More recently a British observer, Roger Matthews, after a review of the critical literature, has concluded that what he calls 'informal courts' (a term mediators would reject) can not only resolve conflicts which would mostly not have reached the courts, but also prevent them and transform them (1988: 23). And in objecting to planning 'from the top down' one has to be clear what is meant. Without it, will anything happen? When a community is in decline, and potential leaders within it have either left or become dispirited, any move to rehabilitate it is likely to require a stimulus from outside. There does not seem to be anything inherently wrong with this, provided that the initiators from outside act only as catalysts, enablers, and involve indigenous people fully from the outset. Raymond Shonholtz emerged from the university, not the community, to found the grass-roots Community Boards Program, and Gloria Patterson, originator of the 'homespun' Community Association for Mediation in Pittsburgh, had been 'thoroughly indoctrinated in mediation' by working for the American Friends' Service Committee (Wahrhaftig 1982: 89, 94). Perhaps there are advantages in initiatives at least from the 'middle' down.

Whose interests are served?

Two criticisms of mediation are that it serves the interests of one of the parties at the expense of the other, and that it benefits the justice system more than either. Can true mediation take place where one party has much more administrative or economic power, or personal dominance, than the other, or is physically violent? This could happen where an individual had a dispute with a large company (as customer or employee), a local authority (perhaps as a tenant), or an aggressive member of the family. The answer will depend on circumstances. The essential prerequisite is that both sides are willing to negotiate in good faith, and not use mediation to legitimize an unfair solution. To some extent it is possible for the mediators to redress the balance, for example by allowing each side roughly equal speaking time, by discreetly helping less articulate people to express their point of view, and by not calling some 'Mr' or 'Mrs' and others by their first name (unless they are children, of course). Mediators can also use information elicited from the weaker party during a private session to stiffen his resolve, or they can discourage him from concluding an agreement that does not give him his due. Some mediation schemes have a policy of excluding such disputes: for example rather than let landlords (municipal or private) 'divide and rule' their tenants by negotiating with some individuals while continuing to exploit the less assertive ones, it might be better to encourage all the tenants to take collective action or go to law. Mediation initiatives, if they are alive to this, can act as centres for the collection of such information, so that individual grievances can be transformed into effective political action (Merry 1982: 188–9); thus they can help a demoralized community to rehabilitate itself. Mediation between even quite large groups is possible, however, provided each can agree on a small number of spokespeople. In cases where a child is at odds with a school, there is certainly disparity of power; but where deadlock has been reached over some breach of school rules, or simply non-attendance, mediation can let both sides off the hook, provided always that both are genuinely willing to negotiate. This can be helpful to the school, in finding out the real cause of the child's resistance; the child can ask the school to agree to make some change, which shows that it cares about the child, and may benefit other pupils as well. Sometimes power is only apparent. Fisher and Ury, in their best-selling guide to the use of mediation *Getting to Yes*, give the example of a wealthy tourist who wants to buy a brass pot from a vendor at Bombay railway station: the vendor, though poor, knows the market, but the tourist is in a hurry and may not know whether it would be difficult, or more costly, to buy a similar pot elsewhere (Fisher and Ury 1987: 106–7).

A substantial strand of criticism is based not so much on mediation in itself as on the relationship of some projects with the established judicial system. Critics like Harrington see Neighborhood Justice Centers as not so much a non-adversarial, problem-solving approach to disputes, offering welcome relief from the delays and protocol of the official system, as an informal 'shadow justice' which 'expands the capacity of the justice system to manage minor conflicts' and attempts to persuade people to seek consensus at the expense of their legally enforceable rights (Harrington 1985: 170, 173). In the same vein Abel takes informal justice apart. It is coercive, and adds to social control of the economically, socially and politically oppressed (Abel 1982: 271–4). Neighbourhood justice is a myth, because there are few neighbourhoods (1982: 277). Abel does not see mediation offering a way of resolving disputes which people find hard to handle, but 'state informal control' undermining time-honoured informal social controls such as gossip, boycott and self-help (does he mean taking the law into their own hands?), and perpetuating the 'theft of the conflict' identified by Christie (1977). In relation to disputes between customers and merchants, employees and employers, informal procedures 'neutralize conflict that could threaten state or capital,' for example by increasing the proportion of claims paid so that almost every claimant gets something, but reducing the amount paid to each (Abel 1982: 280–1). 'The proponents of informalism seek to reduce conflict by curtailing demands, never acknowledging that just as much conflict would be eliminated if those to whom the demands are addressed would accede – cease discriminating, polluting, exploiting, oppressing' (Abel 1982: 285).

These criticisms cannot be ignored, but they cannot be accepted without question. Some mediators might wonder if they are working in the same movement as Harrington and Abel describe, with their references to coercion, penalties and judgment (Abel 1982: 270–1, 274). Mediation can operate in different ways. Some projects are court-based, the agreements reached are court-enforceable, and disputants cannot get access to the courts without attempting to reach agreement first. Others are independent, agreements are not court-enforceable, and they provide an alternative for those who prefer not to litigate. Mediators recognize that there are some disputes which are not suitable for mediation; it might be more appropriate, for example, for tenants to combine and take legal action against a negligent landlord. Abel himself asks rhetorically whether informal methods equalize or aggravate inequalities, increase or curtail popular participation, accelerate or delay the process, and so on, and concludes that 'The answer to virtually every question will be – both' (Abel 1982: 270). Many users like informal procedures (1982: 283), and Abel concludes that informalism is not an 'evil to be resisted'; it expresses values such as the preference for harmony over conflict, mechanisms that offer access to the many, quickly and cheaply, and achieve substantive justice rather than frustrating it in the name of form. Abel's views can be taken as a salutary warning of how mediation projects could be, and in some cases have been, absorbed into the existing system's values and power structure (though not as universally as he implies). That leaves two other possibilities: that the formal system should adopt the best values of mediation, as Abel would prefer, and/or that independently based mediation offers a method that is preferable because it is nearer to the people it serves, spreads knowledge of a different approach to handling conflict, and may help a little to re-create local communities.

Domestic violence

Domestic violence is particularly hard to handle, and there is concern that, for example, a battered wife may 'mediate her rights away' and be persuaded to return home where her husband will soon break his agreement and assault her yet again. This is an important question, and worth considering in some detail. In one of the large New York mediation schemes, the problem is tackled by modifying the neutral role of the mediator. It is impressed on mediators at the IMCR in New York, for example, that mediation does not necessarily lead to reconciliation, but may be a more human way of agreeing to end a relationship (as in a case I observed there – Wright 1982: 248–9). Mediators there are trained to do some counselling as well as mediating, and to make sure that the complainant is informed of all the options available to her before she agrees to anything, and especially before she agrees to return to a husband who has been violent (as I was told by Chris Whipple, Director of Mediation Services at the Victim Services Agency in New York). The project does however, try to screen out cases where there is evidence of chronic violence, for example at the pre-mediation meetings which are held with complainants and respondents separately. Whipple said: 'We also train mediators not to be neutral with respect to violence, and to play a policing, warning role before the session, to warn a wife-abuser that violence is illegal and inexcusable. They remind him that the complainant can request criminal charges at any point, and all the existing sanctions are available as a deterrent.' In keeping with the usual mediating practice, the man is not asked to admit having been violent; but he is warned 'not to do it again'.

At the Brooklyn Mediation Center itself, I was told by its director, Mark Smith, that every case is followed up to see if reparation has been paid, premises vacated, and so on. 'But if there is any violence, we do not play games: the case is sent straight to the District Attorney's office.' Counselling services are also available as part of the follow-up; there is a human response to offenders but they are reminded of the consequences of any violation of their agreement. In New York, according to Smith, 80 per cent of murders involve relationships, and the Center believes that it may be preventing some by helping parties to resolve their differences at an early stage.

Particular attention has been paid to the issue of domestic violence by the Salem Mediation Program, Massachusetts, which started in 1979. Its former director, Suzanne Goulet Orenstein, studied the results of a hundred domestic violence cases handled over thirty months (about one-sixth of the project's mediations). She found that conventional court proceedings are 'brief, formal and narrowly focused, giving the parties little opportunity to express their feelings on the full range of their needs', or to become less angry. On the contrary, the court order, even if obeyed, often arouses resistance which is expressed in indirect ways: by not paying maintenance, or picking arguments over access to the children. Mediation helps to lessen that resistance and its consequences.

One response to violent partners, especially in the United States, has been the introduction of mandatory arrest laws, in which police are *required* to make warrantless arrests in certain domestic violence cases. It is suggested that this is more effective in preventing recidivism than other methods. In a study reported by Humphreys and Humphreys (1985) and Edwards (1989: 192–3) police officers responded to cases either by arrest, or by sending the man away for eight hours, or by giving 'some sort of advice or mediation.' Allocation was by lot. It was found that repeat violence was less among the men arrested, but there are problems with experiments of this kind. Random allocation means that there is no means of even attempting to select the appropriate disposal for particular individuals. The removal of discretion from the police, apart from being unpopular with them, is likely to lead to its reappearance elsewhere, for example in decisions by prosecutors. A fair assessment depends on the alternative, such as the quality of the 'advice or mediation' offered by the police officers, as Edwards (1989) points out. However, with such a serious type of offence, it is essential to keep all options open, and coercion is likely to be necessary in some cases if not all.

Some of these approaches imply an either/or response, but other possibilities are '. . . or else' and 'both/and'. An example of the former is the police early intervention scheme in Streatham, London, where men who have inflicted 'minor' injuries are arrested for a few hours' cooling-off period. If the man admits the offence and has no record of previous assaults on his partner, and she does not wish to press charges, the decision to charge or caution him is deferred for two months. (This period could be used for counselling, a self-help group or mediation, where suitable and available, for example to agree on access to children if the couple separates. The mediation would need to be done in a proper setting, not by a police officer on the doorstep; any counselling should be of a high standard.)

In this project's first few months only four out of seventy-seven men reoffended. But one of these offences involved serious violence; the director of Chiswick Family Rescue, Sandra Horley, therefore says that 'Giving violent men a second chance puts women in danger', and calls for a policy with a 'known measure of success': arrest, charging and prosecution, and 'realistic sentences for men so that the violence is not repeated' (Horley 1990). Unfortunately there is no conclusive evidence that this produces a lower failure rate: it may discourage reporting, and it is also possible that if they had been imprisoned, a larger number would have committed serious violence after release. It does seem that early police intervention can significantly deter repeated abuse and homicide (Edwards 1989: 192), but other things being equal, a policy with potential for developing insight and leaving the parties on speaking terms, even if separated, would appear to have advantages over one based solely on deterrence, not least because of the inseparable counter-deterrent effects.

A parallel may be drawn with another form of violence. The former Home Secretary, Mr David Waddington, has described how the incidence of assault in a Glasgow housing benefit office was reduced: not, as one might have expected, by installing extra security measures but by removing some screens and improving a waiting area. Making the office less forbidding and the staff more approachable resulted in less aggressive behaviour. Similarly the Abbey National building society and bank, valuing customer contact, installed pop-up bullet-proof screens, which can be in place in 0.2 seconds, rather than erect barriers; since they were installed there has been no successful raid or hostage-taking of a customer (*Victim Support* June 1990).

There may be advantages in the 'both/and' approach, combining the force of the law with mediation. Under the Massachusetts Abuse Protection Act 1978 (sec. 209A) a victim of family violence, including forced sexual relations, can apply for an emergency order that the alleged perpetrator must refrain from abuse, or leave the premises, initially for five days. Among the cases where '209A orders' were made, more than half the men, but few women, initially stated that their aim was reconciliation; in the whole sample only nine agreements called for reconciliations or trial reconciliations. In this way, contrary to Auerbach's assertion (1983: 120), the woman loses none of the protection of the law, but gains the opportunity to end (or resume) the relationship on a basis agreed by the two partners personally. Often the judge makes a referral to mediation immediately after making the 209A order. Orenstein (1982) suggests that the mediation helps the man to accept that the woman does not want to return; they can then begin to make decisions about children, property and so on. Over 80 per cent of these agreements are kept for at least the programme's three-month follow-up period. (Figures for a longer period are unfortunately not given.)

Where the couple had already been separated for some time, fewer said they wanted reconciliation. Usually there was no 209A order, because the problem was not an emergency but intermittent harassment. The results here are slightly less good than with the 209A cases, but even so 74 per cent of those referred agree to mediate, and 60 per cent of the agreements were kept for at least three months.

When an agreement has been broken (or was made for a limited period in the first place) a second session can be arranged: these have so far always ended in agreement. Alternatively the woman can return to court and apply for existing remedies.

In short, for a woman to 'mediate her rights away' would not be impossible, but it can be guarded against, both by the way mediation is conducted and by preserving the existing protection of the law. Many women, I was told, are clear about what they want – for example to continue the relationship provided the man will stop being violent, or to end it even if he cannot afford to pay maintenance – and do not want to be pushed by lawyers into making a lot of extra demands. Where mediation is successful it provides a less hurtful way of resolving the situation; even where no agreement is reached, organizers told me that to meet and discuss things in a structured setting helps participants to a better understanding of each other's feelings. One aspect of inequality is that the weaker party could be under pressure to accept too little, in the hope of obtaining

an agreement and being left in peace. Some mediators might be tempted to
encourage a person to settle for less than his or her rights, in order to 'chalk up'
another agreement. This has to be weighed against the common complaint that
lawyers often push their clients into demanding everything possible, when one or
two key items would be enough; mediators, too, might be protective of disadvantaged clients and urge them to ask for more than they want. It has been suggested
that if maintenance were negotiated by mediation, a husband could fare better
than in court, because mediators lack the lawyer's power to require disclosure of
assets (Weigend 1981: 33). But respondents who are in a strong economic position, even if their case is weak, can in any case wait out complainants' (costly)
efforts to sue them in court.

The advocates of mediation offer various answers to such charges. One is to
train mediators to compensate for inequalities, for example by the methods outlined on p. 68, and by making it clear that certain behaviour, particularly violence, is non-negotiable. Second, where the rights of a spouse, tenant or
employee are at issue, the complainant should be encouraged to check the negotiated agreement with a lawyer before signing it. For example, the director of the
Dispute Settlement Center in Cambridge, Massachusetts, John Mack, told me in
1983: 'We would advise the tenant and give him a list of places to go and find
out about rights. For divorce cases we practically require them to see a lawyer,
or at least we give time to consult, say a relative.' Similarly, a leaflet of the
Family Mediation Service (FMS) in Washington, DC, states

> Participants must be assured that their legal rights will not be compromised
> in any way. At FMS each party is urged to consult with his or her own
> attorney at the beginning and end of the mediation process. Parties may
> consult any attorney of their choice or may choose from a list of names pro-
> vided by FMS.

At Salem Mediation Center, if there was any suggestion of violence, a woman
would obtain an injunction to restrain a man: mediation was used to complement
the law, not as a substitute (Orenstein 1982).

The third safeguard practised by some projects is simply not to accept certain
types of cases. It has therefore been proposed, notably by Professor Frank
Sander (1976/1982: 37), that mediation, courts and other services could be
housed in a 'multi-door courthouse' so that applicants could be referred to the
appropriate service within one building. The first such centre, the Tulsa,
Oklahoma, Citizens Complaint Center, was opened in 1984 (*Tulsa Daily
Business Journal and Legal Record* 24 October 1984); others were established in
Houston, Texas, and Washington, DC. All are backed by the legal profession,
and by 1986 an assessment had found that they were handling from 120 to 600
cases a month; over 80 per cent of users were satisfied and would use them again
(*Dispute Resolution* (American Bar Association) 1986 (20): 6–7).

Is mediation an appropriate technique in cases of racial harassment? Where
this arises from deliberate politically motivated persecution, it is difficult to

envisage. But in a neighbour dispute with racial overtones, the position of victims has parallels with that of battered women. If they involve the police or the local authority housing department, that in itself could aggravate the ill-feeling while waiting for action such as prosecution or a compulsory transfer of the harassers, which requires proof and takes time. In mediation, on the other hand, it is not necessary to establish the precise facts, and the process of meeting has potential for increasing understanding and casting doubt on stereotypes. While it may not be appropriate for all cases, therefore, it is worth considering as a first step.

Second-class justice for the poor?

Some critics fear that mediation is a way of providing second-class, low-cost justice for people with low incomes, particularly in the United States where the State provides little financial support for litigation (e.g. Marks *et al.* 1984: 51–2). Some projects, which have not arisen from a secure base within the community, appear to be operating largely as a safety-valve easing the pressure on the courts. Provided the cases referred are the most suitable, this creates no problem for a mediation project. Another suggestion, however, is that cases referred by police or courts may be those which no one else wants: the mediation project becomes a 'dumping ground'. This could also 'widen the net', if the agreement is court-enforceable; when it is broken, and a sanction is imposed, the offender is worse off than if mediation had not existed. This danger could be avoided either by making mediated agreements not enforceable in court, and relying on persuasion; or by defining types of offences, such as assaults, harassment, and theft and property damage among parties known to each other, where mediation would normally be available in preference to courts (Weigend 1981: 45–8), or where an attempt at mediation would be required before the case could proceed to the criminal court, as in the *Schiedsmann* (official mediator) system in the Federal Republic of Germany. This is a form of coercion *into* mediation, but Professor Sander considers that 'modest pressure' of this kind can be regarded as acceptable: it is coercion *within* mediation that must be avoided (Sander 1984: 106–7). In civil proceedings, rather more than modest pressure is now applied by *Schiedsmänner* in North Rhine-Westphalia: since 1 January 1984, when one party lodges a complaint, both must appear at a hearing before the official mediator, on pain of a penalty. The number of cases dealt with before the *Schiedsmänner* has gone up, with no reduction in the proportion settled; thus those who appear under penalty are not less willing to reach agreement (*Schiedsmannszeitung* 1989 (4): 49–56). Like the coercion in criminal cases in Brooklyn (see p. 58) however, this is likely to arouse suspicions of excessive social control among both radical legal critics of mediation and its grass-roots activist supporters.

Mediation has to co-exist, for the time being at least, with the courts. The nature of this relationship is a further subject of debate. For some, the courts are there as a safeguard, to deal with cases not suitable for mediation or to enforce mediation agreements that have not been kept. Others see this as an example of the courts' reluctance to let go; Merry, for example, thinks that 'mediation programs could be more creative in developing non-court forms of pressure' to observe agreements, and finds it ironic that the mediation movement, which was set up to offer a more appropriate mechanism for resolving conflicts, relies heavily on the courts to generate referrals and to enforce agreements (Merry 1982: 180).

In Australia the charge of 'second-class justice' to which low-income groups are 'shunted' (Tomasic 1982: 246) has been robustly answered by Kevin Anderson, Deputy Chief Stipendiary Magistrate of New South Wales: 'In 35 years in magistrates' courts administration, I have not seen many examples of first class justice' (Anderson 1982: 246). In the United States, people who can afford to choose are using professional mediation; indeed there is a counter-assertion that privately financed dispute resolution systems could become a 'luxury class justice' accessible only to large corporations and other major litigants (Marks *et al.* 1984: 52–3). The answer seems to be that mediation has great potential for resolving at least some kinds of disputes; the fairness or otherwise depends on whether it is available to anyone who could benefit by it.

Is mediation succeeding?

Advocates of mediation maintain that it offers a way of resolving disputes for people who would otherwise have to choose between passive endurance, private retaliation or the vagaries of the courts; and that in so doing it can empower not only those individuals but also whole communities. Critics question whether the agreements reached are always more satisfactory to the weaker party than would have been achieved in court; they also suggest that mediation projects have often been co-opted by the courts, first into easing pressure on the official system by accepting its overload, and second into allowing courts to retain the final say in the disposition of cases.

As always in evaluating initiatives of this kind (including reparation, see pp. 45–7), it is necessary to agree not only on the principal aims but also on their order of priority if there should be competing interests. Then ways have to be found of assessing the attainment of these, and not merely of subsidiary ones which happen to be easier to measure, unless that is the only feasible approximation. The primary aim could be regarded as the 'product', the subsidiary ones as aspects of 'quality control.' For example if a project aims primarily at satisfying its participants, some extra expense may be tolerable, but exorbitant costs would invalidate it, even though the primary aim was achieved. Conversely if a project set saving costs or relieving the traditional system as its primary aim, it could be invalidated if individuals were highly dissatisfied or their rights infringed.

There is a lack of agreement on the primary aim of mediation. Is it to divert part of the caseload of the criminal justice system, or to provide a service to ordinary citizens (Marshall 1985: 76)? Is the project aiming to be a mediation programme or a community programme?

If the basic concern is particular participants and the failure of the criminal justice system to meet their needs, the mediation services ought to be provided by a small number of experienced, highly motivated and closely supervised mediators. If on the other hand, mediation is seen as an aspect of a community's struggle to settle its own quarrels, to take responsibility for its own social control and its own fate, then the base of mediators must be broad, even at the cost of less effective individual mediations (Felstiner and Williams 1980: 122–3): These aims were balanced in one project in a Hispanic area of New York by recruiting community leaders and opinion-formers for the first intake of mediators, so that they would spread the word about mediation; for later intakes, selection was primarily on criteria of suitability as mediators (interview with Dana Vermilye, Washington Heights, NY, October 1983). Advocates of community mediation would argue that trained lay mediators are in some ways better than professionals at individual mediation. They are more readily available out of working hours. They tend not to become 'case-hardened' because they undertake fewer cases; with their community contacts, they spread knowledge of mediation among friends and colleagues. They need supervision and support; but in a good project, with regular feedback and monitoring, they probably receive more than, for example, lay magistrates.

Other possible benefits are listed by McGillis (1982: 62, 74):

1 *Benefits for individuals in dispute:* a better way of handling conflict because disputants can explore underlying problems, without lawyers and the restrictions of legal procedure; and improved access to this service.
2 *Benefits to the community:* enhancement of community power *vis-à-vis* the authorities, by teaching citizens a new technique for solving problems collectively; improving the quality of life through increased citizen participation in major life decisions; reducing community tensions through effective conflict resolution.
3 *Benefits to the justice system:* diverting cases from the courts, freeing them to attend to more serious cases.

Many projects would claim to work towards all three of these, but there are bound to be circumstances where one aim can be achieved only at the expense of another. Projects could be evaluated more clearly if each would define its priority: indeed this would help the mediation movement itself to work towards a consensus.

In practice, the needs of the judicial system, as a criterion for 'success', have taken precedence over those of individuals and the community, and many projects have acquiesced in this because they depend on the justice system for an adequate supply of referrals, according to Professor Sally Merry. She found (1982: 181–90) that evaluations tend to focus on caseload data such as numbers, speed and costs.

As regards access to justice, clearly this is not much improved if a project obtains most of its referrals from the court: the participants will by definition already have found their way there. But if the primary claim for mediation is that it is superior to traditional adjudication, at least for certain types of case, then a transfer of such cases from the latter to the former can be counted as success. The quality of the process itself is harder to assess, which may be why Merry found no study that had investigated it (1982: 187). It is impossible for researchers to determine what would be a just result in each of the cases examined, and then measure the proportion in which the actual outcome coincided with it; they are therefore thrown back on assessing users' satisfaction. Some disputants may be satisfied with something less than justice, either because they are unaware of their rights or because the process of mediation is more congenial and makes a less-than-ideal outcome acceptable. There is of course no guarantee that they would have fared better under the traditional system. Also some criteria can be monitored by day-to-day record-keeping in the project, while others require special research.

The criterion of empowering the community appears to be regarded, for example by Wahrhaftig (1982), as much the same as empowering individuals: the latter leads to the former. If anything, he seems to put the interests of the community first, implying that a project is failing in its task if it does not collect and collate information about community problems, in addition to helping individuals with disputes. Wahrhaftig suggests as criteria: Has the project acted as a mechanism for community fact-finding? Is it run by the community served or by a more educated elite? Has the community changed since the project started, and would any difference be noticed if it stopped? (See for example his comments on IMCR and other projects – Wahrhaftig 1982: 80–1, 85, 87.) There are various indicators of community involvement in a project, such as whether the community's social, ethnic and linguistic composition is reflected among the members of the management committee and the volunteer mediators; actual influence would have to be inferred from events which demonstrate whether members of the community had acquired, or regained, the capacity to negotiate with the local authority, large landlords, local firms, and the like, about matters of communal concern.

The direct impact on the justice system, if any, could ultimately be mainly in the form of a numerical reduction of caseload, although only the large US projects closely integrated with the traditional system have achieved this so far. It is also possible that mediation projects may have an indirect effect on its procedures. As Tony Marshall, director of FIRM, comments (1988a: 50), the idea of 'co-operative problem solving', in the eyes of many of its advocates, 'could, if it attracts widespread adherence, constitute a reform of fundamental proportions in the nature of society.' The effect on the number of cases, whether civil or criminal, transferred from the courts to mediation, is limited by the basic premiss that all involve some form of relationship between the parties. The impact on the system, as well as on individuals, is considerably widened if mediation is introduced in criminal cases where there was no prior relationship (this development will be considered in Chapter 5).

The return of the victim
to the criminal process

Mennonites are a Protestant church, with a strong tradition of social service; they are active in Ontario, Indiana, Pennsylvania and elsewhere. In 1968 the Mennonite Central Committee (MCC) of Ontario appointed a study committee to seek a concept for dealing with offenders without bricks and mortar. It considered how forgiveness and making a fresh start, without forgetting the past, 'could be a central concept in an alternative to the criminal justice system as it was operating'. (This summary is based mainly on accounts by Bender 1984, 1985, and Peachey 1989.) It took note of, among other initiatives, the Night Prosecutor Program in Columbus, Ohio, and the community service orders, which started to operate in Britain in 1973.

This chapter will trace how that initiative, in North America and Britain, brought together the ideas of reparation by offenders and conflict resolution through mediation, and led to the development of victim/offender mediation projects. It will attempt to classify these projects, outline some of the main evaluations so far published, and then consider some critiques of the theory and practice, including the views of a number of practitioners in Canada and the United States.

The Canadian prototype

In 1974 a Mennonite probation officer, Mark Yantzi, suggested to the MCC group that, in a current vandalism case in the nearby town of Elmira, it would be a good idea for the two teenage offenders to meet their victims. He dismissed his own idea as impractical but, challenged to pursue it by an MCC-supported volunteer, Dave Worth, he suggested to the judge that 'there could be some therapeutic value in these two young men having to personally face up to the victims of their numerous offences'. To everyone's surprise the judge, Gordon McConnell, agreed. Yantzi and Worth set off to visit all the twenty-two victims (except two who had moved) with the offenders, who had each been ordered to pay, within three months, a fine of $200 and compensation to the victims for their uninsured losses. This amounted to $550 for each youth and was duly paid.

The following year, with support from the MCC, the Ontario Ministry of Corrections and the Area Probation Officer John Gaskell, the Victim/Offender Reconciliation Project (later Programme) was set up, and known by its acronym VORP. Three noteworthy features were present from the start. The impetus came originally from the search for alternatives not only to the use of custody but also, more radically, to the criminal justice process itself; reconciliation, rather than mere reparation, was a primary concept (although reparation would often be its symbolic expression); implementation was dependent on gaining the interest of the court, which was achieved by stressing advantages such as the 'therapeutic' effects on offenders, which were thought likely to appeal to courts but were not necessarily first in the project's own order of priorities.

Later, Yantzi and Worth assimilated the idea of Christie (1977) that the State and professionals had 'stolen' the conflict from the participants, who should be empowered to resolve it themselves. Another significant force in the development of VORP was its Christian inspiration, stressed by Mennonite writers such as Howard Zehr (1982, 1990). This was, however, not in the retributive tradition of Christian writers like Kant, nor even of more humane ones like Sir Walter Moberly, whose book *The Ethics of Punishment* (1968) explores the disadvantages of punishment but in the end reluctantly concludes that it can be justified. Zehr on the other hand points to the rabbinical tradition that Old Testament justice is based on the limitation of retaliation (*not more than* an eye for an eye), on reparation (*the value of* an eye for an eye), and on the restoration of *shalom*: peace combined with justice, harmony and right relationships. The New Testament goes further: Jesus and his apostles repeatedly called for a non-judgemental response (for example to the woman taken in adultery, *St John*: ch. 8), and appeared to reject the idea of just, or proportional, rewards and punishments (in the parable of the labourers in the vineyard, *St Matthew*: ch. 20). He emphasized unconditional love, forgiveness and reconciliation as a way to persuade people to change, rather than coercion (Zehr 1982: 5–6, 16–18). Zehr was also one of those who focused on the position of victims, and the 'second victimization' which many of them experience at the hands of the criminal justice system. The contrast with popular conceptions is illustrated by an incident which Bender recounts (1985: 6): a television producer heard of VORP at a conference on restitution and filmed a victim/offender meeting, but the film was not used because there was no fiery confrontation – just people sitting down working out an agreement.

Meanwhile the idea of VORP spread over the border to the Mennonite community in Elkhart, Indiana. Edgar Epp, an adviser to the Mennonite Central Committee, formerly superintendent of two prisons and deputy minister of corrections in British Columbia, was invited to speak there in 1976. The following year a member of the probation staff was appointed to spend half her time organizing a VORP for juveniles. In order to expand, however, it was felt that a base in the community rather than the probation service was needed, in keeping with the project's growing use of volunteers as mediators. A Mennonite organization for ex-offenders released Howard Zehr, its director, half-time to run it. In 1979 it moved to its own office on a shoestring budget, and in 1984 under a new director, Mark Chupp, it severed its link with Prisoners and Community Together (PACT) and became the Center for Community Justice.

Both in Canada and the United States VORP remains, however, inevitably in a close relationship with the criminal justice system. In Canada the courts could order that an offender should attempt to come to mutual agreement with the victim regarding restitution, or else be referred back to court. But in 1982 the Ontario Court of Appeal found that courts had no power to delegate the decision in this way (in the case of *R.* v. *Hudson*), and the number of referrals, and of VORP programmes, in Ontario has been in decline. The dependence of the Elkhart VORP was exemplified in 1983 when it obtained a grant of $86,000 under Indiana's Community Corrections Act. The purpose was 'providing an effective alternative to imprisonment at the State level'. To achieve this, VORP was given a strong incentive to persuade judges to pass non-custodial sentences: its grant would be cut each time a person was sentenced to a state prison, except for specified serious offences where courts could not be expected (or even permitted, under Indiana's severe law) to pass anything but an immediate prison sentence (circular letter from David Rathbone, Director of Court services, Elkhart, to local judges 10 November 1983). This is a more restrictive variant of the California Probation Subsidy system, under which probation projects received grants in proportion to the reduction in the number of offenders received into prison (R. Smith 1972; Wright 1982: 152–6).

On the basis of his experience in VORP, Zehr (1985, 1990) has proposed a new paradigm. The traditional assumption, he writes, is that 'We define crime as an offense against the state. We define justice as the establishment of blame and the imposition of pain under the guidance of right rules.' But, drawing an analogy with Copernicus, he points out that this is not the only possible paradigm. He draws on the Old Testament concept of *shalom*, making things right, living in peace and harmony with one another in right relationship. Crime is a wound in human relationships, and creates an obligation to restore, to repair. Thus Zehr's new paradigm defines crime as a conflict not between the individual and the State, but between individuals. It encourages victim and offender to see one another as persons. The old paradigm's focus is on blame-fixing for the past; the new one, while encouraging responsibility for past behaviour, looks to the future, problem-solving, the obligations created by the offence:

> Instead of 'paying a debt to society' by experiencing punishment, accountability would mean understanding and taking responsibility for what has been done and taking action to make things right. Instead of owing an abstract debt to society, paid in an abstract way by experiencing punishment, the offender would owe a debt to the victim, to be repaid in a concrete way.
>
> (Zehr 1985: 15)

This view is taken a step further by Professor Herman Bianchi, of the Free University, Amsterdam. He points out that traditional justice is based on the consensus model of the State, in which there is assumed to be a uniform culture and system of norms. He says that except in penal law an 'assensus model' operates, in which there is no unanimity but a constant discussion of basic norms and values. An implication of this is that crimes against other individuals would be treated as torts. Recognizing that serious acts could put the perpetrator at risk from other citizens, he proposes a reintroduction of the ancient practice of sanctuary: the perpetrator would be able to go to a place of safety from which he would negotiate appropriate reparation (Bianchi 1978, 1980).

Victims meet offenders in Britain

In Britain initiatives for involving victims in the reparative process came from most of the principal agencies involved in criminal justice, or at least from individuals within them: the police, probation and prison services, NACRO (National Association for the Care and Resettlement of Offenders) and Victim Support (the National Association of Victims Support Schemes, NAVSS). In the courts, several judges, magistrates and justices' clerks were prepared to support projects once established. To some extent projects reflected their origins. Where the initiative came from the police, projects tended to focus on juvenile liaison schemes and use of the police caution. A major concern of probation is to promote alternatives to custody: this was given prominence at the Leeds Reparation Project. In the West Midlands, however, John Harding and his probation colleagues felt that a multi-agency approach would strengthen projects' ability to set their own agenda, on behalf of both victims and offenders, rather than adopt the offender-oriented tradition of the criminal justice system; of the three West Midlands projects one has an independent committee (Coventry), one was based on a voluntary organization (The Crypt), and Sandwell, after an ill-defined start, has an independent elected committee (Cowell 1989: 49–50).

First in chronological order had been the work of Philip Priestley, of NACRO's South Western Region (which was also instrumental in creating the first victim support scheme). In 1969 Priestley set up a discussion group with victims, offenders and others associated with criminal justice. The participants suggested that the existing system did not provide emotional support for victims, nor an opportunity for offenders to experience the feelings of their victims towards them (which might be bitter or constructive). Those offenders who wished to make reparation could not do so, apart from the 'clumsy provisions of a restitution order' (Priestley 1970: 3). Priestley made a plea for positive justice based on restitution and reparation, rather than negative justice based on retaliation and retribution (Harding 1989). One person receptive to these ideas was John Harding, who had directed one of the first community service order schemes, and held senior probation posts successively in Devon (at the time of the Exeter initiative), the West Midlands and Hampshire. He went to the United States in 1975 and 1980 and described reparation projects there, although the ones he visited made little use of mediation (Harding 1980; 1982).

In Devon the police, social services and probation departments offered juveniles the opportunity to make an apology and sometimes reparation, after the police had decided to caution rather than prosecute the offender. The reparation scheme of the Exeter Joint Services Youth Support Team, begun in 1979, is still in operation. Offenders are diverted into the project only where the offence is admitted by the offender, both parties (and the juveniles' parents) agree to it after having it explained, and the experience is likely to be beneficial to them. Usually a fairly simple meeting, with an apology by the offender, takes place, but there is a more conflict-resolving form of mediation in a few more serious cases such as assaults (Harding 1989; Veevers 1989).

This was followed in 1981 by a similar policy in the Juvenile Liaison Bureaux of Northamptonshire to increase the use of police cautions, in the spirit of the Children and Young Persons Act of 1969. Reparation, with or without contacts between victim and offender, was only one part of this, and it was offender-oriented – its aims contain no mention of victims (Northamptonshire County Council 1985: 4). Nevertheless, 77 of the 492 people referred in 1981/82 took part in offence resolution (Blagg 1985: 268). Of these, 48 offenders met their victims; the remainder made indirect reparation through a community task. Blagg concludes that face-to-face meetings work better when conducted with a personal victim as opposed to the representative of an organization such as a shop or factory, but his sample was small, and his findings could mean merely that the managers he came across handled the situation less sensitively than others. Even if that is so, however, the fact that the 'success' of a meeting depends partly on the attitudes and interpersonal skills of the victim is significant for the position of mediation in criminal justice. In 1986 Northamptonshire initiated the first pre-court adult mediation and reparation project in the country at Kettering. Of 127 victims identified in the first year, 104 wanted to involve themselves or wished the Bureau to take action; 25 per cent met their offenders, and a further 50 per cent negotiated an agreement using a go-between (Kettering Adult Reparation Bureau 1986/87).

Another voluntary organization, NAVSS, promoted discussion of the new ideas. Its interest was aroused partly by descriptions of US initiatives by visitors returning from the United States, such as John Harding and a young barrister, Robin Griffiths (Chinkin and Griffiths 1980). In addition, the newly formed NAVSS was approached in 1980 by the Department of Health and Social Security, whose responsibilities include juveniles, with a proposal for a juvenile reparation project. This was not taken up, because NAVSS wanted to concentrate on services to victims, but interest in the idea remained (Reeves, 1989: 45). In 1981 NAVSS invited Professor Burt Galaway to speak (Galaway 1983), together with representatives of the Exeter project. Galaway had helped to establish the pioneering restitution project in Minneapolis (see p. 38), and had published research and books on the subject (e.g. Hudson *et al.* 1980; Galaway and Hudson 1981). NAVSS convened a series of meetings which led to the formation of the Forum for Initiatives on Reparation and Mediation (FIRM); it also compiled the first list of reparation and mediation initiatives in Britain, later updated by the Home Office and FIRM (Reeves 1982; Marshall 1984; Marshall and Walpole 1985; FIRM 1989b). Its director, Helen Reeves, was a founder member of FIRM's executive committee. This is not to say that she, or others involved with victims' support, was an uncritical advocate of victim/offender mediation. NAVSS described reparation as 'a new distraction', and avoided direct involvement which it felt would have diverted attention from the needs of victims (Reeves 1989). It raised the possibility that the process of mediation might subject victims to additional pressures (Reeves 1986), and in FIRM's executive Helen Reeves, representing the concerns of NAVSS, consistently resisted the suggestion that FIRM should actively promote victim/offender mediation before there was evidence that it was in victims' best interests. This assurance now seems to have been given by research findings (*Victim Support* 1989 (35): 6).

The fourth main impetus came from within the probation service. John Harding commissioned a feasibility study in Coventry (Wright 1983), where in 1985 one of the four Home Office-funded projects was set up. (The others are in Wolverhampton, Leeds and Cumbria.) Meanwhile another probation officer, Peter Dixon (like Helen Reeves a Quaker), ran the South Yorkshire Victim/ Offender Mediation Project, in Rotherham and Wombwell, for three years from November 1983. There have been several other projects, mostly also initiated by probation officers; they are recorded by Marshall and Walpole (1985) and in *Mediation* (the newsletter of FIRM) from summer 1986 onwards, but those mentioned above are the most extensively documented.

The probation service, however, was also in two minds about reparation. The National Association of Probation Officers (NAPO) was sceptical of reparation schemes where there is 'implicit coercion' of the offender – rather surprisingly, since probation has always worked on that basis. It also opposed the use of probation resources for the purpose on the grounds, among others, that the service should put concern for offenders first (NAPO 1985: 7, 9). In Hampshire, where John Harding had become chief probation officer, a reparation scheme in Southampton was 'suppressed', 'the victim of NAPO opposition', according to a local law lecturer and magistrate, Alec Samuels (1987); nearby in Totton only five cases were referred by probation officers in the first year of the project's operation (G. Davis *et al.* 1987: 19).

The last major contribution was of a different kind. At the youth custody centre in Rochester, Kent, groups were organized by the chaplain, the Reverend Peter Taylor, and subsequently by the psychologist, Gilles Launay. Offenders serving sentences for burglary met victims (of other burglaries) who had volunteered through the local victims support scheme. The project, named Victims and Offenders In Conciliation (VOIC), is described in more detail on pp. 98–9.

Reparation is a concept which has wide popular appeal, as numerous surveys have shown. One survey found that 85 per cent thought it was a good idea to make some offenders do community service instead of going to prison, and 66 per cent wanted to make them pay compensation to their victims. In another, 93 per cent thought offenders should 'make good the consequences of their crime wherever possible.' The second British Crime Survey found that victims were not more punitive than others, but that they want offenders to make some redress (Wright 1989: 264–9). Victims were asked whether they would have accepted the chance of meeting the offender in order 'to agree a way in which the offender could make a repayment for what he had done', and 49 per cent said they would; a further 20 per cent would have liked such an agreement without a meeting. The main reasons spontaneously given were 'to know why he did it' or, among burglary victims, 'to see what he was like'. When possible reasons were suggested, they also wanted 'to give him a good piece of your mind', 'to arrange for offender to pay money in compensation', and to let him 'see the effect the crime had on you' (Maguire and Corbett 1987: 227–31).

The concept also wins support from most parts of the political spectrum. In the 1970s there was disillusionment among the supporters of rehabilitation, yet even politicians of the Right, once in office, could not fail to see that the overuse of prisons was costly and unproductive (see for example the opening paragraphs of the Conservative government's Green Paper *Punishment, Custody and the Community* – Home Office 1988b). All could agree on concern for victims, and on the desirability of holding offenders 'accountable' (though for some that word has retributive overtones). Thus the Parliamentary All-Party Penal Affairs Group (PAPPAG), which has always had close links with NACRO and the probation service, was attracted to the idea, and produced a report advocating it (PAPPAG 1984). The then Home Secretary, Mr Leon Brittan, was so interested in the report (of which he had received an advance copy) that he made its ideas the theme of a widely publicized speech on the night before its publication (Brittan 1984). Legislation was considered (Home Office 1985a), and a two-year programme of demonstration projects was introduced (Marshall and Merry 1990). A consultative document was issued, but in it the ideas of reparation and mediation were somewhat confused (Home Office 1986). Respondents almost unanimously pointed out that mediation and reparation were possible within existing legislation, and that a new Act would be premature.

The Criminal Justice Act 1988 accordingly confined itself to promoting compensation by offenders, by requiring courts to give reasons if they omitted to make a compensation order. In February 1990 the White Paper *Crime, Justice and Protecting the Public* (Home Office 1990a: 24) stated that the victim/offender mediation schemes 'showed that there was often confusion whether [mediation and] reparation were for the benefit of the victim or a means of rehabilitating the offender'. There was some truth in this in the late 1980s but probably less now, as attention has been drawn to the problem. The White Paper also states that 'Victims felt under pressure to co-operate', a response which the research carried out so far has seldom encountered. It concedes that 'It may be helpful for mediation . . . , or reparation, to be arranged informally by the probation service', but does not mention independent projects. The White Paper also concludes that 'reparation to victims should not be a requirement of orders made by the courts'; if this means 'reparation by means of mediation' as the context suggests, most reparation and mediation workers would probably agree.

Organization

Victim/offender mediation projects can be categorized according to the way they are structured and their style of operation. Structural factors are, first, whether they operate within or independently of the criminal justice process, and second, the independence or otherwise of their management. Operationally they may be oriented primarily towards the victim, the offender or both, or to the requirements of the criminal justice system. Their methods of working may be categorized according to whether they work with individual victims and offenders or with groups, face-to-face meetings or an intermediary, the types of cases which they accept or exclude, and whether mediation is done by volunteers or only by staff.

Relationship with the formal system

The most significant structural factor affecting victim/offender mediation is whether the offender, and hence also the victim, is independent, relatively independent, or subject to the jurisdiction of the criminal justice system.

The same project may work at more than one level. A project is 'independent' of the formal structure when participants are referred directly by community or voluntary organizations such as Citizens' Advice Bureaux, or approach it directly rather than report their case to the police; the case is then treated as a dispute rather than as a crime. This is a possibility wherever the 'victim' knows who the 'offender' is (quotation marks are used because in many disputes each party has offended against the other). The 'victim', sometimes referred to in mediation jargon as 'Party A', may prefer this route in order to avoid the drawbacks and delays of the criminal process (described in Chapter 2) or when the victim does not want 'Party B' to be exposed to the risk of punishment, but merely wishes to control his or her behaviour. This may be because the victim regards the likely sentence as excessive, or fears that when the punishment is over the offender will retaliate against the victim for having brought it about. This could occur in a dispute between neighbours, or a theft by a child living next door; it is also possible in the case of more serious acts of violence between the partners in a relationship. In such cases the parties retain autonomy over the decisions they make, which are not court-enforceable, but it is important that the rights of both are safeguarded, particularly where the parties are unequal.

Mediation will be 'relatively independent' when a case has entered the criminal justice process, but is referred to the project unconditionally. This can happen at almost any stage. A police officer called to a dispute between neighbours may suggest it to the parties. If an offence was committed, the police may decide to issue a formal caution instead of prosecution, and then recommend mediation; there is no sanction for not taking part, but if the offence is repeated, further action can be taken. It is possible in England and Wales for the prosecutor or the court to discontinue (but not apparently to defer) the case in the preliminary stages and make a similar recommendation, though as yet it does not appear to have been done; the accused can require prosecution to continue (Prosecution of Offences Act 1985, sec. 23 (3), (7)). A Scottish reparation and mediation project operates on the basis that the Procurator Fiscal defers the prosecution of cases that have already been considered of sufficient seriousness to merit prosecution. This power derives from the common law of Scotland (Mackay 1988: 69 and personal communication.) Finally, the case could go through the system and be referred at the end. Mediation could then be suggested by a probation officer, but with no disciplinary threat if the offender declined to take part. It could be offered during a prison sentence, with no promise that the outcome would affect release on parole; this could be to help victims overcome the effects, or give them the opportunity to negotiate with offenders an agreement that they would keep their distance after release (Reeves 1986: 4). The referring agency would not retain any control over the people involved, whether or not they reached an agreement: in all these cases there is no further sanction if the agreement is not kept, other than an attempt at further mediation. But there would have been none without mediation either, and there is reason to hope that at least in some cases an agreement made personally between the people concerned, rather than an order imposed by a court, will mean more to the victim and be more likely to be observed by the offender.

Other projects, however, are 'dependent' on the courts, because they offer mediation at a point when the criminal justice process has not yet run its course. Police could make the decision to caution conditional upon successful mediation, and the prosecutor could do the same with the decision not to prosecute. The court could adjourn the case *sine die* on the same understanding. In England, three of the four projects in the Home Office research programme operate after conviction in court but before sentence, at the stage where cases are commonly remanded for pre-sentence reports. This has implications for the voluntariness of participation and the criteria for 'success' (see pp. 88–92).

Structure

The second basis for classifying projects is their organizational structure. Projects can have autonomous management or be under the aegis of a voluntary organization, while still having to work closely with the system in order to obtain referrals (Coventry and Wolverhampton Reparation Projects, Boston

Municipal Court Mediation Program, Elkhart VORP). There are also projects entirely managed by a criminal justice agency, or statutory agencies, such as the Exeter Joint Services Youth Support Team and the Juvenile Liaison Bureaux in Northamptonshire, established by the police and other agencies, and the probation-based projects in South Yorkshire and Leeds.

Operational policies

There are five main operating styles, according to whether the service is oriented towards victims or offenders, whether meetings are between individuals or groups, whether participants meet face-to-face or communicate through an intermediary, the types of cases they accept, and whether mediation is carried out by trained volunteers or staff. Often there is no hard-and-fast policy, and it is a question of where the emphasis lies.

The first distinction is between projects which are primarily oriented towards the needs of the victim, or those of the offender. English projects were considered by G. Davis and colleagues (1987: 25) to base selection on offence and offender characteristics, rather on victims' needs. Some of them passed information to the court only when it was favourable to the offender, although it would not be hard for courts to infer that no news was bad news (G. Davis *et al.* 1987: 35–6. 63). In Leeds there was an explicit policy of basing selection on the seriousness of the current offence or the offender's previous record, so there was no commitment to the victim's *right* to reparation (1987: 51, emphasis in original). Davis and colleagues suggest (1987: 46) that if the main aim of the project is to benefit the offender, through mitigation of sentence, and perhaps also to ease the pressure on the system by keeping him out of court or out of prison, it should not be called a reparation scheme. As Reeves (1986: 3) has pointed out, by policies such as accepting only the less serious offences, they are giving the conventional values of the criminal justice system precedence over the wishes and needs of some victims. Sometimes the nature of the mediation process leads to the exclusion of some victims; in the Canadian VORP studied by Dittenhofer (1981), for example, cases were not referred where there was excessive animosity, nor where the victim was considered not to have adequate verbal skills. Surprisingly this project also avoided cases where there was a prior relationship, on the grounds that this could lead to potential conflict in the meeting (Dittenhofer 1981: 23, 72).

In all these projects, it is usual for victims to meet their 'own' offenders individually; but in a second type of scheme, groups of victims take part in discussions with 'unrelated' offenders. This happens in Victims and Offenders in Conciliation (VOIC – see pp. 98–9). Launay (1985) suggests that it is helpful for both victims and offenders to challenge each other's prejudices, stereotypes and rationalizations, and that this is better achieved in groups than in the VORP model, although this does not preclude bringing the individuals together to consider how offenders can make amends for the damage they have done. VOIC also has the advantage that it can provide for the victims (the majority) whose offenders are not caught, and for those offenders whose victims do not wish to take part.

Third, in some projects mediators act as go-betweens, where victims do not wish to meet their offenders face-to-face, or project workers consider this undesirable. Alternatively non-victims may act as 'advocates'. Some Victim Support co-ordinators and volunteers have met groups of prisoners or probationers (*Victim Support*, March 1990, 4–5). In some ways similar is a project in the prison at Hameln, FRG, where female volunteers, who have not themselves been victims, act as non-professional therapists, discussing with convicted rapists the effects of their actions on the lives of their victims. The aim is 'to lead the young offenders to sexuality experienced as a partnership.' In exceptional cases the offender can meet his own victim (Dünkel and Rössner 1989: 167; Tügel and Heilemann 1987).

The other two categories are self-explanatory. As regards types of cases, projects normally make policy decisions as to the types of cases they will accept. There may be limitations in the interests of participants, for example because of mental disorder, or a shortage of experienced mediators; if a project accepts only cases below or above a certain level of seriousness (the petty or the prison-bound), it may be giving priority to relieving pressure on the courts or the prison system respectively. A project may have to pay a price for being 'independent' (as defined above) in that only relatively minor cases are likely to be referred or self-referred.

Lastly, mediation may be carried out by staff or by trained volunteers. The latter policy implies a commitment to involvement of the community, and thereby spreading understanding of restorative principles more widely.

Evaluation

It was some time before Canadian and American VORPs were systematically evaluated; in Britain by contrast, researchers were busy almost before some of the projects had established themselves. In studying the role of victim/offender mediation it is necessary to consider not only the findings but also the criteria selected as a basis. This section will review some research in Canada, the United States and England, and a small survey of practitioners' attitudes; the next section will attempt to identify some of the issues raised.

The original VORP in Kitchener, Ontario, operates through probation orders in which the court stipulates restitution, more than half of them specifying VORP. Although independently managed, it is therefore dependent on the criminal justice system for the referral of cases. The only substantial research into its operation is by Dittenhofer (1981), later summarized by Dittenhofer and Ericson (1983).

The findings were based on the forty-five cases handled during eight months of 1980; the potential number of eligible cases is not stated. Fifty-one offenders were involved, with an average age of 22. Almost one-third had one or more previous convictions, nearly all for indictable offences. There were 159 victims, two-thirds of them (mostly small) business establishments, and 5 per cent corporate. There was relevant insurance cover in 13 per cent of cases, but in 76 per cent there was none. In 85 per cent of cases offenders had no prior relationship with victims.

Of the cases concluded at the time of the study, victim/offender contact was arranged in about half (eighteen), but in sixteen it was not, mostly because the victim or offender refused, though an amount of restitution was determined in seven of these. Twenty-nine amounts of restitution had been settled, totalling $12,958, the highest being $4,000. Two cases were settled by small donations to charity. In nine cases insurance companies were to be reimbursed (with meetings in four cases). The staff had misgivings about this, but felt that it could lead to a better deal for the offender than being sued by the insurance company.

A minority of the offenders had been assessed as 'prison-bound'; in the event, two in every five received additional sentences – community service orders, fines or jail. Whether there were fewer jail sentences than there would otherwise have been is not clear; judges and Crown attorneys had mixed views about whether VORP should be an alternative to jail. One probation officer, however, estimated that 60 to 75 per cent of the VORP offenders would have been imprisoned if the project had not existed. This study did not assess victims' or offenders' satisfaction with the process, nor reconviction rates. Community involvement was less than had sometimes been claimed in descriptions of VORP; volunteer mediators were used in only 46 per cent of cases. It was found that both victims and offenders were under some pressure to take part.

The question of the primary aim of the project was confused. Staff, when interviewed, generally affirmed that reconciliation was the main goal. The training manual for volunteers, however, stated that this word should not be used in gaining the support of the victim: a discussion, and payment for losses, were to be given as the reasons for a meeting (Dittenhofer 1981: 56). A similar approach is given in the *VORP Volunteer Handbook*, issued a little later in Elkhart, Indiana: the policy is 'to make room for it [reconciliation] to happen, but we don't insist' (Zehr 1983: 7).

In practice, the focus appeared to be chiefly on restitution, and this sometimes led victims to expect more than offenders could pay. Descriptions of VORP, the researcher found, gave a number of objectives: restitution, reconciliation, helping to reduce the victim's trauma and danger by disclosing the real nature of the offender, demonstrating to the offender the actual harm caused, and avoiding the use of jail. Publicity also stressed punitive aspects such as the difficulty of meeting a victim and of paying compensation. When interviewed, judges and Crown attorneys tended to appreciate the potential benefits of meeting, though they would also assess it in terms of their traditional concern for punishment or rehabilitation of the offender. The authors concluded that the project was 'only partially obtaining its goals and departing substantially from the picture painted by most descriptions'.

It was not until 1985 that research into the American VORPs appeared, based on experience in Elkhart, Indiana (where the project started in 1978) and some newer projects in Indiana and Ohio. In these VORPs cases are usually referred by the court at sentencing, although referrals may also be made when an offender has already been placed on probation or (for juveniles) when the case is being diverted from the court process. For 80 per cent of the sample, VORP was part of their sentence. Coates and Gehm (1985, 1989) evaluated the assessments of VORP made by victims participating (thirty-seven) and not participating (twenty-six), and by the seventy-three mainly juvenile, white, first offenders referred during 1983 and a matched sample of those not referred. Also interviewed were twenty-seven criminal justice officials and twenty-two members of VORP staff and mediators. Twenty-three offenders had taken part in face-to-face meetings. No estimate is given of the number of eligible cases and the proportion actually referred to VORP.

There were 163 victim/offender combinations with the potential for a meeting (excluding those where the dispute had already been settled), and of these 98 (60 per cent) resulted in face-to-face meetings; 45 (28 per cent) did not, because the victim was unwilling. Where a meeting did take place, a contract resulted in every case but two. The great majority of contracts involved monetary compensation (forty-nine), work for the victim (twenty-seven) or other work (three). Half the monetary compensation was for $71 or less, but the highest amount was $10,000; 82 per cent were completed. The average number of hours of service was thirty-one, with 90 per cent completed.

Of participating victims 59 per cent were 'satisfied' and 30 per cent 'somewhat satisfied' with the VORP experience. All but one (97 per cent) would do it again or recommend it to other victims of crime. After the session, they said the thing they found most satisfactory was meeting the offender; receiving restitution was in second place, followed by the offender's expression of remorse and the mediator's care and concern (a function increasingly filled in the United Kingdom by Victim Support groups).

Reasons given by victims for not wanting to meet were, first, that the hassle of involvement was not merited by the loss, and second, fear of meeting the offender. Some had already worked out a settlement; others felt there had been too much delay.

Many of the offenders were apprehensive about meeting, but all, given the chance, would take part again. They, too, valued the meeting most, as well as the prospect of avoiding jail and the opportunity to pay back (although some victims complained that payments were not maintained). Paradoxically though, some offenders listed meeting the victim as both the most satisfying and the least satisfying part of the experience.

As an alternative to imprisonment, VORP had only partial success. Offenders referred to VORP were given custodial sentences in the same proportion (about

20 per cent) as those not referred, but for a much shorter average period (38 days, as against 212). The project did not claim that it could affect the rate of reconviction, and this was not studied. It did, however, aim to involve the community in the process, and two thirds of the meetings studied were conducted by trained volunteer mediators. The quality of mediation was not directly studied, but 79 per cent of victims and 78 per cent of offenders felt that justice had been served in their cases – justice being defined by them in terms such as 'making things right', 'holding the offender accountable', and 'fairness in settling disputes'. Nearly half the victims and offenders changed their attitudes, for example seeing each other as 'real people'. Some victims were moved by what they believed to be sincere remorse on the part of the offender; offenders were surprised by the meaning attached to the items they had stolen.

The project was not without its problems. Participation is supposed to be voluntary, and restorative rather than punitive, but although victims did not feel unduly pressured to take part, most offenders were ordered to do so by the court, and felt that they were being punished. It is not clear, however, whether the mediation itself, as distinct from the reparation, was seen as punishment, because in 87 per cent of cases VORP was combined with community service, probation or jail.

As so often, a major difficulty was that different participants defined the project's aims and priorities differently. Staff and mediators wanted primarily to humanize the criminal justice process, with several subsidiary aims such as increasing the offender's accountability, involving victims and providing restitution, victim/offender reconciliation, increasing community understanding, and providing an alternative to incarceration. Victims' first priorities were to recover their loss and to help the offender out of trouble. Offenders hoped to avoid harsher punishment, get the whole experience finished, and 'make things right'. For criminal justice officials the aims were a selection of these, with 'easing probation load' in addition. Coates and Gehm (1989) do not propose one aim to take precedence, but a choice of one of four models:

1 *'Community conflict resolution'* would work with individuals who had not been arrested; they would bring disputes, some of which have involved criminal acts, for resolution without recourse to the criminal justice system. This would not be 'widening the net' of State control, because participation would be voluntary.
2 *'Diversion'* from the criminal justice process would occur at the point of arrest or before the trial, with the co-operation of criminal justice officers. It would also not be seen as punishment nor as net-widening.
3 As an *'alternative to incarceration'* VORP would operate only with offenders likely to be imprisoned; but if imposed with a package of other measures on those who were not prison-bound, it could lead to net-widening.
4 Finally, a *'justice model'* would place emphasis on the offender's reparation to the victim (or to the community as victim). This could be an alternative to

the other sanctions, or an addition, but the latter possibility does not concern the proponents of this model, according to Coates and Gehm, because it is just for the offender 'to be confronted with the impact of his or her crime.'

The British experimental projects

The most detailed evaluation so far of victim/offender mediation is the study by Marshall and Merry (1990) of the four Home Office funded projects and some other British examples. It is therefore worth reviewing in some detail. Some projects operate at the stage of police cautioning, the others mainly at pre-sentence report stage. The research was based on the records of the four projects themselves, and some others which voluntarily completed the monitoring forms; there were also interviews with offenders and victims who took part (but not with victims who declined to do so). Data are analysed for 326 referrals to police-based projects, and 521 to court-based ones, mostly from 1985 to 1987. Once mediation was considered, there was a high take-up rate.

Police-based schemes were all for juvenile offenders, mostly aged 12 to 16; 69 per cent had a record, but only 14 per cent of these had been convicted, while the remaining 55 per cent had been cautioned only. In court-based schemes 80 per cent were no older than 25, and 80 per cent also had a previous record (almost all of them a conviction). At the Leeds Reparation Project 38 per cent had seven or more previous convictions and 18 per cent between four and six.

As regards victims, two-thirds of those in the police-based projects were corporate bodies (businesses, local authority departments, and other agencies); of the individuals, 43 per cent were adults aged 26 to 59, 12 per cent were 60 or over, and the remainder 25 or under. Just over half were male. In court-based projects only one-third were corporate victims, of whom 60 per cent were commercial firms, shops, garages, car sales firms, and national services; among the non-commercial corporate victims, educational establishments predominated. The age distribution of the individuals was broadly similar to that in the police-based projects, but with more old people, and fewer juveniles.

The proportion of cases where there was a previous relationship between victim and offender was not as high as might be expected: 23 per cent in police-based projects and about half in court-based ones. In cases of violence, however, the proportions who knew each other were much higher: 76 per cent and 64 per cent respectively; the proportions were also high in cases of fraud. Marshall and Merry (1990) suggest that the parties to a dispute who see themselves as 'victims' may feel they have more to lose by 'reducing' their status to that of a disputant on more or less equal terms with the offender.

The offences most often referred to police-based projects were theft (53 per cent) and criminal damage (32 per cent); in court-based projects thefts (39 per cent) were followed by burglary (29 per cent) and violence (20 per cent).

Mediation was offered in about two-thirds of cases in police-based schemes; 90 per cent of 208 juvenile offenders agreed to take part and 79 per cent of 211 victims. In both groups the majority were at least 'moderately keen' to do so. A meeting took place in 47 per cent of all cases referred. In court-based schemes it was offered in a greater proportion of cases (84 per cent). Nearly all the offenders agreed to take part (95 per cent), with 57 per cent 'very keen' and 39 per cent moderately so. Only 51 per cent of the victims agreed, perhaps because these projects dealt with adult offenders, for whom there may have been less sympathy than for juveniles. But of these, two victims in five were 'very keen' to meet their offenders; 21 per cent, however, were 'not keen'. It appeared that victims were less happy to meet the offender when the crime had caused them emotional distress, for example where there was racial harassment or the offender was related by kinship, but the research did not explore whether some victims were embarrassed at merely being asked and having to decide whether to take part. Female and elderly victims were less enthusiastic, while those who were employed in non-manual jobs, and those who had suffered nuisance offences, were more so. Meetings took place in 34 per cent of cases; there was indirect mediation in a further 21 per cent.

As has been found generally, an agreement was reached in the great majority of cases where mediation took place. Agreement was recorded in 79 per cent of cases in police-based schemes; there was full agreement in most cases, but this was less likely when offenders were not under threat of official legal action. The total proportion was similar in court-based schemes, but full agreement was much less likely where no face-to-face meeting took place.

The researchers note that the projects undertook hardly any follow-up of their own, and suggest that they should, on the ground that it would be 'good manners' to show that degree of concern to participants, who should be treated as partners. Victims who have tried to be helpful should be informed of the offender's progress (with the latter's permission). Some of the victims and offenders whom they approached, however, preferred not to resurrect the matter, but these were more likely to be those who were involved only in indirect mediation.

Meeting the offender was felt to be valuable by 82 per cent of victims, including 22 per cent whom it had helped to relieve their worries about the offence, and others who hoped it might help to reform the offender. Victims who had received reparation were more likely than those in the control group to think that compensation would be a sufficient sentence (40 per cent as against 13 per cent), and less likely to want the offender to be sent to prison (10 per cent as against 48 per cent). Almost all the offenders said they had been glad they met their victims. In one project, after having met, only 17 per cent of offenders gave mitigation of sentence as one of the benefits, whereas 57 per cent had given it as the reason for first taking part. 'Offenders were generally surprised at the positive reception they got and were often visibly affected by the victim's generosity in accepting them as individuals in spite of what they had done.'

As with other mediation projects, the reduction of recidivism was not expected to be high on the list of goals, although in the unlikely event of a substantial increase the project might be called into question. It is too soon for the Home Office projects to be fully evaluated in this respect, but a survey was made of small samples at Coventry and Wolverhampton, based on before-and-after calculations of the number and seriousness of offences. Those who took part in direct mediation showed a slight improvement, and those not involved, a slight deterioration. Cases in which there was indirect mediation, or individual discussions between the offenders and project workers, however, showed different results in the two projects, and these have not been satisfactorily explained.

One advantage that has been claimed for mediation projects is that they can involve members of the community, and many US VORPs have made a considerable investment in the training of volunteer mediators. In Britain that is not yet usual, except in the Leeds Reparation Project, which does use volunteers and pays them a sessional fee; this is felt to enable the project to expect more commitment on their part.

Marshall and Merry (1990) have drawn attention to the importance of the *quality* of mediation. It should be fair, with both parties aware of their legal rights and able to exercise them fully. It should be impartial; in those residual cases where a conflict of interest cannot be resolved, a court will have to decide. There is as yet little research on how mediators can best achieve equal treatment of the participants when one party is much less powerful or articulate than the other.

It is generally agreed that there should be no pressure on victims to take part, beyond explaining the potential advantages which might arise for them or for the offender. But if the operation of the criminal justice system is in any way conditional upon mediation, some degree of coercion is unavoidable for both victims and offenders. Victims may feel that they do not want the anxiety of being even indirectly responsible for the fate of another human being. Unlike magistrates and judges, they did not volunteer for this role. It could be argued that victims who do not really want to devote time, trouble or nervous energy to a meeting may reluctantly agree, for example because they do not want to feel that their refusal contributed to another person's prison sentence, or, more ominously, because they fear retaliation. There is no evidence of such a response yet: the great majority of those who took part have been glad of it, and a substantial number have shown themselves able to decline the invitation. Again, may some of those who refused have found the decision itself stressful? This did not appear to be a problem in the small sample of victims who had refused mediation, surveyed by D. Smith *et al.* (1988: 125–6); their worst fear appeared to be to look silly by accepting a possibly insincere apology. Only one of those who did meet her offender felt that this had made matters worse (1988: 134), and they did not feel pressured into making the decision (1988: 128).

Mediation projects are aware of this problem. Some approach the offender first to save troubling the victim if the offender does not want to take part; offenders who are willing are told that the victim will be consulted and 'other enquiries' made, indicating that the decision will not be the responsibility of the victim (Kettering Adult Reparation Bureau 1986/87: 12). Others contact the victim first; if he or she refuses, the accused does not hear about it, and at least one victim said this was important (Mackay 1988: 71, 37). Another possibility is that the fear of retaliation would become more real as mediation was offered in increasingly serious cases. But the position of victims after declining mediation is no worse than their position when deciding whether to report an offence, press charges and give evidence under the traditional system, where some victims are so intimidated that they incur imprisonment for contempt of court, rather than give evidence against the accused (e.g. Michelle Renshaw and Stephen Samada, *Guardian* 13 and 21 June 1989).

In other words, under the traditional system, if there is any fear of retaliation the victim's only way of avoiding it is not to pursue the case (short of moving, or seeking police protection); a reparation agreement offers the victim, depending on the circumstances, the chance to negotiate amends, tell the offender personally about the consequences of the offence, end (or prevent) feuds, pre-empt retaliation, improve or restore relationships, and (if pre-trial) avoid the inconvenience of court appearances (Mackay 1988: 38).

Offenders often take part in the hope of being released with a caution or being given a lighter sentence. There is no reason in principle why there should not be at least an incentive to offenders to meet, as Marshall and Merry (1990) suggest, but pressing them to make an insincere apology will not be likely to improve their attitude; even if it is genuine, the victim will not always be able to be sure that it is. If there is a meeting, the victim will often feel able to judge whether the offender is sincere; if the offender makes a tangible act of reparation, this may be a sign of that the offender is genuinely sorry, or, failing that, the victim may feel 'I can't make him feel sorry, but at least he did something to make up for it'. A proportion of offenders agree to take part for the 'wrong' reasons, but emerge with a greater understanding. Some examples may show, better than theoretical discussion, how the process can work in practice (Coventry Reparation Scheme 1986; 1987).

Malicious wounding of policewoman

A young man entered a supermarket at night through an already broken door. As he left a police car drew up; he panicked and threw a bottle, which broke a window and caused cuts to a policewoman's face and legs. He had never intended the consequences of his action; he had not been in trouble before. The offender was grateful to the victim for allowing him to meet and apologize, and she felt that she had had a 'good experience'. Sentence: conditional discharge, compensation and costs.

Burglary

A woman aged 57 was burgled; property valued at over £900 was stolen. The offender turned out to be a 15-year-old boy. The victim wanted to hear more about what had occurred, and felt that he should be made more aware of how it felt to experience a burglary. He clearly warmed to the victim, whose fair and valid points encouraged him to think about his own behaviour. For the victim the meeting appeared to reassure her as regards the boy's future behaviour at least towards herself. He offered, without prompting, to do a practical task to make amends, but she could not think of one. Sentence: supervision order and compensation.

Criminal damage

Returning to the car park on a foggy night, a young couple found that their car's headlights had been smashed. Their journey home was difficult, and repairs cost over £100. The offender was a 19-year-old who had been drinking. The victims were impressed that he was willing to meet them and apologize; his parents, who were worried about his behaviour, were also reassured by this. He had saved sufficient money to pay for the damage, and handed it over at the end of the meeting. Sentence (for this and other matters): community service order, sixty hours, plus costs.

Section 47 assault

Victim and offender were both aged 16; the offender struck the victim after hearing from classmates that the latter had made derogatory remarks about his mother. At the meeting they were able to discuss the influences of their friends directly, and determined to be seen communicating directly in future. The victim's father, a Sikh, was concerned that the assault could have been racially motivated, but the boys did not interpret their problems in this way and the victim was reassured by the offender's apology. Sentence: conditional discharge and costs.

Aims

A further test of a mediation project is its ability to maintain its original aims, and not be co-opted into giving primacy to those of the criminal justice agencies: diverting offenders out of the system, or rehabilitating them, or punishing them, all of which put the offender back in the centre of the stage, leaving the victim once again in the shadows. The police-based reparation projects, which in any case emphasize reparation rather than mediation, have so far tended to provide another way of dealing with offenders, rather than offering a service to victims. In at least one project it is reported that there is 'obvious "coaching" of victims in preparation for a meeting'. This could be regarded as another example of the conflict being 'stolen', but it is not necessarily so, if the victim's reason for taking part is to make an impact on the offender.

To evaluate a project, its aims must be defined, as Marshall and Merry (1990) emphasize; it must be decided whose interests should have priority if there is a clash. If for example the primary aim of mediation were to persuade offenders not to reoffend, by drawing attention to the human effects of their actions, victims should be selected who had been markedly affected by the crime, were articulate, but were not so angry as to alienate the offender altogether. This was in fact the commonest reason given by victims for taking part. A few felt towards the offender as they might have felt towards their own sons or grand-sons, some of whom had also been in trouble. But if the primary aim was service to victims, one should select those whose needs would be met through media-tion, including those with serious needs; at present, however, many of these are excluded, because most projects take relatively minor crimes. Marshall and Merry (1990) suggest that overall, mediation should serve victims *and* offenders, though not necessarily both in every case, but in all issues such as the timing of the intervention the victim's interests should be the determining factor. This means weighing the interests of the victim not only against those of the offender, but also against those of the criminal justice system.

Since a basic principle of mediation is that the outcome is determined by the parties themselves, with as little influence as possible from the mediators, Marshall and Merry (1990) argue that a project cannot properly set itself any particular outcome as a criterion for success, such as the number of apologies or the amount of reparation paid. The aim should be to facilitate the meeting, they suggest, or at least to help the parties 'to a constructive, revealing and influential experience that relieves the pain of victimization on one side, while it assists self-realization and behavioural reform on the other'. This conclusion has also been reached by the Coventry project, which defined its primary aim as 'to help both Parties come to terms with the aftermath of crime and discuss issues relat-ing to it'. An agreement about making amends is given as an additional aim. The VORP in Minneapolis does not conceive reconciliation to be its goal, but merely to increase opportunities for reconciliation, that parties may use or not as they wish, as Galaway (1985) has said. The primary measure of the project's effec-tiveness then becomes the number of cases where two parties, who wished to meet, were enabled to do so. The proportion of victims who agree to participate is thus one measure of success. Others include the proportion of negotiations that result in agreements, and the extent to which the terms of the agreements are ful-filled. Finally, 'a society is strengthened if its citizens – both victims and offend-ers – perceive that they have been dealt with in a fair manner'; this may be assessed through short questionnaires (Galaway 1985: 13).

Relationship with criminal justice

If there is to be mediation, and there is also a traditional criminal justice appara-tus, the relationship between the two has to be considered. Marshall and Merry (1990) analyse the difficulties. Should it make a difference to the way offenders are dealt with if they take part in mediation, or make reparation, or both? Mediation can be independent of the court, a meeting between two people who hope that it will be helpful to themselves or each other. But the researchers found that it was not independent: offenders who had taken part in mediation and reparation tended to receive reduced sentences, and the expression of forgiveness by the victim made it difficult to impose a harsh sentence unless 'necessitated' by the offender's previous record. They suggest that although it may be reasonable enough that a positive performance by the offender reduces the chance of custody, it is disturbing that an antagonistic victim more than doubles it (unless this can be explained by the assumption that the victim is more likely to be antagonistic if the offence was a serious one – Marshall and Merry 1990: 141).

Marshall and Merry attempt to square this circle by suggesting that mediation projects should be 'independent of too great pressure to manifest an impact on sentences' (1990: 226), so as to make for a higher quality of victim and offender involvement, but that a report to court should be made, because it might 'be influential in reducing the punitiveness of the disposal in recognition of the offender's atonement' (1990: 226). They found that victims were 'far happier' when compensation had been given or offered before mediation occurred (1990: 248); they suggest that mediation could be offered *in any case where the parties were willing* (1990: 225, emphasis in original), and could then concentrate on feelings and possible atonement and forgiveness. The court, in turn, could take account of the reparation offered by the offender, but need not be influenced by any mediation that might or might not have taken place. Thus no pressure would be placed on the victim, because his or her participation would not affect the sentence.

Victim/offender groups

One-to-one mediation between victims and their offenders is not the only option. In a project called Victims and Offenders In Conciliation (VOIC), groups of four to six victims of burglary met groups of a similar number of young men aged 15 to 20 serving sentences for burglary at the Youth Custody Centre at Rochester, Kent. The victims were recruited mainly from the local Victim Support Scheme (VSS). Almost all the offenders approached wanted to take part. They generally had many earlier convictions, and often had previously been in penal institutions. Sessions were video-taped for analysis. The organizers, and representatives of the VSS and of the police in the initial sessions, also took part. Each group met for three sessions of one and a half hours, at weekly intervals. There were structured discussions, at which for example victims told the offenders that not everything is covered by insurance, and that even commercial theft can cause individuals to suffer, as when the theft of specialized equipment led to the loss of a contract and hence to employees being laid off. This can compel the offenders to abandon both their excuses (e.g. 'it wasn't really my fault because I was unemployed/drunk') and their justifications (e.g. 'I did it but it wasn't really wrong because the victim was insured/deserved what I did to her'). Role-plays and simulated mediation meetings were also used, with victims and offenders taking their own roles and each other's. The project continued for a time under the local probation service, after the youth custody centre's conversion to a prison for adults (Launay 1985; Launay and Murray 1989).

Victims rated themselves less anxious and angry after the meetings and, with the exception of elderly women victims, rated burglars as more friendly and likeable. Offenders similarly rated victims more positively after the meetings, and knew more about the impact of a burglary on its victim; but they felt some of those who had previous dealings with offenders to be patronizing.

Launay suggests that in some ways these meetings are actually preferable to the one-to-one mediation approach. The victims who volunteer are mostly those whose burglaries were not cleared up, so that they would not have had the chance to take part in mediation and may be more in need of help. Group dynamics may make the sessions less tense than one-to-one encounters. The timing of the meetings is flexible: they can be held when the participants are ready to meet, and are not dependent on the operation of criminal justice. The interaction of victims and offenders is the clear primary purpose, not complicated by questions of reparation, sentencing or diversion from the system. There is scope for discussion and further action research as to which approach works better with particular types of victims and offenders; clearly meetings of this kind are of potential benefit to victims whose 'own' offenders are not caught – the majority, in the case of burglary – and to offenders whose victims do not wish to meet them. Launay considers that, while reparation is desirable, a primary objective for a victim/offender meeting should be to allow both parties to challenge each other's prejudices and rationalizations, and group meetings were better suited to this (Launay 1985). But the project, like others, was not suitable for all – not for hardened professional burglars, for example, nor for elderly women victims (Launay and Murray 1989).

Further issues in mediation and reparation

In addition to the issues raised in these evaluations, some further questions have been asked about mediation and reparation, and their relation to criminal justice. A small-scale survey has been undertaken among co-ordinators in mediation projects, and mainly like-minded criminal justice practitioners in Canada and the United States. The respondents were either asked to fill in a questionnaire or interviewed with a tape recorder. The numbers were small, and so the views should be regarded as indicative rather than representative; this account therefore deliberately does not emphasize the numbers or percentages of those who expressed particular views, nor does it correlate opinions with types of respondents. The survey intended only to discover some of the views held by a number of people who had given thought, from various professional standpoints, to the issues, and should be regarded as an exercise in picking their brains, rather than as a representative survey. They included leaders of mediation/reparation projects in Canada and the United States, judges, prosecutors and others involved in criminal justice. Further details of the twenty-four respondents are given in an earlier article (Wright 1985), where some of the responses summarized below were first published. The issues affected victims, offenders, the criminal justice system, and society in general.

Victims

It was generally agreed that, as one respondent said, 'a major emphasis should be reconciliation, dealing with feelings, and bringing healing. Though this includes money, that should not be the only issue.' It follows that, particularly for victims, mediation should be available in the more serious cases of violence, including sexual assaults, because it was here that reconciliation was most needed. It was potentially to victims' advantage to give them the opportunity (which of course they need not accept) to 'take ownership of their disputes', 'vent their anger and ask questions', gain emotional relief, and be personally involved in deciding how to resolve matters. But in Britain Victim Support has warned that victims should not have the responsibility of deciding the offender's future, and Helen Reeves, director of Victim Support, believes that most probably do not want it (Reeves 1984).

As for the financial aspects, most respondents did not feel that it is a problem if victims may settle for less compensation, after meeting the offender, than they might have received from a court; or that victims of similar crimes might receive different amounts. But one mentioned that the fairness of the result may depend partly on the mediator.

Offenders

Opinion was divided as to whether it could be unfair that different offenders would be asked to pay different amounts after similar crimes, but any unfairness was thought to be no greater than existing sentencing disparities, or indeed the rest of life – 'not so much unfair as bad luck'. With independently reached agreements there would not be objective consistency, but there could be subjective fairness meeting the circumstances of the individuals concerned. The mediators have some influence over this, and in court-based projects the judge can exercise control; offenders themselves can refuse. It was pointed out that the offender risks the consequences, which may include having an unsympathetic victim. One respondent thought, however, that black offenders would probably more often face refusal by white victims to meet them.

Supposing mediation is looked at in relation to criminal justice? When a new intermediate sanction is introduced, there is a danger that it will be used in place of some less restrictive non-custodial sanction, thus 'widening the net' of social control by the State, or that it will be added on to existing measures, rather than used instead of them – 'strengthening the net'. On both of these, too, opinion was divided. Some felt that 'mediation is usually already the least restrictive sanction around', and that even if it is used as an 'add-on' it has the advantage of educating the offender in responsibility 'without hurting too much'. Coates (1985: 17–22) made a similar point, and added that it also gives the victim the opportunity to be involved. To resolve the problem one project was considering using a pre-trial or non-criminal dispute resolution centre and post-conviction victim/offender mediation in tandem. Most cases involving a personal relationship, and the less serious crimes by strangers, would be referred to the former, but efforts would be made to secure the referral of an increasingly serious level of crime; only those too serious for this pre-trial diversion would go to court, and could be referred to victim/offender mediation after conviction.

Programmes which divert defendants from the criminal process, provided they admit the offence, have long been subject to concern that they offer offenders an inducement to forgo the right to defend themselves. One critic has said that mediation 'had been refurbished as a coercive form of juvenile plea-bargaining, with pressure for a guilty plea' (Auerbach 1983: 127). They may admit something they didn't do and agree to do whatever the diversion programme requires, rather than face the delay and hassle of a trial. Alternatively they may have committed an act, but be entitled to acquittal on grounds such as self-defence or lack of criminal intent. Comments were invited on the statement: 'There is a risk that mediation may infringe the rights of the offender, for example by requiring him to admit guilt before he is offered the chance to take part.' Among VORP projects which took the majority of their referrals after conviction, most disagreed: in practice most offenders admit complicity long before they hear of VORP. (No mention was made of the small minority who protest their innocence even after conviction.) In one project the volunteer mediators, when they first encounter the offender, ask 'What did you do?' (Presumably the mediation session itself could provide another opportunity to discover if the defendant was not involved or if there were extenuating circumstances.) This respondent said that he could not recall any case where they said 'I didn't do it', though they might say 'I was there but I didn't take the stuff.'

All the pre-trial projects disagreed with this statement: they had clearly thought about it. One enclosed the form which all defendants sign: it expressly states that by participating, they are neither admitting nor denying guilt. It informs defendants that on successful completion of the agreement, which includes several conditions of the type usually associated with probation (to be of good behaviour, report change of address, etc.), the prosecution will be discontinued or the case dismissed. It is then stricken from the record. Defendants must waive their right to a trial, but if they fail to comply with any condition of the agreement the prosecution is reinstated, and so are their rights. This and another project stated that participation is voluntary, but without going into the question of whether consent is truly voluntary in the circumstances. Another asked for an admission of civil responsibility, i.e. that something happened but not that it constituted an offence: this leaves open the possibility of denying criminal intent if the case comes to court.

The criminal justice system

There is a danger that projects such as mediation can be marginalized by the criminal justice system, if it refers only minor cases to the project, or uses it as a 'dumping ground' for those that are difficult but not serious. But such a practice calls into question the project's claim to give priority to the needs of the victim. Respondents were asked whether 'Provided it is accepted by those concerned or their relatives, and the public, mediation and reparation could be appropriate in even the most serious cases.' Several agreed in principle but thought that it would be a long time, if ever, before the public would accept it for the most serious crimes: one referred to the still persisting 'Wild West' tradition of simple retribution – 'You did it, you go to jail'. Others were in full agreement; one had just heard the feelings of victims of violent crime at a conference, and believed strongly that 'victims begin to heal only when they can let go of their fear and anger, and that mediation can assist this process'. Far from being excluded, victims of crimes such as assault and sexual assault often have a real need for reconciliation. A start could be made with drunk driving: in one project a drunk driver had indeed met the victim whom he had paralysed. It should be remembered that the questionnaire was filled in by project leaders, not by victims; on the other hand mediation in this context is relatively new, and victims who had not experienced it would not be well placed to answer questions about it.

Although the primary aim of criminal justice (as has been argued) is denunciation, and reparation can achieve this, it is sometimes criticized for not achieving the subsidiary aim of deterrence. But nearly all respondents disagreed with the suggestion that 'Mediation and reparation are not a sufficient deterrent for the offenders concerned, or for other potential offenders', mainly on the ground that punishment is not effective either. The question was intended to distinguish individual and general deterrence, but evidently did not do so clearly enough, and only a few replies could be taken as referring to the latter. Some regarded the criminal justice *process* of arrest, conviction and sentence as a deterrent, particularly for first-time offenders; as one said, those who have been through it have either learnt to manipulate it or become 'calloused towards any guilt feelings'. One judge considered that it deters 'winners', the competent, responsible people who have something to lose, but not the 'losers', who haven't.

In several answers the word 'deterrence' was used loosely – not in its strict sense of frightening people into conformity, but referring to any means of inducing people to change their ways. It was felt that mediation could be effective in doing this, not by instilling fear, but by making offenders accountable when they are confronted with the human cost of their behaviour through putting a face to the victim.

Those who do not have full confidence in this approach sometimes suggest that it should be combined with deterrence. Similarly since at least the end of the nineteenth century, courts have espoused both punishment and rehabilitation, a bigamous relationship in which one partner always suffers when, as is inevitable, the other is given precedence. To flirt with reparation as well could be to court disaster. Confusion of this sort has caused inconsistency and even injustice in the application of community service orders. To sound out the views of practitioners, the statement on which they were asked to comment was put in a rigorous form: 'Reparation between victim and offender should not be accompanied by any punitive or rehabilitative sanction, because they are based on different principles which conflict with the aims and effects of reparation.'

Only a minority agreed. One felt that 'jail and reparation are ideologically incongruent, especially when one follows the other'. Another qualified his agreement with the comment that being arrested, charged and convicted is already a sanction of sorts. One respondent, although she felt that one process cannot meet all the needs of an offender, wrote:

> I would like to see mediation and reparation used and valued on their own, not as 'add-ons'. We tell the parties that they are empowered to resolve their conflict, but then negate that statement by inclusion of other sanctions. . . . Mediation holds a unique place in the debate over whether treatment or punishment are an appropriate response to crime. . . . The characteristic of *responsibility* would seem to be appealing to everyone. Thus, when necessary to 'sell' the idea, the exponents of mediation can tailor their descriptions to suit their audience.

This is an understandable position, and most advocates of reform have probably adopted the tactic described at some time. It does however evoke a strong reminiscence of the paragraph in the Wootton Report (Advisory Council on the Penal System 1970a: para. 33) which listed several possible justifications for community service orders, to suit all tastes. This may have assisted the introduction of the measure, but it has confused its use, as different courts, probation officers and work supervisors have different conceptions of what they are trying to achieve.

The replies hardly referred to implications for the victim, except indirectly by mentioning reparation. For the offender, there was a feeling that reparation could be combined with other demands: some would add it to punishment, others to community service. 'There should be some small sanction over and above the restitution in order to demonstrate that an offender can't break laws of peace and security without paying some retribution to society', one said. Another summed up his view of the proposition in one word: 'Ridiculous'.

Victims, offenders and the rest of society

We have to consider, first, whether the response to crime should be entrusted to the State or to the individuals directly involved, and second, what impact, if any, mediation makes on society in general.

Is the State or the victim the victim? Some writers (Christie 1977; Barnett 1977) imply that this is an 'either/or' question: the State has taken over the conflict, and it ought to be restored to the victim and the offender. In practice, however, the line is not hard-and-fast: in some jurisdictions, for example, there are offences that can be prosecuted only at the victim's instigation. Moreover the individual victim is not the only person affected: the actions of an offender make other people feel threatened, according to G. Davis and his colleagues (1987: 9), and they need reassurance. Therefore they (or the State on their behalf) should 'have a voice in determining what would reassure'. (But this argument needs further examination. First, it could in theory apply to civil disputes, because others could need reassurance that the defendant will not commit a tort against them too; but there the State does not find it necessary to intervene except by providing courts to adjudicate if requested. Second, it applies only to crimes against strangers: if a man uses violence against his wife or underworld rivals, people who are neither do not personally feel threatened. Third, the measures imposed by the criminal justice system are so ineffective that the reassurance offered is somewhat illusory; whereas words such as 'reassurance' repeatedly occur in the case histories from mediation projects, like those from Coventry cited on pp. 95–6.)

To explore this question, respondents were asked to comment on the categorical statement that 'The State's duty to punish should take precedence over the victim's right to reparation, if the two are in conflict'. It is seldom expressed in this form, but is implicit when, for example, prosecutors refuse to withdraw a prosecution although the victim wishes it, or courts impose a custodial sentence which makes it virtually certain that the offender will have neither the ability nor the inclination to make reparation. Nearly all disagreed. Some went the whole way and said that the victim should come first: 'The State is not the *real* victim'. One reply dismissed the idea as 'self-evidently rubbish! Concrete reparations are better than abstract "justice".' Others challenged the duty of the State to punish: its duty is to organize life in the community, and to make the offender responsible, which is 'not in conflict with mediation and reparation'. The relatively conventional view, held by (among others) most of the legal respondents, was that the system could include both: reparation for the less serious offences, punishment for the more serious, or even a combination: if the court did not consider reparation adequate, punishment could be added.

A drawback of offering mediation only in the less serious cases is that any advantages it offers may be denied to the victims of the most serious offences. One project leader felt, in reply to another question, that involvement of victims would lead to greater understanding, and hence (using Christie's phrase) less demand for 'pain delivery'.

This leads to the question of the effect of mediation on society. First, could it even be regressive? Although many victims are themselves poor, needy offenders do often steal from affluent victims, and requiring them to pay back might be thought to reinforce the unequal distribution of property. Only one person agreed with this: it had been a concern of his, and he felt that the mediator should be an advocate on behalf of the weaker party if necessary.

Some disagreed on straightforward ethical grounds: if you take, you should pay back. There was consideration for the victim who has experienced loss and possibly pain: 'a victim is a victim', and should not have to do without the reparation, even if he or she could afford to, 'merely because someone who might need the material possession more decides it'. Reparation should be made, but it could be in the form of a symbolic payment, a gift or service. Moreover, in such cases the need for reconciliation may be greater. There was also concern for offenders, and the need for them to face their accountability was again stressed. Two replies suggested that other court decisions, especially jailing offenders, reinforced the status quo just as much; at least mediation gives the offender some say in how reparation should be made. Of those involved with the criminal justice system, two had 'no problem' with this issue: 'to do otherwise would be to tell people that it's OK to steal'. One prosecutor thought the question was 'a can of worms'. And one judge said: 'Sounds like a socialist made up this question. Just don't steal from the rich then.'

Second, could mediation play a part in changing attitudes? Criminal justice is often assumed, despite the lack of conclusive evidence, to spread various messages among citizens. It is supposed to reassure the law-abiding that malefactors are being dealt with, and to warn them not to become malefactors themselves, nor to take the law into their own hands. It could be open to other interpretations, such as that the State uses force against those who do things which it does not permit, and that citizens may therefore feel entitled to behave similarly. All these are based on what is done to convicted offenders. Does the involvement of victims in mediation affect their outlook on life? It is a very personal experience, and can open the eyes of the victims to the offenders' circumstances as well as vice versa: does it for example lead them to recognize a link between social inequality and crime? To answer would really require a survey of victims, but respondents were asked for an impressionistic response to the statement: 'Despite occasional success stories, middle-class or affluent victims seldom significantly change their attitudes to social policy, or their life-style, as a result of meeting an offender'.

Hardly anyone had considered the point, and when asked, most expressed qualified disagreement. Of those who agreed, that is felt that attitudes are *not* affected, some indicated that this was not a goal they had set themselves; one said he was more concerned with the victim's response to the individual offender and personal conflict resolution. Others cautiously thought that after mediation people might 'maybe understand why the offence was committed', and 'possibly lead the victim to be a little more charitable', or, more positively, that 'attitudes towards social policy do change as a result of victim/offender meetings'. Increased support for alternative sentencing policies, changes in welfare, and confidence in the criminal justice system, were all mentioned. One project reported 'numerous cases' in which the victim became a victim counsellor. A lawyer pointed out that it was a 'two-edged sword': if there was a less than repentant offender, the victim's attitudes towards offenders might be reinforced. But she did not cite instances, and was not aware of this happening often. This may be a testimony to the preliminary screening process of VORP, which is intended to reduce the likelihood of such occurrences. A 40-year-old professional burglar would probably not be invited to mediation, for example; neither would a victim who seemed unlikely to give the offender a chance to make amends.

Since this survey, Coates's study of VORPs has found that about one-third of victims and offenders felt their attitudes had changed: 'the common refrain was, "We see them now as real people".' This seems to indicate change at individual level, but does not suggest new insights into the effects of inequalities built into the structure of society; one respondent to another question, however, criticizing the fact that 'his' offender was sentenced to jail as well as to VORP, said that 'the system caters to the affluent' (Coates 1985: 10–12).

Finally, an open-ended question was asked about the future of mediation, and problems which it might face. Some saw a danger that it could become 'captured' by the existing system, professional and political, losing its commitment to the involvement of volunteers, and operating for the convenience of courts; it would be regarded as 'just another punishment', and restricted to the less serious cases. It might need continuing funding from the State, although that would make it harder to preserve independence of philosophy and management. But there was a feeling that, combined with preventive methods, it had prospects for spreading the values of non-violence and forgiveness, even in the more serious cases, and that this would help to 'restore wholeness to the community'.

Towards restorative justice

Looking back at the traditional criminal justice system, we see a structure with much internal logic, and many additions reflecting new ideas and to meet needs that have become apparent over the years, like a stately home that has been enlarged in different styles by successive generations. Safeguards for the offender have been added, and then in some cases removed. It has not however taken much account of the psychological reactions of offenders to punishment, the social origins of crime, or the needs of victims. Recently awareness of the latter has developed, although little has been built into the statute book (restrictions on the cross-examination of rape victims are one example), and the statutory right to criminal injuries compensation, for which the Criminal Justice Act 1988 provides the framework, has been shelved for the time being. Compensation by the offender is characteristically often regarded as an extra punishment for offenders, as well as showing recognition for victims. Punishment has until now remained the basic principle of sentencing. A century ago there was a major change in thinking, in which rehabilitation was added to punishment as an aim of the system; there are now proposals for another change, of Copernican proportions, in which restorative justice would become the central principle.

This concluding chapter will review the ethical and practical problems which we have noted in the current criminal justice system, and recent moves towards introducing a restorative and participatory approach. It will consider the basic principles on which a restorative system of justice might be developed from these beginnings, how they might be put into practice, and some of the social and political implications.

Crime and punishment

The boundary between crime and other harmful actions is an artificial and constantly changing one. Crimes are not necessarily different in kind from other actions by which people harm each other. If a neighbour claims a strip of land by moving the fence, the conflict is treated as a civil one; if a thief lays claim to a car, it is defined as a crime, but is still essentially a conflict over ownership. The theft is usually committed by a person who is a stranger to the victim; there is no inherent reason for dealing with the two incidents in different ways, and indeed crimes do also constitute civil wrongs. There are, however, advantages in defining which actions are forbidden, which might be described as *prohibita quia mala,* provided that this is not widely taken to mean that all other actions are acceptable. Crimes are actions by which people cause certain types of harm, prohibited by law, and for which, if a person is convicted of them in court, a sanction may be imposed. There are also regulatory offences, such as failure to display a tax disc correctly in a car, which do no harm but cause administrative inconvenience (Durkheim 1893/1964: 83–4; Tench 1981), and their enforcement is therefore a burden on the community. The sanction is assumed, in conventional definitions, to be punishment. A government minister, asked for evidence that an increase in the average length of prison sentences is effective in reducing the total volume of crime, replied: 'The main purpose of a prison sentence is to punish the offender. The courts and prisons can make only a limited contribution to reducing crime' (Mr John Patten, *Hansard* [HC], 10 November 1988). In other words, punishment is justified as retribution and denunciation, regardless of whether it reduces crime. Therefore, if a more constructive method of achieving these objects can be found, it should be acceptable. The old doctrine *nulla poena sine lege* (there should be no punishment except for a legally defined crime) implies that it is only the existence of punishment that requires the individual to be safeguarded by spelling out precisely the conditions on which punishments can be imposed. (Punishment is here used to mean the deliberate imposition of pain on offenders; other court orders, which are not deliberately painful although this may be a side-effect, are referred to as measures or sanctions.)

The enforcement of the law also left victims out of account. They have commonly not been kept informed; criminal procedure aims at determining guilt or innocence, with little or no thought as to whether the *process* is helping victims to recover, or offenders to consider the human consequences of their actions. There have been improvements recently, but the procedure is still oriented primarily towards dealing with offenders. We need to consider whether punishment is an appropriate response to crimes, and whether the process by which the response is decided needs to be improved.

An ethical response to crime

The appropriateness of the response depends not only on whether it achieves its purpose but also, as is often omitted from the discussion, on ethical considerations and on whether there are unacceptable side-effects. The ethical question is whether it is ever right for the State deliberately to inflict measures designed to cause suffering, as opposed to those which do so as an unfortunate side-effect (Christie 1982). Can the end justify the means? Certain extreme forms of pain are called torture and are outlawed, even if they 'succeed' for example by producing confessions – whose value is in any case doubtful. At what point can a line logically be drawn between torture and punishment? Should a just society tolerate the use of the death penalty, mutilation, fetters, solitary confinement, restrictions on family contacts, overcrowding, enforced inactivity, and lack of sanitation, or forbid them unequivocally?

The moderate reformist view accepts punishment on certain conditions: first, that it is not cruel, inhuman, degrading or excessive, second, that it achieves legitimate objectives, and third, that these could be achieved in no other, less damaging way. Supposing that the first group of conditions were met (which in most countries is far from being achieved), the next step is to consider objectives. One of these is to reduce the level of crime through general deterrence. That general deterrence operates to some extent cannot be excluded, but it is widely held that deterrence through enforcement (probability of being detected) counts for much more than deterrence by harsher punishments, which of themselves create a less desirable society in which to live. Whatever is done to the minority of offenders who are caught will have at best a limited effect on those who think they are going to get away with it, or do not think about the consequences at all.

This view is gaining acceptance, for example in the recent Green and White Papers (Home Office 1988b; 1990a), and there is a consequent shift of emphasis towards community-based crime prevention measures. Nor has it been demonstrated that no other method would work. Rewards can be more effective in promoting desirable behaviour than punishment in suppressing the anti-social; this includes intangible ones like praise and social acceptance. Legal theorists appear to be unaware of the findings of psychology which show that punishment is effective in controlling behaviour only under limited conditions: it has to be prompt, consistent, not excessive, and combined with opportunities for learning and adopting different behaviour. It may elicit more aggressive behaviour (Atkinson *et al.* 1987; Morgan and King 1971). Punishment provides little opportunity for commendable behaviour other than, say, enduring prison courageously or paying fines punctually. Rehabilitative measures, by contrast, offer the prospect of approval and acceptance when they have been successfully completed, and reparative ones begin to earn this reward while they are still being carried out. In keeping the peace and maintaining justice, it may be said that esteem (including self-esteem) and tangible rewards for the law-abiding stand in the same relation to deterrence as, in recruiting for the armed forces to fight a war, patriotism and good pay to the press-gang. There is a case for preferring general incentive to general deterrence as a social policy.

As regards convicted offenders, the problem is threefold. It is unethical to inflict more punishment on them than they deserve in the uncertain hope of affecting the behaviour of others over whom they have no control. Offenders' own behaviour is in many cases more likely to be influenced by persuading and enabling them; punishment often has counter-productive side-effects, such as increasing stigma and alienation, damage to family relationships and employment prospects, and the temptation to try to escape it, often by committing a further crime. This could be called 'counter-deterrence'.

Punishment is also imposed with the symbolic aim of retribution. This has few advantages, except that it can to some extent be made proportionate to the offence; any equivalence between an offence and a given level of punishment is arbitrary.

In relation to the third condition, that the aim can be achieved in no other way, the tangible effects can be produced by crime prevention measures, and the symbolic one (denunciation) by reparation (this concept will be explored on pp. 114–117).

Part of the reason why punishment persists is that it fulfils a function in society. It enables 'us' to blame 'them', and thus to avoid recognizing, finding time for, and paying for, the tasks and social reforms which could alleviate the extent and seriousness of crime. Social Darwinism draws a parallel between human behaviour and that of animals, which drive deviants out of the herd, but this is not an acceptable model for human society – it would also permit the exclusion of, for example, disabled people. Durkheim commented that punishment is a 'passionate reaction' which maintains the intensity of the collective sentiments which the crime offends; like crime, it promotes the cohesion of society (Durkheim 1893/1964: 90, 106; 1895/1938: 96). But elsewhere he pointed out that it is not the only kind of sanction. Sanctions are of two kinds: some consist essentially in suffering, or at least a loss, and are called repressive, while the other type 'does not necessarily imply suffering for the agent, but consists only of *the return of things as they were*' (Durkheim 1893/1964: 69, emphasis in original). Sanctions have their place, but the degree of development of a society can be correlated with less use of penal, more of restitutive ones (1893/1964: 144–5).

It is commonly assumed that punishments must be maintained at a high level because public opinion and victims demand it. It is true that, as long as the amount of punishment is the only yardstick by which the gravity of crimes is denounced, people feel that, particularly for serious offences, a substantial sanction should be imposed; as to the type of sanction, surveys have repeatedly shown strong support for reparation to the individual or the community, in many cases instead of imprisonment, not in addition (Wright 1989).

Aid for victims

A move towards assistance for the victim is now gaining a place beside the traditional uneasy mixture of punishment of, and concern for, the offender. This operates in different ways. First there is the community response, through Victim

Support and similar groups, in which members of the community voluntarily offer the victim emotional or practical support. Next there is the State response, through compensation to victims of violent crime, medical care, in countries which have a national health service, and social security assistance (in Britain now largely limited to loans) to some of those suffering great hardship as a result of property crime. If offenders are convicted, there is increasing pressure on the courts to order them to pay compensation. Offenders can also make indirect reparation, not to the victim but to the community, through the community service order; this can be particularly appropriate when the victim does not wish to receive compensation, or where there is no individual victim. Lastly, information should be gathered from the offences that are resolved, to assist in improving crime prevention and social policies.

Procedure: adversarial or reconciling

In earlier times the procedure for responding to wrongdoing involved victims directly (and in other cultures it still does); however, bringing prosecutions became burdensome, and was later taken over by the police and ultimately the Crown Prosecution Service. That left victims on the margin. The court process has been blamed as being too adversarial, formal, uncertain, slow and often inaudible; it may even, because of the stigma it imposes, be criminogenic (West and Farrington 1977). Only recently is it beginning to be accepted again that the individual victim, where there is one, should be kept informed about the case and not treated as just another witness (see e.g. the *Victims' Charter* – Home Office 1990b). The problem has been made worse, it is suggested, by the fact that the system is based on punishment. The more serious the punishment, the more safeguards are needed for the accused, which can lead to acquittal of a guilty person, or conviction on a lesser charge, both of which leave the victim (and justice) unsatisfied. This in turn is countered by restricting the defendant's rights. Again, defendants often try to secure acquittal, or a reduction in penalty, by blaming the victim. This is contrasted with the attitude in Japan, where accused persons, if they admit the offence, are encouraged to make reparation so that the judge need not impose so much punishment (Haley, 1989).

Some different models suggest possibilities for making the process more constructive. In the Scottish juvenile court system, the Reporter meets the juvenile and whenever possible one of the parents, for a discussion to try to agree on voluntary action, including the possibility of putting right what the child has done. Where the Reporter feels that compulsory measures are necessary the case can (if it is not contested) be transferred to a hearing before a children's panel, but here too the emphasis is on discussion, until the final stage when the panel decides the outcome (Martin *et al.* 1981).

The practice of Inland Revenue and Customs and Excise shows an interesting way of applying the existing criminal law and procedure. They do not normally prosecute, with a view to conviction and punishment, but use the possibility of prosecution as a lever, with a view to obtaining payment (Marshall 1985).

One response to the widespread criticisms has been the development of mediation, particularly in cases (civil or criminal) where there is a relationship between the two parties. Legal systems tend to concentrate on the 'result', with little regard to the effects of the process on participants. Adversarial proceedings tend to make one party the 'winner', the other the 'loser', so that their relationship is often worse than before. Rather than risk this, many people, in the absence of an alternative, suffer in silence; some take the law into their own hands. Mediation derives from a much older tradition, studied by anthropologists, some of whom have been active in promoting its application in modern western societies. The concept has several strands, not all of which are found in all the projects.

The process itself should help to promote understanding; the aim is to agree an outcome acceptable to both parties. The participants, not a court, decide what is relevant, and are able to tell the 'whole truth' as they see it; there is no necessity to establish the 'facts', because the purpose is not to allocate blame for what is past, but to secure agreement as to future conduct. There is often a philosophy of involving, and hence empowering, the community, by recruiting mediators from the local population. In practice the community involvement and autonomy vary. Some projects are integrated into the court system in a coercive way, both in the manner in which cases are referred, and in the fact that agreements are enforceable at law. Those who see mediation as a way of strengthening the community resist these tendencies. ('Community' here is generally taken to mean people who live or work locally and may be affected by the offender's crime or any reparative actions, including members of local organizations, and elected representatives in local government.)

A new model has been proposed in which the response to crime would be, not to add to the harm caused, by imposing further harm on the offender, but to do as much as possible to restore the situation. The community offers aid to the victim; the offender is held accountable and required to make reparation. Attention would be given not only to the *outcome*, but also to evolving a *process* that respected the feelings and humanity of both the victim and the offender. This can include offering both parties the opportunity to be involved personally in resolving the incident, rather than have it dealt with by professional proxies. Where these projects have been evaluated, the great majority of participants, both victims and offenders, have found the experience helpful.

The emergence of the restorative model

These parallel developments, reparation as the outcome and mediation as the procedure, came together in the 1970s with the establishment of the Victim/Offender Reconciliation Programs (VORPs), which developed the idea of bringing together the injured party and the wrongdoer even if they were strangers to each other previously (Chapter 5). A new criterion for evaluating the process is introduced: that it should be satisfactory for both parties, not only the victim but also the offender. The model is not based on meeting offenders' needs (though that can be part of it) nor punishing their deeds; rather it builds on their good qualities by requiring them to make amends. It is not a 'battle model' against an 'enemy of society' but a 'family model' with the offender as 'wayward child'. The ultimate objective is spoken of in terms not of deterrence and coercion but of healing and reconciliation.

The reparative approach is not without its critics. Traditionalists regard it as lenient, and inadequate to deter crime; they are as yet unfamiliar with the concept of expressing denunciation in a currency other than punishment. From the liberal reformist viewpoint, there is a danger that this approach will increase, not reduce, the apparatus of social control. Even independently managed projects may be under the control of the courts, and reparation can be an 'add-on' to punishment, not a replacement. On behalf of victims there are fears that mediation may prove a burden; others say that there is little or no evidence of that, and that it is possible to be overprotective towards victims, who often find it helpful. Even where they have agreed to it only because as conscientious citizens they hope to influence the offender, this can be a step towards regaining autonomy over their own lives.

The victim/offender mediation projects in particular have been criticized for confusion as to their aims. The prototype was called a Victim/Offender *Reconciliation* Programme, but in order to gain acceptance projects of this kind have proposed a variety of goals, such as reducing the prison population, easing the pressure on the courts, re-educating the offender and securing reparation for the victim. In fact the proportion of all cases in which the offender has probably been diverted from prison has been modest, although there is a tendency towards shorter sentences, and some projects have concentrated on relatively serious cases. Courts have tended to forgo a reduced workload in the interests of retaining control, but some projects divert cases before they reach court. Some offenders' attitudes do seem to have been influenced; there is no significant evidence yet as to whether they also modified their behaviour (Marshall and Merry 1990: 193–7). Finally, by no means all victims have shown that substantial reparation is what they want most; they often seek symbolic reparation, an opportunity to try to persuade the offender not to offend again, and, where the parties are related, a resolution of the underlying dispute.

In criticizing reparation and mediation projects for lack of clarity about aims, it should be remembered that the existing system is open to the same charge. Some measures may be intended both to punish and to prevent crime; those intended to rehabilitate are seen as inadequate to denounce the crime, and so on. Since the 'stolen' conflict is being restored to its owners, some lack of clarity of aims is inevitable. The aim of the criminal justice system would then be not to impose a specific outcome in every case, but to enable the parties to work towards their own. A starting-point for a new model may be to distinguish the different aims of social policy in relation to crime, and to propose specific measures designed to achieve them. What might be the basis of a new model and how might it be put into practice?

Basis for a new model

The first step in planning a new system is to define the task and to consider how its aims may be achieved, with as few harmful side-effects as possible. It should be taken as axiomatic that the methods must be ethical, and not transgress the values they are meant to uphold. This section, building on the thinking and experience described earlier, will outline a possible structure for putting such a policy into effect.

To avoid contradictions, such a system should have one primary aim, qualified by subsidiary aims or limiting factors. A subsidiary aim is one which is desirable, but is subordinated to the primary aim if the two are incompatible. A limiting factor is an operating condition which must not be overstepped in the pursuit of the aims. Within the broad aim of maintaining a just society, and one that is as fulfilling and rewarding as possible for all its citizens, the primary tasks of a social order policy are to try to reduce the harm which people cause to each other, the community and the environment, and, when harmful acts are committed, to see that the damage is restored as far as possible.

It is traditionally assumed that the prevention of the acts defined as crimes is, in England and Wales, achieved principally by preventive measures (the responsibility of the Home Office), apprehending offenders (Home Office), imposing penalties (Lord Chancellor's Department) and implementing them (Home Office). The main methods employed are general deterrence and situational crime prevention, that is prevention focused on the individuals or things which are the objects of the criminal acts. A problem-solving approach would also include social crime prevention, focused on the circumstances and pressures acting on potential offenders. This would therefore involve all departments of government, especially housing, education, employment, recreation and social security. To make the point, let us assign the functions to two hypothetical new ministries, although they could be carried out within the existing structure.

A Department of Crime Prevention would be responsible for co-ordinating the preventive aspects of this work, just as for example the Department of the Environment is concerned with the effects of other ministries' policies on pollution. Since deterrence through punishment has at best a limited role in crime reduction (Zimring and Hawkins 1973; Colson and Benson 1980; Beyleveld 1979), crime control would concentrate on deterrence by enforcement, thus maximizing the probability of detection. Since the policy would not be based on fear, the word 'deterrence' would not be appropriate; it would be better to speak of 'disincentives', ensuring that crime did not pay because of the reparation that offenders would be required to make. The reparative measures would be a disincentive, because they could require the offender to spend as much time and effort, or pay as much money, as punitive ones, but their aim, the spirit in which they were applied, would be different.

Under the ethical imperative that the means should not contradict the end, there would be no place for general deterrence by exemplary punishment, based on fear of harm deliberately inflicted by the State. In its place would be the principle of general incentive, in which the aim would be in line with that of general social policy: to provide an adequately fulfilling life for all, without resort to crime. It would be backed up by disincentives: probability of being caught and having to make reparation. There is no evidence that this would be less effective than a policy based on fear, and it would be likely to have fewer undesirable side-effects – although it might be harder to put into practice.

A separate Department of Justice would be responsible for making a just and constructive response to crimes when they are committed. It would be responsible, first, for services to victims. It would fund Victim Support and similar agencies, and this would enable it, with consultation, to agree standards of service, while preserving their autonomy. They could further enhance their independence by obtaining part of their funding from elsewhere. Second, it would be responsible for the Criminal Injuries Compensation Board, and ideally also for compensation for crimes against property, at least for people unable to afford private insurance.

Third, it would facilitate the development of autonomous mediation and reparation services. These, like Victim Support, would not only offer assistance to victims, but also constitute a substantial involvement of members of the community. Their operation will be considered on pp. 117–23.

Fourth, the department would be responsible for the administration of justice through the courts. The organization would not be substantially altered, but the sanctions imposed, in accordance with the restorative principle, would be based not on ensuring that those who cause harm should suffer in return, but on the principle of restoration combined with individual incentive: that they should make up for the harm, and would be given credit for doing so. Although their reparation could, in serious cases, be onerous, it would not be imposed for that reason, but for its benefit to the victim or the community. The concept of reparation is perhaps most easily visualized in relation to crimes where there is an identifiable victim (individual or corporate); where there is not, or the victim does not want compensation, the offender could make amends to the community, and fines could be so regarded (the French word for fine is *amende*); this might be emphasized by making the payments to a local charitable trust rather than to the Exchequer. In addition, the proceeds of the offence should be forfeited; the Drug Trafficking Offences Act 1986 and the Criminal Justice Act 1988, following the Howard League report *Profits of Crime and their Recovery* (1984), have established this principle and ways of strengthening its enforcement are being developed. It has been suggested that confiscated assets of drug users should be used to provide drug education and rehabilitation services; this would strengthen the reparative element. If there was concern that offenders with money could make amends more easily, there could be a requirement that they, too, would have to undertake some community service.

Although based on the principle of holding the offender accountable, and imposing a sanction proportionate to the offence, restorative justice would not inflict punitive 'just deserts'. The reparation would be related to offenders' ability to pay, or translated into service, and it could include co-operating with such counselling, training or other support as they might need. In this way offenders would not be objects of punishment or treatment, but partners in over-coming any factors which made them prone to commit crime; some could also co-operate in crime prevention research. Unlike some concepts of rehabilitation, this would not tend to exonerate offenders, nor to allow them (short of psychia-tric disorder) to deny their accountability for the harm caused by their actions to others, by attributing blame for their behaviour in a deterministic way to hered-ity, upbringing or social conditions. Nor, however, could the community absolve itself by putting the sole blame on the offender: it would have responsibility to provide the training and treatment (and where necessary accommodation and employment) and to accept the implications for prevention, some of which could require the Department of Crime Prevention to press for considerable revision of social policies.

Thus the primary aim of the Department of Justice would be to see that the victim's previous condition was restored as far as possible and, in cases of hard-ship, improved. Subsidiary aims would include holding offenders accountable, requiring them to make amends, and enabling them to earn reacceptance into the community as contributing members. Denunciation would be another secondary aim; it would be achieved not only by the reparation required of the offender, but also by the amount of compensation and other assistance provided by the State and the community to the victim in those cases where the offender could not make full reparation, or was not convicted. (Other questions, such as deciding the amount of reparation, and enforcement, will be considered on pp. 124–7.) For this department, crime prevention would be only a limiting factor: the poli-cies would not be expected to reduce crime, but would have to be reconsidered if they could be shown to increase it. Other limiting factors would be human rights, cost and public acceptability. The latter could be influenced by the way the new practice was explained, for example by showing that denunciation is still included although in a different way. But care would be needed not to subvert the principles in order to make them acceptable; for example it is true that repar-ation can be onerous, but to advocate it *for that reason* would be to undermine its restorative philosophy.

If the aim of the system is to restore the victim's former state, the primary cri-terion for the system's performance would be the extent to which this was done. It would include the extent to which support and compensation were provided by the community and the State, as well as reparation by the offender.

Assessment of mediation, on the other hand, would not be primarily by the outcome, since there is no yardstick for a successful result; that depends on whether the individuals concerned are content with it. The first criterion here is whether the option of participation, one-to-one or in a group, has been made available to as many victims as wish to take part: 'The evaluative question is to what extent does the program provide opportunities for reconciliation, rather than to what extent does reconciliation occur' (Galaway 1985: 11–14). The second, which should be applied also to the traditional process, is whether the process itself was such as to make both individuals feel that it was a helpful way of resolving the incident. Although the satisfaction of offenders would, in the event of competing priorities, take second place to that of victims, it is in the interests of respect for the law that they should feel fairly treated.

The principles of restorative justice may be summed up as: for the victim, support and reparation (with mediation if required); for the offender, reparation to the victim or the community, including co-operating in any needed rehabilitation, with restrictions or detention only if necessary. This would, it is suggested, have an integrative effect on the local community, whose members would have the right and the duty to participate in the process as much as possible.

Restorative justice in practice

A system based on restorative justice would be similar to the present one, with one change in procedure, one significant addition, and one major change. Precedents for all of these are already in existence.

The change in procedure, whose precedent is in the practice of the Inland Revenue and Customs and Excise, is that except in serious or persistent cases, or those where the act was denied, prosecution would proceed only where adequate reparation was not forthcoming from the offender.

The addition would be local mediation services. Several of these have been established in the United Kingdom and their experimental stage has been researched. They have been operating for some time in North America (Marshall and Merry 1990; FIRM 1989c; US Association for Victim/Offender Mediation 1989). Restorative justice could be administered without them, but they would facilitate its operation, and this account will include them.

The major change would be that the primary purpose of the courts would be restoration of the community and the individual victim, where there is one, rather than punishment of the offender. Functions traditionally attributed to punishment would be carried out in other ways: prevention of crime would be allocated to a separate department, denunciation and disincentives to crime would still be present though not primary, and incentives to acceptable conduct would be explicitly incorporated into public policy. There are already restorative features in the response to crime: compensation orders, especially when used as a sole sanction, and adjuncts to the system such as Victim Support and criminal injuries compensation.

How could this be made to work in practice? First, a few general comments. The following scenario is obviously only one of many possible variants, and in some cases more than one will be proposed. It would be subject to change in the light of monitoring and feedback. For simplicity it will concentrate on crimes where there is an individual victim, but a representative could act on behalf of corporate bodies, and where the victim did not wish for reparation, or the crime was committed against the State, reparation could be made to the community. At some points there is a tension between aspects which have to be balanced (but the same is true of the existing system): for example the victim should be involved but should not be burdened with responsibility, and mediation services should be autonomous but have to work with police, probation, prosecutors and courts. These are matters of balance and working relationships.

Certain assumptions will be made. First, many offences arising out of private disputes can be resolved through the independent mediation service alone, but those which have led to serious crimes, and most crimes by strangers, have a public aspect and should as a safeguard be referred to the criminal justice system, even if it then exercises discretion not to proceed. Second, offenders would be given the chance to offer reparation voluntarily, even if the voluntariness is constrained by the knowledge that the decision to prosecute or the court's sanction may be influenced by it. Third, the court's sanction should take account of the reparation offered, but should *not* be affected by the victim's acceptance or otherwise, nor by his or her decision as to mediation. The victim would thus be unconstrained by any concerns about what sanctions the court might impose on the offender, and would have more confidence that any apology was genuine.

Harmful acts would be divided into private ones, which do not necessarily involve the criminal justice system, and those with a public aspect, such as burglary, which does not affect only the direct victims but causes fear among other citizens. The former could be resolved privately, if both sides agreed; the latter should be overseen by the agencies of criminal justice.

For non-criminal harmful acts and disputes, and for those which could otherwise lead to private prosecutions or criminal charges up to a certain level of seriousness (for example actual bodily harm) a local mediation service could be available. Cases thus resolved need proceed no further. This would not constitute widening the net of the justice system, because the mediation service envisaged here would be offering citizens an extra resource in handling everyday problems. It would not be under the control of any criminal justice agency, it would have no powers, and agreements would not be enforceable at law. They would be 'without prejudice'; if no agreement were reached or fulfilled, or if either party did not wish to use mediation at all, the normal legal remedies would be available.

Although the mediation services envisaged here would have to work with the criminal justice system, they could retain considerable autonomy by having independent management committees, which could include representatives of the main relevant agencies, and by being funded from more than one source.

For crimes by strangers up to a similar level, there could also be a step towards decriminalization: if full reparation were made, the court need make no order (as in the Federal Republic of Germany); if it were made before the offence was notified to the police, no crime would be deemed to have been committed (following the Austrian model). The mediation service could facilitate such offers. Mediation, direct or indirect, would be available but not insisted on. If the victim did not wish to receive reparation, or could not be traced, the reparation could be made to a charitable fund or through community service.

For more serious crimes committed by strangers, where a suspect was discovered by the police and admitted the act, the suspect would first be given the chance to offer reparation. The victim would have the right to request mediation if he or she felt it would be helpful. The case would then be returned to the criminal justice system to consider whether the public interest required any further reparation, and whether any form of restriction or detention was required.

Where the victim and offender were known or related, a serious case could if appropriate be taken first to the mediation centre, where the private aspect could be dealt with, before being referred to the criminal justice system.

In either case, if there was a grave risk of repeated violence, a restriction could be ordered immediately (for example ordering a partner accused of domestic violence to stay away, but there would be an opportunity for mediation to agree on practical aspects of separation), or in the most serious cases detention.

Case example 1: burglary

The process may be illustrated by two case examples, which will also show what mediation consists of in this context. There are of course many possible combinations of punishment, rehabilitation and reparation, but we will use mainly 'pure' examples to indicate the effects of traditional measures, and then the lines on which a restorative approach can be followed. The first involves burglary. Ms Turner, an office worker, divorced, suffered a burglary in which a beer stein of sentimental value was broken, and a £700 video which she had borrowed was stolen and later dropped, damaging it beyond repair. It was not covered by insurance. Mark, aged 20, was charged with the offence. He had already served three years in custody as a juvenile for burglary, and was currently on probation for taking a motor cycle without consent, possession of a weapon, and two other offences. (Case summarized from Marshall and Merry 1990: 80; names have been changed.)

Traditional justice

Punishment   Mark, with his record, would have been likely to get a custodial sentence or at least a fine. This would give the victim nothing, and would be unlikely to give Mark insight into the effects of his behaviour on victims.

Rehabilitation If, despite his record, the court decided that he needed help with personal problems, he could have been placed on probation. This could have helped, but there would have been a risk that it would have allowed him to blame his conduct on his problems. In terms of 'just deserts' it would have appeared 'lenient'. Again, the victim would receive nothing.

Restorative justice

Mixed traditional and reparative What in fact happened in Mark's case was that Ms Turner, when approached by the reparation project, was keen to meet him. Her own son had been involved in petty crime, and she wanted to ask him why he intruded into people's homes, and to tell him the effect of this violation on her. A meeting was arranged, and she did so. Mark, who did not have a close relationship with his parents, responded to her willingness to talk to him, and explained that he had been drinking on the night in question. The mediator suggested that he might make a payment to Ms Turner as reparation. She and Mark agreed to this, although his earnings were small, and he regularly paid £5 a week. The case then came to court, whose sentencing options included disregarding the private arrangement and imposing punishment, which would have been disillusioning for Mark; or taking it into account, which could have been seen as unfair on other offenders whose victims were not willing to take part. In the event the court did apparently take note of what had happened, and put Mark on probation.

Reparative To avoid putting pressure on victims by making the sentence dependent on their decisions, the chance to offer reparation would be provided at the beginning of the process to all offenders like Mark who admitted the alleged act. If victims wished to meet offenders as well, as Ms Turner did, they could do so unconstrainedly, to express feelings, discuss the amount of reparation, or both. For those who did not wish the offender to pay them in person, other arrangements would have to be made. Offenders would still be subject to the element of deprivation which most advocates of punishment regard as necessary, but it would not entail inflicting pain for its own sake. In this case a good relationship developed, so that taking a weekly payment to Ms Turner was not as hard as it might have been. This probably strengthened the effect on Mark, but it would have weakened a punitive impact, had that been the intention.

Where there was no individual victim, as in the case of speeding through a village or vandalizing a school or housing estate, reparation could be paid into a fund for the benefit of the community concerned. If desired, a meeting could be arranged with a representative such as the chairperson of the parish council or tenants' association, or the teacher whose classroom was most damaged, but there would be no obligation on a corporate victim any more than on an individual one.

Case example 2: sexual assault

A Victim Support visitor called on Ms White, a young single mother who had reported a burglary. She revealed that the burglar had also indecently assaulted her, and spontaneously said she would like to meet the man who had done this to her. (Case summarized from *Mediation* 6(2): 11–12.)

Traditional justice

Punishment   The usual sentence for Dave, aged 18, would have been youth custody. He would have emerged labelled as a sex offender, which could potentially damage his prospects both in obtaining jobs and in relationships. Although Ms White would receive help from Victim Support, she would not be able to meet the offender as she wished, and would get nothing from the criminal justice process itself; if Dave chose to plead not guilty, she would have to relive her ordeal in court.

Rehabilitation   As in Mark's case, if Dave were placed on probation this would appear lenient, even if he had problems with which he needed help; again, there would be no benefit to the victim. Traditional probation focuses on offenders' problems rather than on the impact of their actions on the victims (though this is changing).

Restorative justice

Mixed traditional and reparative   Victim Support put Ms White in touch with Leeds Reparation Service, a mediator visited her and Dave to check that it was in both their interests for a meeting to be arranged, and it took place. Dave tried to apologize, but this was not acceptable to Ms White at this stage. She told him forcefully about the effects of the offence on her. Afterwards she said that she felt 'marvellous'. Dave explained that although he had previous convictions for burglary, he had not committed an offence like this before, and did not see himself as a sex offender. He had been high on drugs at the time. Afterwards he was frustrated at not being able to make reparation, but with her permission he was told how his participation had helped her. This may have helped him to feel better about himself; also it was the first time he had had to face up to someone he had harmed by his behaviour. When the case came to court, however, he was sentenced to two years' youth custody.

Reparative   When Dave was willing to make reparation, but Ms White did not want it, a reparative system would have provided the opportunity to make reparation to the community. A meeting could still have taken place to enable her to express her feelings. Dave would not have been imprisoned, because his record did not suggest that he was likely to commit such a serious offence again; his reparation could have included tackling his use of drugs, as well as the meeting itself. He would then have emerged not as a person who had served a two-year sentence, but as one who had done what he could to make up for his offence.

Examples could be multiplied, including more serious cases. But until experience has been gained with moderately serious cases, and the idea has become familiar to the public, it is not to be expected that a fully reparative approach could yet be adopted across the whole range of offences. It should be remembered, however, that the victim's needs are potentially greatest when the offence is serious; restorative justice could then be more, not less, appropriate.

At each stage of the formal process there would be, as now, defined discretion whether to proceed: the police could caution, the prosecutor could discontinue, the court could adjourn in contemplation of dismissal, or remand pre-sentence, or defer sentence. At each stage the victim would be kept informed. The authority concerned would take into account whether the offender had made, or shown a convincing intention of making, adequate reparation (to the victim or the community). This is an extension of the principle which is already applied to deferment of sentence. Adequate reparation to the victim could be regarded as meeting both the private and the public aspects of the offence; in some cases further reparation to the community would be required to meet the public aspect.

The offender would of course have to admit the act, as is already the case with a caution. (For this purpose offenders would not have to admit *guilt* in the legal sense. They might for example admit that they had harmed the victim but deny that they had intended to do so. If offenders alleged that the victim was in any way to blame, the victim would be given an opportunity to discuss this, if he or she wished, in mediation.) Offenders would have the right to advice in drawing up a reparation plan, which might include a rehabilitative programme. The decision whether to discontinue the proceedings, or to defer them conditionally, would be based on this proposal, not on the victim's response, although the justice agencies making the decision would be aware of the latter. This is in order to protect victims from any pressures that might be placed upon them if they were in a position to influence the decision-making process. But they would have a role. The most serious crimes would be regarded as having a substantial public aspect, so that they would have to go to court even if full reparation had been made to the victim. If offenders made no move towards reparation, the case would proceed in the normal way, which could still include a caution or discontinuance if prosecution was not warranted; if offenders denied the act, they could insist on a trial.

Besides ordering reparation, where it was not arranged voluntarily, courts would still retain powers to impose restrictions on offenders where this was necessary for the protection of the public. These have been described as 'natural consequences' (Wright 1982: ch. 10). They would not be intended punitively, but to restrain certain offenders from certain activities which had been associated with their offences – such as driving a car, running a company, working with children or handling cash – until they had regained the trust of fellow citizens.

Where there was a serious risk of further grave harm, detention could be imposed, but this too would not be intended punitively. It would probably be used very little: the number of prisoners currently in the highest security category, 'A', in England and Wales is fewer than 400; even the next highest, Category 'B', has fewer than 5,000. The duration of such restrictions will be considered on pp. 126-7.

It may be objected that offenders could be under pressure to pay more in reparation than they would have done in fines under the present system, but they would receive guidance to keep this within reasonable limits; in any case one criticism of existing practice is that they are not held accountable for the harm they have caused. Reparation does not have to be in cash. It is also said that they might admit guilt falsely, in order to escape worse consequences if they pleaded not guilty at the trial and were not believed. This is not uncommon now, however, and the criticism applies to all forms of diversion from the system; where a case went to mediation, there would be an improved chance of discovering that the guilty plea was wrongly made. If a person is nevertheless wrongly convicted, it is possibly less painful to make reparation for something one did not do than to be punished for it.

The victim's role

When the offender had made an offer of reparation at any stage of the process, the victim would have several options. In countries like the United Kingdom, where Victim Support services are well developed, a volunteer could be available to discuss the choices if required. Victims could simply accept the offer, or consider it inadequate and ask for mediation with the offender regarding the amount. They might accept, but ask for mediation at which to express feelings, ask questions, and perhaps seek an apology. They might refuse the offer (which would then be made to the community), but still ask for mediation, or they might refuse outright. In each case they would have had an opportunity for personal involvement, with the aid of trained mediators, but if they declined, or did not accept the reparation agreement offered, this would not affect the decision reached in the criminal justice system.

At each stage, if the offender did not offer reparation, the case would proceed to the next one. There would be an opportunity for a victim who particularly wanted mediation to request it, but it would have to be voluntary on the offender's part, and would be possible only where the offender had admitted the act. When the victim wanted reparation, and the offender had still made no offer when the case came to court, the court would ask for full information as to the loss or harm suffered by the victim, just as it does now when making a compensation order.

For offenders whose victims did not wish to take part, and for victims whose offenders were not caught, another possibility could be made available: to enable both to take part in groups of 'unrelated' victims and offenders on the model of Victims and Offenders in Conciliation (VOIC – see pp. 98–9).

Deciding and enforcing the restorative sanction

The deferment of prosecution, conditional upon reparation, would substantially reduce the number of cases that came to court. It would be possible, as an interim phase, to operate it while courts still followed a retributive philosophy, although that would inevitably lead to contradictions. This has been found in some of the experimental projects operating within the existing system, where sentences on contrite offenders have included a conditional discharge for attempted murder (admittedly in exceptional circumstances) and a custodial sentence for two burglaries (Marshall and Merry 1990: 253–6). Let us assume, however, that such a hybrid phase has been successfully worked through, and that courts have been persuaded of the advantages of making restorative justice their primary aim. How are they to apply it?

The question of quantum is a complex one in all forms of compensation. The effects of crime may involve financial loss (property stolen or damaged, time off work as a result of injury), and inconvenience, shock or lasting trauma. There is also the more intangible question of how to quantify reparation to the community for the public aspect of an offence.

As regards financial loss, clearly if offenders are able to repay it, they should. But most cannot, or could do so only in instalments over a disproportionately long period. If offenders are unemployed the period will be longer still. There is a case for saying that if society expects them to repay, it should make it possible for them to do so. The 'Earn-It' scheme in Massachusetts provided employment for this purpose (Wright 1983). It was criticized for giving offenders precedence in the queue for jobs; its proponents replied that to have to work and pay all one's disposable income as reparation is not much to be coveted, and many of the jobs were temporary; admittedly some led to permanent employment. The scheme was also said to provide cheap labour for some unscrupulous employers; the organizers would therefore have to stipulate that fair wages should be paid by participating employers. Some might feel that such schemes should be organized by a statutory body, or a government-funded voluntary organization such as NACRO or the Apex Trust.

When an offender makes payments by instalments, the victim receives them by instalments, which greatly diminishes their practical and psychological value. It has been proposed that the court should advance the money and collect it from the offender later (Home Office 1988b). A non-statutory alternative is to set up a charitable debt regulation fund for this purpose (see p. 37; Wright 1988). The advantages are that terms can be negotiated, perhaps by probation officers or ancillary workers, for repayments of the other debts which many offenders have, and that this would put pressure on the offender to pay so as not to deplete the fund; the disadvantage is that it would be practicable only for 'good risks', and indeed it might not survive the cultural transplant from the Federal Republic of Germany, where it originated.

For victims' pain and suffering there is no 'conversion table' for deciding an appropriate amount of reparation. It would however be possible to borrow from the day-fine system. For a particular degree of suffering a period of time could be determined during which offenders would make reparation through their disposable money or time. This is analogous to retributive sanctions, and the duration would admittedly be somewhat arbitrary, but it is not punishment within the definition used here, because the *purpose* is not that offenders should suffer but that they should make a contribution of value.

At present both fines and compensation are generally scaled down to what an offender can reasonably pay in one or two years. Similarly community service orders are in practice restricted to 'disposable time' for about a year, and probation orders to a maximum of three years. If, however, reparative measures are to be imposed even for the most serious crimes, and are to be served in the community except where there is a major risk of further grave offences, then considerably longer periods will be required in the interests of natural justice and public acceptability. This will indeed be burdensome, and will require a substantial degree of supervision during the period of enforcement. If this task were given to the probation service, it is not one that many probation officers would welcome, but it is surely preferable to the continued use of imprisonment on its present scale. It is already the practice in the United States to require long periods of community service. This could open the door to long community sanctions for minor offences; statutory safeguards to prevent this would be needed.

In the last resort some form of restriction might also be necessary to ensure that reparation was made; in keeping with the reparative ethic, the principle behind this would be to ensure that the offenders made reparation, not to punish them for failing to do so. There would be less pressure to default if reparation payments were proportionate to the offender's means. It is anomalous to use imprisonment to enforce a non-custodial sanction, and although the ultimate sanction for non-payment of fines in many countries remains imprisonment, there is pressure to minimize its use, down to 0.2 per cent of cases (13 offenders) in Sweden and 0.1 per cent (160 offenders) in Japan (Grebing 1982: 148, 273). There are moves towards civil-law processes of enforcement; in Italy the Constitutional Court has ruled that when a fine is not enforced on account of an offender's insolvency, it is unconstitutional to convert it into default imprisonment (Grebing 1982: 266).

At the other end of the scale is a problem concerning the reparative principle. Suppose the cost of the harm is much *less* than the offender can easily afford to pay, as in the case of successful professional shoplifters, or the large company producing adulterated goods or illegal pollution. If shoplifters are caught, they will hand back the stolen items: have they then made full reparation? If so, is the concept of deterrence through enforcement still tenable? Assuming that they are no longer concerned about their reputation, they have nothing to lose by continuing to steal if the worst that can happen is that they return the goods. One approach is to apply the principle of *caveat mercator* (let the merchant beware): a company whose business involves certain risks, whether through shoplifting, high seas or any other peril, has a duty to take reasonable precautions; in this case, the provision of enough shop assistants to supervise the temptingly displayed stock adequately. If it does not, the argument runs, it should not be able to use the criminal justice agencies as a less expensive substitute. At the least it could be required to bring prosecution privately if it wished to do so. Denmark is even firmer in requiring the shops to take care, because there is no right of private prosecution in such cases (Wright 1982: 213). Critics would say, however, that this argument comes close to 'blaming the victim', even if the victim is a supermarket. An alternative would be to extend the concept of reparation, for example to cover a proportion of the cost of preventive measures made necessary by the behaviour concerned. In the case of the delinquent company, it would pay compensation to individual consumers, workers or local residents, but it could also be required to make reparation for the public aspect of the offence by contributing to the medical, social and enforcement costs of its actions, or to a charitable fund.

How long for?

When reparation includes rehabilitative activities, there will be some questions to resolve in relation to their duration. If, for example, they include attending a day centre or staying in a hostel, it could be considered fair that they should not last so long as if the offender continued to live at home and have a job. One suggestion is that offences should be graded on a scale from 1 to 100, as has been done with unit fines: for each point the appropriate amends might be a week's day-payments or a day's community service; a week's attendance at a day centre, since it involves greater restriction of liberty, might be worth two points (Wright 1982: 261). These assessments would admittedly be somewhat arbitrary but, being proportional to the harm done, they would fulfil one function at present performed by punishment without its harmful side-effects. They would not, on the other hand, bear any relation to the length of the training or counselling which individuals might need to overcome their condition; they would set a limit to the period required by the reparative order, after which any continuance would be voluntary. The proportion of people who continued voluntarily because they needed further help would be one measure of the value of the programme offered.

The question is more acute when the restriction of offenders' liberty is not for their benefit but for the protection of the public. The courts would retain the power to impose appropriate restrictions, and in serious cases detention. How long should they last? For non-payers and non-compliers it would be until their reparation was completed. But there would be a maximum, proportionate to the offence; this would be reduced if additional restrictions on the individual's liberty were involved. Again, the actual duration would have to be to some extent arbitrary, like the existing tariff, but could take as a starting-point the degree and duration of reduction of the quality of life of victims.

For those considered dangerous, detention would have to remain an option. Conditions would not be punitive; like conditions outside, they should enable the offender to make reparation. Even so, deprivation of liberty is a serious matter. If they were detained until they had completed reparation, some might be released while they were still dangerous, whereas those who would not or could not co-operate might be kept in for life, which for most offences would be disproportionate. Attempts to assess continuing dangerousness are notoriously likely to lead to the detention of those who would not in fact reoffend, as well as the occasional release of those who are still dangerous (Floud and Young 1981). A compromise seems inevitable: a period with upper and lower limits proportionate to the offence, between which offenders could be released when the risk of their committing further serious crime was considered sufficiently low. The procedure should take account of the fact that the risk does not depend solely on the offender: there would be a duty on the relevant agencies to take adequate measures to enable the offender to be released to a situation which would not be conducive to reoffending. For the exceptional cases where offenders, on reaching the upper limit of their sentence, were considered to be still highly dangerous, but could not be placed in a secure hospital because they were not mentally ill, there could be a procedure for applying for an extension; this would require detailed safeguards.

Public and professional acceptability

Changes need the support of the public and of the professionals who are to implement them (including lay magistrates in the present context). Public opinion is much less punitive, and more in favour of reparative measures, than is generally supposed, at least for common offences. In Britain, 85 per cent of a sample of 988 thought that it was a good idea to make 'some offenders' do community service instead of going to prison, and 66 per cent wanted them to compensate their victims. In another poll, 93 per cent thought offenders should have to 'make good the consequences of their crimes wherever possible', although there was often an assumption that the reparation would be accompanied by punishment (for a review of public attitude surveys see Immarigeon 1986; Wright 1989). A recent international survey found that in western Europe, the most appropriate sentence for a recidivist burglar aged 21 was considered to be community service, chosen by 41 per cent (from 60 per cent in the FRG to 33 per cent in the UK). Prison was favoured by 28 per cent. Except in the United States, people with a higher level of education were more likely to opt for a community service order and less likely to choose a prison sentence (Mayhew 1990: 13, 14; Van Dijk et al. 1990: 82).

It has not generally been found that victims themselves are more punitive than the general public. The British Crime Survey's large sample found that what many victims want is that offenders should make some redress (Hough 1985; Hough and Moxon 1985: 169, 170). This is consistent with anecdotal evidence from Victim Support workers that many victims want some good to come of their bad experience, and with the willingness of many to take part in mediation even when they expect little or no personal benefit (Marshall and Merry 1990). The international survey did find, however, that victims of burglary were more likely to favour imprisonment (Mayhew 1990: 14). Maguire and Corbett found that victims visited by Victim Support volunteers were much less punitive, and more likely to take part in mediation, than a matched sample of victims not contacted by Victim Support (1987: 170). About half of a much larger sample in the British Crime Survey said they would have accepted the chance of meeting the offender in order 'to agree a way in which the offender could make a repayment for what he had done', and a further 20 per cent would have liked such an agreement without meeting the offender, making 69 per cent in all. Of these, 30 per cent said that if an agreement was reached, that would have been sufficient: they would not have wanted the offender prosecuted and punished as well (Maguire and Corbett 1987: 227–9). The survey was carried out in 1984, before the idea of reparation and mediation was widely known; it is consistent with the suggestion that many victims want not retribution, but a sufficient recognition of what has happened to them. The commonest spontaneous reasons for wanting to meet were 'to see what the offender was like' or to 'know why he did it'; when further reasons were suggested, victims said that they wanted to give offenders a good piece of their mind, to arrange for compensation, or to let offenders see the effect the crime had on them (Maguire and Corbett 1987: 230–1). Projects will however have to give thought to winning the support of the public and the media. They could follow the experience of the introduction of community service orders, where the media reported cases such as a non-violent cannabis-using student (Pease 1981: 12) and a woman whose community service consisted in playing the piano in an old people's home; cases like these struck a chord with the public and community service soon became accepted.

The response of those professionally engaged in the administration of justice has been mixed. In the Home Office projects, 38 per cent of the magistrates, justices' clerks, probation and police officers and defence solicitors expressed a favourable attitude and 9 per cent were unfavourable, but 44 per cent had mixed views; the great majority of both groups (78 per cent), however, thought that the projects should continue (Marshall and Merry 1990: 163–4). It is possible to secure high levels of co-operation: in Coventry Reparation Scheme 93 per cent of the 144 cases in two years were referred by the courts, and at Leeds Reparation Project 98 per cent of 218 by the probation service (Marshall and Merry 1990: 76-7). In some areas, it has to be said, very few cases were referred, so that co-operation can by no means be taken for granted. Support was lowest among the police, whose co-operation would be important; in some areas, however, the police have taken the lead (Exeter and Northamptonshire, for example). Reparation and mediation services would have to work to replace the stereotype that 'the police catch offenders so that they will be punished and the probation service tries to get them off' by a consensus that both services want the offender to be accountable, to make amends, and to be reaccepted into the community.

There is a tendency for professionals to resist the reduction of their responsibilities, despite being overloaded. The scheme proposed should be acceptable on this score, because it would require cases with a 'public' component to be referred into the system, while providing an opportunity for 'private' ones to be filtered out. Police, prosecutors and courts would thus retain considerable discretion. For some, who see victim/offender mediation programmes as having already conceded too much control to the formal system, this proposal may appear to do the same. But at the present level of development only gradual change seems feasible; there would be scope for the dividing line between 'private' and 'public' offences to be progressively raised as confidence was gained.

New measures run the risk of unacceptably widening or strengthening the net of social control. 'Net-widening' means bringing more people under the influence of the system. For mediation, this does not appear to be a problem so long as projects are community-based and help people to reach agreements that are not legally binding; disputants are offered a resource which would not otherwise have been available, while in relation to crimes by strangers, it offers some offenders the opportunity to negotiate the amount of reparation.

With reparation, there is a possibility that, under the proposed conditional diversion, offenders will be under pressure to make reparation where previously they would have received a caution or a nominal penalty, such as a fine, amounting to less than the reparation. Under the traditional system, offenders usually have to be either punished or treated leniently; reparation provides another option, by which they are held accountable, but in a constructive way. Offenders would be offered guidance as a safeguard against feeling under pressure to offer an unreasonable amount, and reparation would not necessarily be in the form of cash.

The possibility of 'net-strengthening' occurs when cases go to court, and an offender finds that reparation does not replace punishment but is added to it. This is the danger of which Stanley Cohen has warned in *Visions of Social Control* (1985). It is a potential problem with hybrid schemes where both punishment and reparation are in use. There can be no certainty about what courts would have done in the absence of the scheme, but it appears that where offenders were referred to a reparation project (whether or not there was successful mediation) there was a tendency for courts to impose fewer fines and custodial sentences, and more compensation orders alone, community service orders, discharges and probation (Marshall and Merry 1990: 136–40). In the United States there was a reduction in the length rather than the number of custodial sentences (Coates and Gehm 1989: 258–60).

A system with the single primary aim of restoration would be less subject to this problem, because the entire sanction would be reparative; in principle, it should add up to the same total whether it consisted of reparation to the victim, to the community, or a combination.

If restorative justice were adopted as official policy, would there be a guarantee that courts would apply it as intended? Reparative sanctions such as compensation and community service orders can be imposed with punitive intent, and restrictions and detention would be prone to being used punitively rather than for the protection of the public only. This would undermine not only the advantages of reparation but also respect for the law, because people on the receiving end are quick to perceive hypocrisy. It would be 'the ultimate treason: to do the right thing for the wrong reason'. For Eliot's Thomas à Becket, the danger was to stand firm in order to gain a martyr's crown rather than because it was right; in the case of courts, it could be to require offenders to pay or work because that was unpleasant rather than because it helped to repair the harm. The ideal would be to secure the support of courts for the principle of restorative justice. Changes in attitudes cannot be achieved quickly – perhaps it is not right that they should. The first step would be legislation to require courts to use reparative sanctions; this would be combined with legal and judicial training and public opinion-forming to ensure that the new principles were understood and to bring about a gradual change. This could be reinforced by the results of monitoring, if they were as favourable as the advocates of the new approach believe; if they were not, it would be necessary to consider whether it was being implemented properly, or whether it should be revised.

Another objection has been that reparation could preserve the inequitable status quo. If a person living in poverty steals from an affluent one, and is then required to pay back, the inequality will remain. But in a democracy, even those who favour redistribution of wealth cannot accept theft as a method of achieving it. Reparation, moreover, does not have to consist of full restitution; often it is a token amount, a present, or an effort at self-rehabilitation, and if mediation takes place it offers an opportunity for the affluent to deepen their understanding. It should be remembered, also, that many crimes are committed by the poor against the poor; others, such as harassment of tenants to force them to move, or contraventions of health and safety laws, by the powerful against the weak.

As to political acceptability, reparation has had a small but growing place on the political agenda during the last ten years. It was mooted in a Conservative White Paper (Home Office 1959); compensation orders and community service orders were recommended by an Advisory Council on the Penal System appointed by a Labour government, and implemented by a Conservative one in the Criminal Justice Act 1972. Compensation as a sole sanction was introduced in the Criminal Justice Act 1982, and compensation was taken further in the Criminal Justice Act 1988, both under Conservative governments. The latest White Paper is guarded, saying that 'it may be helpful for mediation between victim and offender, or reparation, to be arranged informally by the probation service'; it states that 'victims should not feel obliged to co-operate and a court's decision in sentencing an offender should not be influenced by a victim's decision to accept reparation' (Home Office 1990a: 24). Current policy does emphasize crime prevention, although there is a bias towards security rather than social measures. As regards punishment, 'its role must not be over-stated', but the philosophy is still that it 'has a major part to play in reducing crime'; the implication is that punishment is imposed for retributive reasons, even compensation and community service orders being seen as punishments (Home Office 1990a: 2).

The Labour Party moves some way towards restorative justice, stating that 'reparation should be an important feature of criminal justice policy, provided that the effect on the victim is kept at the forefront. *We support the concept of mediation between victim and offender* and will encourage and monitor further experimentation' (Labour Party 1990: 12, emphasis in original). The party puts much less emphasis on punishment (prison, for example, 'should be used as a last resort for those convicted of serious offences'); all its proposed sentencing reforms are in the direction of limiting punishment, and crime prevention, including social crime prevention, forms a major part of the policy. Thus it can be said that both main political parties in Britain have at least some reservations about punishment and some commitment to reparative measures.

Conclusions

To transform the response to crime to one based on restorative justice would be a change at least as great as the adoption of a rehabilitative philosophy in the Gladstone Report of 1895. Current thinking has moved some way towards it, and a somewhat lesser distance away from punishment, although the public is not as punitive as is often believed. The adoption of restorative justice as the primary aim would clarify criminal justice policy. Retribution would be omitted, but other traditional aims of the system, denunciation, crime prevention, disincentive, containment, would be included or achieved in other ways. Not all problems would be resolved; the amount of compensation, and the duration of any restriction or detention, would have a more logical base but would retain a degree of arbitrariness.

The question is inevitably asked, could the restorative approach be applied even to the worst offenders? In principle it could: in the extreme case, a lifetime's reparation could be at least as appropriate as a lifetime's punishment. As Howard Zehr has pointed out, there are exceptional cases to which it is harder to apply restorative principles, at least until they have been further developed and put into practice, but that need not hinder efforts to apply them in the more usual, less serious cases (Zehr 1990). If it fulfilled expectations, it could be extended. It has been argued that the more serious the case, the greater the potential benefit for victims in overcoming the trauma; if this is shown to be the case, victims should not be denied the opportunity merely because the State sets a limit on the types of crimes eligible. They should have a right to meet their offender if they wished and the offender agreed.

Among the positive advantages would be the recognition that the process is important, as well as the outcome. The ethical problem of exemplary punishment would be avoided, and there should be less counter-deterrence. Members of the community would be empowered, that is enabled to share in making and carrying out decisions within an acceptable framework of principles. Victims would be able to be involved in decisions as to reparation, but not punishment. Measures used would as far as possible build on offenders' good qualities, and not accentuate their bad ones. The State's intervention in the lives of its citizens, including those who have broken the law, would be kept to a minimum, and it would be providing an opportunity for voluntary solutions before resorting to coercion. There is a precedent for this in the fact that an offender's consent is required before being placed on probation. Coercive measures, including restrictions and detention, should not be disproportionate to the harm (or potential harm) which gives rise to them. In a small number of cases detention is not ruled out; in accordance with the restorative principle it would be imposed not punitively, but only for the protection of the public from a grave risk of serious harm, and possibly for the enforcement of last resort for reparative measures.

The traditional theory is that to prevent people taking the law (i.e. the infliction of retribution) into their own hands, the State will do so on their behalf, even to the point of punishing those who illegally punish others. But this, while an improvement on anarchy and private vengeance, is itself flawed. It puts the State in the position of saying 'Don't do as I do, do as I tell you'. The democratic State would, according to the model now being proposed, enhance its moral authority and its keeping of the peace by setting an example. It would use the same methods in relation to its citizens (and in their name) as it requires them to use between each other. This would be one term in the social contract. Another would be that the democratic State would not so much seek to use the threat of punishment to compel people to behave well, but rather would aim to provide the social, economic and educational infrastructure to encourage and enable all its citizens to obtain a reasonable quality of life without illegal or harmful behaviour.

Beyond that, the next stage in giving people greater power over their own lives is a further progression: from arbitration, in which the citizens surrender to the State, through the courts and other authorities, the task of adjudicating on their disputes and transgressions, towards mediation, in which the State returns to them the opportunity to resolve their own conflicts – but by negotiation, with the help of mediators if necessary, not by force. The state's duty would be to ensure that such negotiations were fair, and it would retain residual powers in respect of those who tried to abuse the process or did not wish to participate.

How does a restorative model compare to the existing rather imperfect system? The first, fundamental point is that its premises are different. It challenges the traditional assumption that the issue is: Which method of dealing with offenders (the minority who are caught) is most effective in reducing crime? It offers a new paradigm which recognizes that a crime reduction strategy relying heavily on deterrence has not worked well; crime reduction should concentrate on reducing the opportunities for, and pressures towards, crime, while increasing incentives for avoiding it. The old, retributive message is 'Go and stand outside till you learn to behave properly'; the meaning of integrative or reparative justice is 'Join us in putting things right again' (Marshall 1988a: 47). There would still be deterrence, relying primarily on the probability of detection, but the prospect of reparation would be a substantial additional disincentive. To make 'general deterrence' effective, the State relies on the increasing use of prisons; to give credibility to a 'general incentive', it would have to devote resources to more constructive social investment.

By rejecting the assumption that sanctions can or should be a major influence in crime control, a restorative policy would force a rethink of crime reduction strategies. It is these strategies which should be judged according to the amount of crime in society; restorative justice should be measured against a different yardstick, namely the extent to which, after crimes do occur, victims are enabled to resume normal life as far as possible, and offenders to gain, or regain, acceptance by the community, including the victims if they are willing, through making amends. The amount of public effort and resources devoted to this would constitute society's denunciation of the crime.

Both the traditional and the restorative approach have their advantages and disadvantages; it is at least possible that constructive, restorative methods have fewer damaging side-effects. The only way to find out is to try them. The proposal is not for a sudden reversal of policy, or an ideal system, but a gradual change of *direction*: reparation as the sole sanction could be introduced for less serious cases, and be extended, as it became accepted, to more serious ones. This process would not go further than was acceptable to the public in general, and to victims and offenders themselves. Victims should have the right to an opportunity to meet their offenders, provided the latter were willing. Offenders should have the right to offer reparation. Offenders and the community would be able to offer help to the victims; the State would both hold offenders accountable and enable them to make up for the offence. In place of retribution against the offender would be a contribution by the offender. As far as possible the conditions before the offence would be restored and even improved. This would be a step towards a society which would not return evil for evil, but drive out evil with good.

References

Abel, R.L. (1973) 'A comparative theory of dispute institutions in society', *Law and Society Review*, 8(1): 217–347.
—— (ed.) (1982) *The Politics of Informal Justice, Vol. 1.1 – The American Experience.* New York: Academic Press.
Advisory Council on the Penal System (ACPS) (1970a) *Non-Custodial and Semi-Custodial Penalties* (Chairman of sub-committee: Baroness Wootton), London: HMSO.
—— (1970b) *Reparation by the Offender* (Chairman of sub-committee: Lord Widgery), London: HMSO.
Alper, B. and Nichols, L. (1981) *Beyond the Courtroom: Programs in Community Justice and Conflict Resolution,* Lexington, Mass: D.C. Heath.
American Bar Association. Victims Committee (1983) *ABA Guidelines for Fair Treatment of Victims and Witnesses in the Criminal Justice System,* Washington, DC: ABA Criminal Justice Section.
American Friends' Service Committee (1971) *Struggle for Justice: A Report on Crime and Punishment in America,* New York: Hill & Wang.
Anderson, K. (1982) 'Community justice centres in NSW', in Sydney University Law School, Institute of Criminology, *Proceedings of a Seminar in Community Justice Centres, 10 March 1982,* Sydney: Institute of Criminology.
Armstrong, T., Holford, L., Maloney, D., Remington, C. and Stevenson, D. (1983) *Restitution: A Guidebook for Juvenile Justice Practitioners.* Reno, Nev: National Council of Juvenile and Family Court Judges.
Ashworth, A. (1983) *Sentencing and Penal Policy,* London: Weidenfeld & Nicolson.
Atkinson, R.L., Atkinson, R.C., Smith, E.E. and Hilgard, E.R. (1987) *Introduction to Psychology,* 9th edn, San Diego, Calif: Harcourt Brace.
Auerbach, J.S. (1983) *Justice without Law? Resolving Disputes without Lawyers,* New York: Oxford University Press.
Bailey, S. and Tucker, D. (1984) *Remedies for Victims of Crime,* London: Legal Action Group.
Baldwin, J. and McConville, M. (1977) *Negotiated Justice: Pressures on Defendants to Plead Guilty,* London: Martin Robertson.

Barnett, R (1977) 'Restitution: a new paradigm of criminal justice', *Ethics: An International Journal of Social, Political and Legal Philosophy*, 87(4): 279–301, reprinted in B. Galaway and J. Hudson (eds) (1981) *Perspectives on Crime Victims*, St Louis: C.V. Mosby.

Basten, J. (1982) 'CJCs – a comment', in Sydney University Law School, Institute of Criminology, *Proceedings of a Seminar in Community Justice Centres, 10 March 1982*, Sydney: Institute of Criminology.

Bender, J. (1984) 'VORP: a beginning'; *VORP Network News*, 3(4): 5–6.

—— 'VORP spreads to the United States', *VORP Network News*, 4(1): 5–7.

Beyleveld, D. (1979) 'Deterrence research as a basis for deterrence policies', *Howard Journal*, 18(3): 135–49.

Bianchi, H. (1978) 'Returning conflict to the community: the alternative of privatization', unpublished paper.

—— (1980) 'The assensus model: a plea to re-introduce the right of internal asylum', transl. Charles Yerkes, unpublished paper.

Birnie, Sir R. (1828) *Report from the Commissioner of Police of the Metropolis. Criminal Commitments and Convictions, 29 January – 28 July 1828* (reference not verified).

Black, D. (1983) 'Crime as social control', *American Sociological Review*, 48: 34–45.

Blackstone, Sir W. (1778) *The Sovereignty of the Law*, ed. by Gareth Jones from 7th edn (1973), London: Macmillan.

Blagg, H. (1985) 'Reparation and justice for juveniles: the Corby experience', *British Journal of Criminology*, 25(3): 267–79.

Blair, I. (1985) *Investigating Rape: A New Approach for Police*, London: Croom Helm.

Blumberg, A.S. (1967) *Criminal Justice*, Chicago, Ill: Quadrangle Books.

Bottomley, A.K. (1979) *Criminology in Focus: Past Trends and Future Prospects*, Oxford: Martin Robertson.

Bottoms, A.E. and McClean, J.D. (1976) *Defendants in the Criminal Process*, London: Routledge & Kegan Paul.

Brittan, L. (1984) Home Secretary's speech to the Holborn Law Society, 14 March (unpublished).

Bryant, M., Coker, J., Eastlea, B., Himmel, S. and Knapp, T. (1978) 'Sentenced to social work?', *Probation Journal*, 25(4): 110–14.

Bush, R.A. (1979) 'A pluralistic understanding of access to justice: developments in systems of justice in African nations', in M. Capelletti and B. Garth (eds.) *Access to Justice, Vol. III: Emerging Issues and Perspectives*, Aalphenaandenrijn: Sijthoff & Noordhoff; Milan: Giuffrè.

Cambridge Dispute Settlement Center (*c*. 1982) *Mediation Training Manual*, Cambridge, Mass: Cambridge Dispute Settlement Center.

Cantor, G. (1976) 'An end to crime and punishment' *The Shingle* (Philadelphia Bar Association), 39(4): 99–114.

Cappelletti, M. (general editor) (1978–9) *Access to Justice*, 4 vols, Aalphenaandenrijn: Sijthoff & Noordhoff; Milan: Giuffrè.

Challeen, D. (1980) 'Turning society's losers into winners', *Judges' Journal*, 19(1), 4–8.

Chesney, S and Schneider, C.S. (1981) 'Crime victim crisis centers: the Minnesota experience', In B. Galaway and J. Hudson (eds) *Perspectives on Crime Victims*, St Louis: C.V. Mosby.

Chinkin, C.M. and Griffiths, R.C. (1980) 'Resolving conflict by mediation', *New Law Journal*, 3 January: 6–8.

Christie, N. (1977) 'Conflicts as property', *British Journal of Criminology*, 17(1): 1–15, reprinted in B. Galaway and J. Hudson (eds) (1981) *Perspectives on Crime Victims*, St Louis: C.V. Mosby.

—— (1982) *Limits to Pain*, Oxford: Martin Robertson.

Coates, R.B. (1985) *Victim Meets Offender: An Evaluation of Victim/Offender Reconciliation Programs*, Valparaiso, Ind: PACT Institute of Justice.

Coates, R.B. and Gehm, J. (1989) 'An empirical assessment', in M. Wright and B. Galaway (eds) *Mediation and Criminal Justice: Victims, Offenders and Community*, London: Sage.

Cohen, S. (1985) *Visions of Social Control: Crime, Punishment and Classification*, Cambridge: Polity Press.

Colson, C. and Benson, D.H. (1980) 'Restitution as an alternative to imprisonment', *Detroit College of Law Review*, summer: 523–98.

Cornish, W.R., Hart, J., Manchester, A.H. and Stevenson, J. (1978) *Crime and Law in Nineteenth Century Britain*, Dublin: Irish University Press.

Coventry Reparation Scheme (1986) *Victim/Offender Mediation and Reparation: The First Twelve Months, 1985–1986*, CRS, 4 Grosvenor House, Grosvenor Road, Coventry CV1 3FZ.

—— (1987) *Report 1985–1987*, CRS (as above).

Cowell, C. (1989) 'Setting up a community mediation scheme', in FIRM, *Repairing the Damage*. Beaconsfield: FIRM.

Crime and Justice Foundation (1988) *Boston Municipal Court Mediation Program (Statistics)*, January – December 1987, September 1980 – December 1987, CJF, 95 Berkeley Street, Boston MA 02116.

Cross, R. (1975) *The English Sentencing System*, 2nd edn, London: Butterworths.

Danzig, R. (1973) 'Towards the creation of a complementary, decentralized system of criminal justice' *Stanford Law Review*, 26(1): 1–54.

Danzig, R. and Lowy, M.J. (1975) 'Everyday disputes and mediation in the US: a reply to Professor Felstiner', *Law and Society Review*, 9(4): 675–94.

Davis, G., Boucherat, J. and Watson, D. (1987) *A Preliminary Study of Victim Offender Mediation and Reparation Schemes in England and Wales*. Research and Planning Unit Paper 42, London: Home Office.

Davis, R.C. (1982) 'Mediation: the Brooklyn experiment', in R. Tomasic and M.M. Feeley (eds) *Neighborhood Justice: Assessment of an Emerging Idea*, New York: Longman.

Diamond, A.S. (1935) *Primitive Law*, London: Longman.

—— (1951) *The Evolution of Law and Order*, London: Watts.

Dittenhoffer, T. (1981) 'The Victim/Offender Reconciliation Program: a message to correctional reformers', MA thesis, University of Toronto.

Dittenhoffer, T. and Ericson, R.V. (1983) 'The Victim/Offender Reconciliation Program: a message to corectional reformers', *University of Toronto Law Journal*, 33: 315–47.

Ditton, J. (1977) *Part-time Crime: An Ethnography of Fiddling and Pilfering*, London: Macmillan.

Duff, P. (1985) 'Crime on offshore installations', *Howard Journal*, 24(2): 118–29.

Dünkel, F. (1984) Victim Compensation and Offender Restitution in the Federal Republic of Germany: A West European Comparative Perspective, Freiburg im Breisgau: Max Planck Institute for Foreign and International Criminal Law.

Dünkel, F and Rössner, D. (1989) 'Law and practice of victim/offender agreements', in M. Wright and B. Galaway, (eds) *Mediation and Criminal Justice: Victims, Offenders and Community*, London: Sage.

Durkheim, E. (1893) *The Division of Labour in Society*, transl. (1964) from 1st edn (1893) and 5th edn (1926), Glencoe: Free Press.

―― (1895) *The Rules of Sociological Method*, transl. (1938) from 8th edn, Glencoe, Free Press.

Edelhertz, H. and Geis, G. (1974) *Public Compensation to Victims of Crime*, New York: Praeger.

Edwards, S.S.M. (1989) *Policing 'Domestic' Violence: Women, the Law and the State*. London: Sage.

Eglash, A. (1958) 'Creative restitution.' *Journal of Criminal Law, Criminology and Police Science*, 48(6), 619–22.

Eser, A. (1983) *Einführung in das Strafprozessrecht, (Introduction to the Law of Criminal Procedure)*, Munich: Beck.

Faulkes, W. (1982) 'Mediators and mediation', in Sydney University Law School, Institute of Criminology, *Proceedings of a Seminar on Community Justice Centres, 10 March 1982*, Sydney: Institute of Criminology.

Felstiner, W.L.F. (1974) 'Influences of social organization on dispute processing', *Law and Society Review*, 9: 63–94.

―― (1975) 'Avoidance as dispute processing: an elaboration', *Law and Society Review*, 9: 695–706.

Felstiner, W.L.F. and Williams, L.A. (1980) *Community Mediation in Dorchester, Mass.* Washington, DC: US Department of Justice, National Institute of Justice.

Fennell, J. (1989) 'Negotiating justice', dissertation for Diploma in Criminology, University of London, Birkbeck College.

Finlayson, A. (1976) 'The reporter', in F.M. Martin and K. Murray (eds) *Children's Hearings*, Edinburgh: Scottish Academic Press.

FIRM (1989a) *Conflict in Schools: Proceedings of a Conference*, Forum for Initiatives in Reparation and Mediation, 19 London End, Beaconsfield, Bucks, HP9 2HN.

―― (1989b) *Directory of Mediation Projects and Conflict Resolution Services*. Beaconsfield: FIRM.

―― (1989c) *Repairing the Damage: The First National Symposium on Mediation and Criminal Justice*, Beaconsfield: FIRM.

Fisher, R. and Ury, W. (1987) *Getting to Yes: Negotiating Agreement without Giving In*, London: Arrow Books.

Fletcher, A.E. (1981) 'Preliminary analysis of a study of the effect on the use and administration of Community Service Orders of different forms of organisation within the Probation and After-Care Service', unpublished paper, University of Manchester, Department of Social Administration.

―― (1983) 'Organisational diversity in community service', MA thesis, University of Manchester, Department of Social Administration.

Floud, J. and Young, W. (1981) *Dangerousness and Criminal Justice*. Howard League for Penal Reform, London: Heinemann.

France (1977) *Code de procédure pénale. Titre XIV: Du recours en indemnité ouvert à certaines victimes de dommages corporels. Loi no. 77–5 du 3 janvier 1977, art. 706–3; [and] Decret no. 77–194 du 3 mars 1977, art R. 50–9, R. 50.10.*

Frank, J. (1949) *Courts on Trial: Myth and Reality in American Justice,* Princeton, NJ: Princeton University Press.

Freedman, M.H. (1966) 'Professional responsibility of the criminal defense lawyer: The three hardest questions', *Michigan Law Review,* 64(8), 1469–84.

Fry, M. (1951) *Arms of the Law,* London: Gollancz.

Fuller, L.L. (1963) 'Collective bargaining and the arbitrator', *Wisconsin Law Review,* 23: 3–46.

—— (1971) 'Mediation: its forms and functions', *South California Law Review,* 44: 305–39.

Galaway, B. (1983) 'Use of restitution as a penal measure in the United States', *Howard Journal,* 22(1): 8–18.

—— (1985) 'Preliminary experiences of an urban victim offender reconciliation project', paper to 5th International Symposium on Victimology, Zagreb.

Galaway, B., and Hudson, J. (eds) (1981) *Perspectives on Crime Victims.* St Louis: C.V. Mosby.

Garlick, J. (1982) 'The Knights of Labour courts: a case study of popular justice', in R.J. Abel (ed.) *The Politics of Informal Justice.* New York: Academic Press.

Gay, M.J., Holtom, C. and Thomas, M.S. (1975) 'Helping the victims', *International Journal of Offender Therapy and Comparative Criminology,* 19(3): 263–9.

Geis, G. (1975) 'Restitution by criminal offenders: a summary and overview', in J. Hudson and B. Galaway (eds) *Restitution in Criminal Justice: A Critical Assessment of Sanctions.* Lexington, Mass: D.C. Heath.

—— (1981) 'Victims of crimes of violence and the criminal justice system', In B. Galaway and J. Hudson (eds) *Perspectives on Crime Victims,* St Louis: C.V. Mosby.

Gibbs, J.L., jr. (1963) 'The Kpelle moot', *Africa,* 33(1): 1–10, reprinted in P. Bohannan, (ed.) (1967) *Law and Warfare: Studies in the Anthropology of Conflict,* Garden City, NY: Natural History Press.

Gibson, E. and Klein, S. (1961) *Murder,* London: HMSO.

Glazebrook, P.R. (ed) (1978) *Reshaping the Criminal Law: Essays in Honour of Glanville Williams,* London: Stevens.

Gluckman, M. (1955) *The Judicial Process among the Barotse of Northern Rhodesia,* Manchester: Manchester University Press.

—— (1968) 'Judicial process: comparative aspects', in *International Encyclopedia of the Social Sciences,* New York: Macmillan, Glencoe: Free Press.

Grebing, G. (1982) *The Fine in Comparative Law: A Survey of 21 Countries,* Cambridge: Institute of Criminology.

Green, J.R. (1888) *A Short History of the English People.* rev. edn, London: Macmillan.

Griffiths, J. (1970) 'Ideology in criminal procedure, or, a third "model" of the criminal process', *Yale Law Journal,* 79(3): 359–417.

Gulliver, P.H. (1969) 'Dispute settlement without courts: the Ndendenli of Southern Tanzania', in L. Nader (ed.) *Law in Culture and Society,* Chicago, Ill: Aldine.

Haley, J.O. (1989) 'Confession, repentance and absolution', in M. Wright and B. Galaway (eds) *Mediation and Criminal Justice: Victims, Offenders and Community,* London: Sage.

Hall, D.J. (1975) 'The role of the victim in the prosecution and disposition of a criminal case', reprinted in B. Galaway and J. Hudson (eds) (1981) *Perspectives on Crime Victims,* St Louis: C.V. Mosby.

Hampton, C. (1982) *Criminal Procedure,* 3rd edn, London: Sweet & Maxwell.

Harding, J. (1980) *An Investigation into the Current Status and Effectiveness of Juvenile and Adult Restitution Programmes in the United States of America*, Exeter: Devon Probation and After-Care Service.

—— (1982) *Victims and Offenders: Needs and Responsibilities*, London: Bedford Square Press.

—— (1989) 'Reconciling mediation with criminal justice.' in M. Wright and B. Galaway (eds) *Mediation and Criminal Justice: Victims, Offenders and Community*, London: Sage.

Harland, A.T. (1978) 'Compensating the victim of crime', *Criminal Law Bulletin*, 14(3): 203–24.

—— (1980) 'Restitution statutes and cases: some substantive and procedural constraints', in J. Hudson and B. Galaway (eds) *Victims, Offenders and Alternative Sanctions*, Lexington, Mass: D.C. Heath.

—— (1981) 'Victim compensation', in B. Galaway and J. Hudson (eds) *Perspectives on Crime Victims*, St Louis: C.V. Mosby.

—— (1982) 'Monetary remedies for the victims of crime: assessing the role of the criminal courts', *UCLA Law Review*, 30(1): 52–128.

Harrington, C.B. (1985) *The Ideology and Institutionalization of Alternatives to Court*, Westport, Conn: Greenwood Press.

Hay, D. (1975) 'Property, authority and the criminal law', in D. Hay, P. Winebaugh and E.P. Thompson (eds) *Albion's Fatal Tree*, London: Allen Lane.

Heinz, A.M. and Kerstetter, W.A. (1981) 'Pretrial settlement conference: evaluation of a reform in plea bargaining', in B. Galaway and J. Hudson (eds) *Perspectives on Crime Victims*, St Louis: C.V. Mosby.

Hentig, H. von (1948) *The Criminal and his Victim: Studies in the Sociology of Crime*, New Haven, Conn: Yale University Press.

Hibbert, C. (1966) *The Roots of Evil: A Social History of Crime and Punishment*, Harmondsworth: Penguin.

Hofrichter, R. (1977) 'Justice centers raise basic questions', *New Directions*, 2(6): 168–72; reprinted in R. Tomasic and M. Feeley (eds) (1982) *Neighborhood Justice: Assessment of an Emerging Idea*, New York: Longman.

Holdsworth, Sir W. (1956) *A History of English Law*, 7th edn, London: Methuen.

Home Office (1959) *Penal Practice in a Changing Society*, Cmnd 645, London: HMSO.

—— (1984) *Criminal Statistics England and Wales 1983*, London: HMSO.

—— (1985a) *Compensation and Support for Victims of Crime*, Cmnd 9457, London: HMSO.

—— (1985b) *Criminal Statistics England and Wales 1984*, London: HMSO.

—— (1986) *Reparation: A Discussion Document*, London: Home Office.

—— (1988a) *Criminal Statistics England and Wales 1987*, Cm 498, London: HMSO.

—— (1988b) *Punishment, Custody and the Community*, Cm 424, London: HMSO.

—— (1989) *Criminal Statistics England and Wales 1988*, Cm 847, London: HMSO.

—— (1990a) *Crime, Justice and Protecting the Public*, Cm 965, London: HMSO.

—— (1990b) *Victims' Charter: A Statement of the Rights of Victims of Crime*, London: Home Office.

—— Home Office and SHHD (Scottish Home and Health Department) (1986) *Criminal Injuries Compensation: A Statutory Scheme. Report of an Interdepartmental Working Party*, London: HMSO.

Horley, S. (1990) 'A caution against cautioning', *Police Review*, 9 March: 484–5.

Hough, M. (1985) 'The impact of victimization: findings from the 1984 British Crime Survey', *Victimology* 10(1–4): 488–97.

Hough, M. and Mayhew, P. (1983) *The British Crime Survey: First Report*, Home Office Research Study 76, London: HMSO.

Hough, M. and Moxon, D. (1985) 'Dealing with offenders: popular opinion and the views of victims. Findings from the British Crime Survey', *Howard Journal*, 24(3): 160–75.

Howard League for Penal Reform (1976) *No Brief for the Dock: Report of the ... Working Party on Custody During Trial* (Chairman: Lady James of Rusholme), Chichester: B. Rose.

—— (1977) *Making Amends: Criminals, Victims and Society*, Chichester: B. Rose.

—— (1984) *Profits of Crime and their Recovery* (Chairman: Sir Derek Hodgson), London: Heinemann.

Hudson, J., Galaway, B. and Novack, S. (1980) *National Assessment of Adult Restitution Programs: Final Report*, Duluth, Minn: School of Social Development, University of Minnesota.

Humphreys, J.C. and Humphreys, W.O. (1985) 'Mandatory arrest: a means of primary and secondary prevention of abuse of female partners', *Victimology*, 10(1–4): 267–80.

Immarigeon, R. (1986) 'Surveys reveal broad support for alternative sentencing', *National Prison Project Journal*, 9, fall: 1–4.

Ison, T.G. (1980) *Accident Compensation: A Commentary on the New Zealand Scheme*, London: Croom Helm.

Jeffery, C.R. (1957) 'The development of crime in early English society', *Journal of Criminal Law, Criminology and Police Science*, 47: 647–66, reprinted in W.J. Chambliss (ed.) (1969) *Crime and the Legal Process*, New York: McGraw Hill.

Jeudwine, J.W. (1917) *Tort, Crime and Police in Mediaeval Britain*, London: Williams & Norgate.

Jung, H. (1987) 'Das Opferschutzgesetz' (The Victim Protection Law), *Juristische Schulung*, 2: 157–60.

Justice (1962) *Compensation for Victims of Crimes of Violence*, London: Stevens.

—— (1980) Breaking the Rules: *The Problem of Crimes and Contraventions*, London: Justice.

—— (1989) *Sentencing: A Way Ahead*, London: Justice.

Justice of the Peace (1980) 'Compensation Orders', *Justice of the Peace*, 144 12 July: 416.

Kettering Adult Reparation Bureau (1986/87) *Report of the First Twelve Months*, Kettering: Adult Reparation Bureau.

King, M. (1981) *The Framework of Criminal Justice*, London: Croom Helm.

—— (1988) *How to Make Social Crime Prevention Work: The French Experience*, NACRO, 169 Clapham Road, London SW9 0PU.

Kirchhoff, G. (1984) 'Die gesellschaftliche Situation der Kriminalitätsopfer und wie wir damit umgehen', (The social situation of victims of crime and how we deal with it), in Akademische Akademie Bad Boll, *Täter, Opfer und Gesellschaft: Konfliktbewältigung durch Resozialisierung und Wiedergutmachung, Tagung 1984*, (Offenders, victims and society: overcoming conflict through resocialization and reparation, Conference 1984), Bad Boll: Akadamische Akademie.

Knudten, R.D., Meade, A.C., Knudten, M.S. and Doerner, W.G. (1977) *Victims and Witnesses: Their Experiences with Crime and the Criminal Justice System*, Washington, DC: US Government Printing Office.

Kurczewski, J. and Frieske, K. (1978) 'The Social Conciliatory Commissions in Poland: a case study of non-authoritative and conciliatory dispute resolution as an approach to access to justice', in M. Capelletti and J. Weisner (eds) *Access to Justice, Vol. II: Promising Institutions*, Book 1, Aalphenaandenrijn: Sijthoff & Noordhoff; Milan: Giuffrè.

Labour Party (1990) *A Safer Britain: Labour's Working Party on Criminal Justice*, London: Labour Party.

Launay, G. (1985) 'Bringing victims and offenders together: a comparison of two models' [VORP and VOIC], *Howard Journal*, 23(3): 200–12.

Launay, G. and Murray, R. (1989) 'Victim/offender groups', in M. Wright and B. Galaway (eds) *Mediation and Criminal Justice: Victims, Offenders and Community*, London: Sage.

Lees, S. (1989a) 'Trial by rape', *New Statesman and Society*, 24 November.

—— (1989b) 'Trial by rape', *New Statesman and Society*, 1 December.

Lubman, S. (1967) 'Mao and mediation: politics and dispute resolution in communist China', *California Law Review*, 55: 1,284–359.

McBarnet, D.J. (1976) 'Victim in the witness box – confronting the stereotype', paper presented at the Second International Symposium on Victimology, Boston, Mass.

—— (1981) *Conviction: Law, the State and the Construction of Justice*, London: Macmillan.

McCabe, S. and Purves, R. (1972) *Bypassing the Jury*, Oxford: Basil Blackwell.

McClintock, F.H. (1963) *Crimes of Violence*, London: Macmillan.

McConville, M. and Baldwin, J. (1981) *Courts, Prosecution and Conviction*, Oxford: Clarendon Press.

McGillis, D. (1982) 'Minor dispute processing: a review of recent developments', in R. Tomasic and M. Feeley (eds) *Neighborhood Justice: Assessment of an Emerging Idea*, New York: Longman.

McGillis, D. and Mullen, J. (1977) *Neighborhood Justice Centers: An Analysis of Potential Models*, Washington, DC: National Institute of Law Enforcement and Criminal Justice.

McGillis, D. and Smith, P. (1983) *Compensating Victims of Crime: An Analysis of American Programs*, Washington, DC: US Department of Justice, National Institute of Justice.

McGinness, R.E. and Cinquegrana, R.J. (1982) 'Legal issues arising in mediation: the Boston Municipal Court Mediation Program', *Massachusetts Law Review*, fall: 123–36.

Mackay, R.E. (1988) *Reparation in Criminal Justice*, Edinburgh: Scottish Association for the Care and Resettlement of Offenders.

—— (1989) 'The resuscitation of assythment', paper to Socio-Legal Conference, University of Edinburgh, April.

Mackey, V. (1981) 'Punishment in the scripture and tradition of Judaism, Christianity and Islam', Joint Strategy and Action Committee Inc., 475 Riverside Drive, Suite 560, New York NY 10115.

Maguire, M. (1980) 'The impact of burglary upon victims', *British Journal of Criminology*, 20(3): 261–75.

—— (1982) *Burglary in a Dwelling*, London: Heinemann.

Maguire, M. and Corbett, C. (1987) *The Effects of Crime and the Work of Victims Support Schemes*, Aldershot: Gower.

Maine, Sir H.S. (1930) *Ancient Law: Its Connection with the Early History of Society and its Relation to Modern Ideas*, new edn, London: Murray.

Maitland, F.W. (1885) *Justice and Police*, London: Macmillan.

Marcus, G.E. (1979) 'Litigation, interpersonal conflict and noble succession disputes in the Friendly Islands', in K.-F. Koch (ed.) *Access to Justice, Vol. IV: The Anthropological Perspective*, Aalphenaandenrijn: Sijthoff & Noordhoff; Milan: Giuffrè.

Marks, J.B., Johnson, E. and Szanton, P.L. (1984) *Dispute Resolution in America: Processes in Evolution*, National Institute for Dispute Resolution, 1901 L Street NW, Washington DC 20036.

Marshall, T. (1984) *Reparation, Mediation and Conciliation: Current Projects and Plans in England and Wales*, Research and Planning Unit Paper 27, London: Home Office.

—— (1985) *Alternatives to Criminal Courts: The Potential for Non-Judicial Dispute Resolution*, Aldershot: Gower.

—— (1986) 'Keeping the alternative in Alternative Dispute Resolution', paper to 3rd National Conference on Peacemeaking and Conflict Resolution, Denver, Col.

—— (1988a) 'Out of court: more or less justice?', in R. Matthews (ed.) *Informal Justice?*, London: Sage.

—— (1988b) 'Informal justice: the British experience', in R. Matthews (ed.) *Informal Justice?*, London: Sage.

—— (1989) 'Future directions', in FIRM, *Repairing the Damage: First National Symposium on Mediation and Criminal Justice*, Beaconsfield: Forum for Initiatives in Reparation and Mediation.

Marshall, T. and Merry, Susan. (1990) *Crime and Accountability: Victim/Offender Mediation in Practice*, London: HMSO.

Marshall, T. and Walpole, M. (1985) *Bringing People Together: Mediation and Reparation Projects in Great Britain*, Research and Planning Unit Paper 33, London: Home Office.

Martin, F.M., Fox, S. and Murray, K. (1981) *Children out of Court*, Edinburgh: Scottish Academic Press.

Matthews, R. (1988) 'Reassessing informal justice', in R. Matthews (ed.) *Informal Justice?*, London: Sage.

Mawby, R.I. and Gill, M. (1987) *Crime Victims: Needs, Services and the Voluntary Sector*, London: Tavistock.

Mayhew, P. (1990) *Summary of Results from 1989 International Crime Survey: A UK Perspective*, London: Home Office Research and Planning Unit.

Mendelsohn, B. (1963) 'The origin of the doctrine of victimology', *Excerpta Criminologica*, 3(3).

Merry, Sally E. (1982) 'Defining "success" in the neighborhood justice movement', in R. Tomasic and M. Feeley (eds) *Neighborhood Justice: Assessment of an Emerging Idea*, New York: Longman.

Miers, D. (1978) *Responses to Victimization: A Comparative Study of Compensation for Criminal Violence in Great Britain and Ontario*, Abingdon: Professional Books.

Moberly, Sir Walter. (1968) *The Ethics of Punishment*, London: Faber.

Morgan, C.T. and King, R.A. (1971) *Introduction to Psychology*, New York: McGraw-Hill.

Morris, N. (1974) *The Future of Imprisonment*, Chicago, Ill: Chicago University Press.

Munn, N.L., Fernald, L.D. and Fernald, P.S. (1969) *Introduction to Psychology*, 3rd edn, Boston, Mass: Houghton Mifflin.

NACRO (1981) *Fine Default: Report of a Working Party*, London: National Association for the Care and Resettlement of Offenders.

Nader, L. (ed.) (1969) *Law in Culture and Society*, Chicago, Ill: Aldine.

Nader, L. and Todd, H. (eds) (1978) *The Disputing Process: Law in Ten Societies*, New York: Columbia University Press.

Napley, Sir D. (1983) *The Technique of Persuasion*, 3rd edn, London: Sweet & Maxwell.

NAPO (1985) *Reparation*, National Association of Probation Officers, 3–4 Chivalry Road, London SW11 1HT.

NAVSS (National Association of Victims Support Schemes) *see* Victim Support (name adopted in 1988).

Newburn, T. (1988) *The Use and Enforcement of Compensation Orders in Magistrates' Courts*, Home Office Research Study 102, London: HMSO.

Newman, G.R. (1983) *Just and Painful: A Case for Corporal Punishment*, New York: Macmillan.

Northamptonshire County Council (1985) *Juvenile Liaison Bureaux: Statement on Philosophy, Objectives and Operation*, rev. edn, Northamptonshire County Council.

Oberg, S. and Pence, E. (1981) 'Responding to battered women', in B. Galaway and J. Hudson (eds) *Perspectives on Crime Victims*, St Louis: C.V. Mosby.

Orenstein, S.G. (1982) 'The role of mediation in domestic violence cases', in American Bar Association, *Alternative Means of Family Dispute Resolution* , Washington DC: ABA.

Packer, H.L. (1969) *The Limits of the Criminal Sanction*, Oxford: Oxford University Press.

Palmer, J.W. (1974) 'Pre-arrest diversion: victim confrontation', *Federal Probation*, 38 (3): 12–18.

—— (1975) 'The night prosecutor', *Judicature*, 59(1): 23–7, reprinted in B. Galaway and J. Hudson (eds) 1981 *Perspectives on Crime Victims*, St Louis: C.V. Mosby.

PAPPAG (1984) *A New Deal for Victims*, Parliamentary All-Party Penal Affairs Group, 169 Clapham Road, London SW9 0PU.

Parker, H. (1974) *View from the Boys: A Sociology of Down-Town Adolescents*, Newton Abbott: David & Charles.

Peachey, D.E. (1989) 'The Kitchener experiment', in M. Wright and B. Galaway (eds) *Mediation and Criminal Justice: Victims, Offenders and Community*, London: Sage.

Pease, K. (1981) *Community Service Orders: A First Decade of Promise*, London: Howard League for Penal Reform.

Pease, K., Durkin, P., Earnshaw, I., Payne, D. and Thorpe, J. (1975) *Community Service Orders*, Home Office Research Study 29, London: HMSO.

Peggs, H. (1990) 'Social security for victims', *Victim Support*, March: 9–10.

Philips, D. (1977) *Crime and Authority in Victorian England: The Black Country 1835–1860*, London: Croom Helm.

Pike, L.O. (1873) *A History of Crime in England*, Vol. I, London: Smith Elder, reprinted (1968) Montclair, NJ: Patterson Smith.

Pollock, Sir F. and Maitland, F.W. (1898) *The History of the English Criminal Law Before the Time of Edward I*, 2nd edn, Cambridge: Cambridge University Press.

Pound, R. (1906) 'The causes of popular dissatisfaction with the administration of justice', *American Law Review*, 40: 729–49, reprinted in S. Glueck (ed.) (1965) *Roscoe Pound and Criminal Justice*, Dobbs Ferry, NY: Oceana.

Priestley, P. (1970) *What about the Victim?*, Regional information paper no. 8, London: NACRO.

Priestley, P., McGuire, J., Flegg, D., Hemsley, V., Welham, D. and Barnitt, R. (1984) *Social Skills in Prison and the Community: Problem-Solving for Offenders*, London: Routledge & Kegan Paul.

Prussia (1816) *Allgemeine Gerichtsordnung für die Preussischen Staaten. Erster Theil: Prozessordnung*, Neue Ausgabe (General courts decree for the Prussian states. Part I: Procedural decree, new edition) Berlin: Reimer.

Purchase, G.E. (1976) 'Ordering compensation', *Magistrate*, 32(10): 148–50.

Ramsay, M. (1980) 'The development of the prison in modern British society as a response to endemic panic about crime, 1750–1850', PhD dissertation, University of Edinburgh.

Ray, L. (ed.) (1982) *Dispute Resolution Program Directory 1983*, Washington, DC: ABA Special Committee on Dispute Resolution.

Reeves, H. (1982) *Reparation by Offenders: Survey of Current British Projects*, London: NAVSS.

—— (1984) *The Victim and Reparation*, London: NAVSS.

—— (1986) *NAVSS Response to the Government Discussion Document on 'Reparation'*, London: NAVSS.

—— (1989) 'The victim support perspective', in M. Wright and B. Galaway (eds) *Mediation and Criminal Justice: Victims, Offenders and Community*, London: Sage.

Reifen, D. (1966) 'Sex offenders and the protection of children', *Canadian Journal of Corrections*, 8: 120–32.

—— (1967/68) 'La jeunesse délinquante et le role thérapeutique du tribunal pour enfants', *Revue de Droit Pénal et de Criminologie* (Brussels), 48(1), October: 771–83.

Rich, J.T. (1981) 'Background notes on community based services for rape victims', in B. Galaway and J. Hudson (eds) *Perspectives on Crime Victims*, St Louis: C.V. Mosby.

Roberts, S. (1979) *Order and Dispute: An Introduction to Legal Anthropology*, Harmondsworth: Penguin.

Roehl, J.A. and Cook, R.F. (1982) 'The Neighborhood Justice Centers field test', in R. Tomasic and M. Feeley (eds) *Neighborhood Justice: Assessment of an Emerging Idea*, New York: Longman.

Rössner, D. and Wulf, R. (1984) *Opferbezogene Strafrechtspflege: Leitgedanken und Handlungsvorschläge für Praxis und Gesetzgebung* (Victim-Oriented Criminal Justice: Principles and Proposals for Action in Practice and Legislation), Bonn: Deutsche Bewährungshilfe e.V. (German Probation Association).

Rudolph, L. and Rudolph, S. (1967) *The Modernity of Tradition: Political Development in India*, Chicago, Ill: Chicago University Press.

Rumbelow, I. (1971) *I Spy Blue*, London: Macmillan. (reference not verified).

Samuels, A. (1987) 'Concerns for courts', *Mediation*, 3(4): 12–13.

Sander, F.E.A. (1976) 'Varieties of dispute procesing', 70 FRD 111–34, reprinted in R. Tomasic and M. Feeley (eds) (1982) *Neighborhood Justice: Assessment of an Emerging Idea*, New York: Longman.

—— (1984) 'Observations regarding the symposium discussion and thoughts about the future of dispute resolution', in Vermont Law School, *A Study of Barriers to the Use of Alternative Methods of Dispute Resolution*, South Royalton, Vt: Vermont Law School Dispute Resolution Project.

Sanders, A. (1985) 'Class bias in prosecutions', *Howard Journal*, 24(3): 176–99.

Schädler, W. (1989) 'Victim rights in the German legal system: a model for reform for the US?', *NOVA Newsletter* (National Organization for Victim Assistance), 4: 2.

Schafer, S. (1960) *Restitution to Victims of Crime*, London: Stevens.

—— (1968) *The Victim and his Criminal: A Study in Functional Responsibility*, New York: Random House.

—— (1970) *Compensation and Restitution to Victims of Crime*, Montclair, NJ: Patterson Smith.

Schiedsmanns-Zeitung (1989) 'Förderung der vor- und aussergerichtlichen Streitschlichtung in Nord-Rhein Westfalen . . . ' (Development of pre- and extra-court dispute resolution in North Rhine Westphalia . . .) *S-Z*, 60(4): 49–56.

Schur, E.M. (1973) *Radical Non-Intervention: Re-thinking the Delinquency Problem*, Englewood Cliffs, NJ: Prentice-Hall.

Sebba, L. (1982) 'The victim's role in the penal process: a theoretical orientation', *American Journal of Comparative Law*, 30: 217–40.

Serrill, M.S. (1975) 'Minnesota Restitution Center', *Corrections Magazine*, 3: 13–20.

Sessar, K. (1982) 'Offender restitution as part of future criminal policy?', paper to 4th International Symposium on Victimology, Tokyo/Kyoto, Japan.

Shapland, J. (1982) 'The victim in the criminal justice system', *Research Bulletin*, Home Office Research and Planning Unit, 14: 21–3.

—— (1983) 'Victim assistance and the criminal justice system: the victim's perspective', paper to 33rd International Course in Criminology, Vancouver.

—— (1984) 'Victims, the criminal justice system and compensation', *British Journal of Criminology*, 24: 131–49.

Shapland, J., Willmore, J. and Duff, P. (1985) *Victims in the Criminal Justice System*, Aldershot: Gower.

Sharpe, J.A. (1980) 'Enforcing the law in the seventeenth century English village', in V. Gatrell (ed.) *Crime and the Law*, London: Europa.

Shaw, S. (1982) *The People's Justice: A Major Poll of Public Attitudes on Crime and Punishment*, London: Prison Reform Trust.

SHHD (1964) *Children and Young Persons' Scotland* (Chairman: Lord Kilbrandon), Scottish Home and Health Department, Cmnd 2306, Edinburgh: HMSO.

Shonholtz, R. (1983) *New Justice Theories and Practice*, Community Board Program, 149 Ninth Street, San Francisco CA 94103.

Shubert, A. (1981) 'Associations for the prosecution of felons 1744–1856', in V. Bailey (ed.) *Policing and Punishment in Nineteenth Century Britain*, London: Croom Helm.

Six Quakers (1979) *Six Quakers Look at Crime and Punishment*, by Janet Arthur *et al.*, Quaker Social Responsibility and Education, Friends' House, Euston Road, London NW1 2BJ.

Smith, D., Blagg, H. and Derricourt, N. (1985) 'Does mediation work in practice?', *Probation Journal*, (32): 135–8.

—— (1986) *Mediation in South Yorkshire*, University of Lancaster, Department of Social Administration.

—— (1988) 'Mediation in the shadow of the law: the South Yorkshire experience', in R. Matthews (ed.) *Informal Justice?*, London: Sage.

Smith, K. (1964) *A Cure for Crime*, London: Duckworth.

Smith, R. (1972) *A Quiet Revolution*, Washington, DC: US Department of Health, Education and Welfare.

Softley, P. and Tarling, R. (1977) *Compensation Orders and Custodial Sentences*, Home Office Research Series 43, London: HMSO.

Stephen, Sir J.F. (1883) *A History of the Criminal Law of England*, London: Macmillan.
—— (1890) *A General View of the Criminal Law of England*, 2nd edn, London: Macmillan.
Stubbs, W. (1880) *The Constitutional History of England*, Oxford: Clarendon Press.
T, Anna. (1988) 'Feminist responses to sexual abuse: the work of the Birmingham Rape Crisis Centre', in M. Maguire and J. Pointing (eds) *Victims of Crime: A New Deal?*, Milton Keynes: Open University Press.
Tallack, W. (1900) *Reparation to the Injured, and the Rights of the Victims of Crime to Compensation*, London: Wertheimer, Lea.
Tarling, R. (1980) *Sentencing Practice in Magistrates' Courts*, Home Office Research Study 56, London: HMSO.
Taylor, L. (1984) *In the Underworld*, Oxford: Basil Blackwell.
Tench, D. (1981) *Towards a Middle System of Law*, London: Consumers' Association.
Thorvaldson, S.A. (1978) 'The effects of community service on the attitudes of the offenders', unpublished doctoral thesis, University of Cambridge.
—— (1980a) 'Does community service affect offenders?', in J. Hudson and B. Galaway (eds) *Victims, Offenders and Alternative Sanctions*, Lexington, Mass: D.C. Heath.
—— (1980b) 'Toward the definition of the reparative aim', in J. Hudson and B. Galaway (eds) *Victims, Offenders and Alternative Sanctions*, Lexington, Mass: D.C. Heath.
—— (1981) *Reparation by Offenders: How Far can we Go?*, selected papers of Canadian Congress for the Prevention of Crime, Winnipeg, Manitoba; Vancouver: Research and Evaluation Unit, Ministry of the Attorney-General, British Columbia.
—— (1983) 'Compensation by offenders in Canada: a victim's right?', paper at 33rd International Congress in Criminology, 'Victims of Crime', Vancouver BC.
—— (1985) *Crime and Redress: National Symposium on Reparative Sanctions, Vancouver BC, 1982: Summary and Overview*, Vancouver: Ministry of the Attorney-General, British Columbia.
Tomasic, R. (1982) 'Mediation as an alternative to adjudication: rhetoric and reality in the neighborhood justice movement', in R. Tomasic and M. Feeley (eds) *Neighborhood Justice: Assessment of an Emerging Idea*, New York: Longman.
Tomasic, R. and Feeley, M. (eds) (1982) *Neighborhood Justice: Assessment of an Emerging Idea*, New York: Longman.
Tügel, H. and Heilemann, M. (eds) (1987) *Frauen verändern Vergewaltiger* (Women Change Rapists), Frankfurt am Main: Fischer.
United Nations (1986) 'Declaration of basic principles of justice for victims of crime and abuse of power' (Annex to General Assembly Resolution 40/34, 29 November 1985), New York: UN Department of Public Information.
US Association for Victim/Offender Mediation (1989) *Directory of Members*, Valparaiso, Ind: US AV/OM.
US President's Commission on Law Enforcement and Administration of Justice (1967a) *The Challenge of Crime in a Free Society*, Washington, DC: US GPO.
—— (1967b) *Task Force Report: Crime and its Impact*, Washington, DC: US GPO.
—— (1967c) *Task Force Report: Corrections*, Washington, DC: US GPO.
US President's Task Force on Victims of Crime (1982) *Final Report* (Chair: L.H. Herrington). Washington, DC: US GPO.
Van Dijk, J.J.M., Mayhew, P. and Killias, M. (1990) *Experiences of Crime across the World: Key Findings from the 1989 International Crime Survey*, Deventer: Kluwer.

Veevers, J. (1989) 'Pre-court diversion for juvenile offenders', in M. Wright and B. Galaway (eds) *Mediation and Criminal Justice: Victims, Offenders and Community*, London: Sage.

Vera Institute of Justice (1977) *Felony Arrests: Their Prosecution and Disposition in New York City's Courts*, New York: Vera Institute.

Victim Support (1984a) *The Victim and Reparation*, Victim Support, 39 Brixton Road, London SW9 6DZ.

—— (1984b) *Victim Support Schemes: The United Kingdom Model*, London: Victim Support.

—— (1988) *The Victim in Court: Report of a Working Party* (Chairman: Lady Ralphs), London: Victim Support.

—— (1989) *Punishment, Custody and the Community: Response [to Home Office Green Paper] of the National Association of Victims Support Schemes*, London: Victim Support.

—— (1990) *Report of the Families of Murder Victims Project*, London: Victim Support.

Von Hirsch, A. (1976) *Doing Justice*, New York: Hill & Wang.

Wahrhaftig, P. (1982) 'An overview of community-oriented citizen dispute resolution programs in the United States', in R.L. Abel (ed.) *The Politics of Informal Justice, Vol. I, The American Experience*, New York: Academic Press.

Walker, N. (1972) *Sentencing in a Rational Society*, Harmondsworth: Penguin.

—— (1985) *Sentencing: Theory, Law and Practice*, London: Butterworths.

Walklate, S. (1989) *Victimology: The Victim and the Criminal Justice Process*, London: Unwin Hyman.

Wasik, M. (1978) 'The place of compensation in the penal system', *Criminal Law Review*, October, 599–611.

Weigend, T. (1981) *Assisting the Victim: A Report on Efforts to Strengthen the Position of the Victim in the American System of Criminal Justice*, Freiburg im Breisgau: Max Planck Institute for Foreign and International Criminal Law.

West, D.J. (1965) *Murder followed by Suicide*, London: Heinemann.

West, D.J. and Farrington, D.P. (1977) *The Delinquent Way of Life*, London: Heinemann.

Wikström, P.O. (1985) *Everyday Violence in Contemporary Sweden: Situational and Ecological Aspects*, Report no. 5, Stockholm: National Council for Crime Prevention.

Williams, G. (1978) *Textbook of Criminal Law*, London: Stevens.

Wright, M. (1977) 'Nobody came: criminal justice and the needs of victims', *Howard Journal*, 16(1): 22–31.

—— (1982) *Making Good: Prisons, Punishment and Beyond*, London: Unwin Hyman (Burnett Books).

—— (1983) *Victim/Offender Reparation Agreements: A Feasibility Study in Coventry*, Birmingham: West Midlands Probation Service.

—— (1984) *In the Interests of the Community: A Review of the Literature on Community Service Orders*, University of Birmingham, Department of Social Administration.

—— (1985) 'The impact of victim/offender mediation on the assumptions and procedures of criminal justice: impact on the victim', *Victimology*, 10: 631–44.

—— (1987) 'State compensation for criminal injuries: a short comparative survey', *Justice of the Peace*, 151, 1 August: 489–91.

—— (1988) 'Out of the morass: a rational approach to debt', *Probation Journal*, 35(4): 148.

—— (1989) 'What the public wants', in M. Wright and B. Galaway (eds) *Mediation and Criminal Justice: Victims, Offenders and Community*, London: Sage, reprinted from *Justice of the Peace*, 151, 14 February: 105–7.

Wright, M. and Galaway, B. (eds) *Mediation and Criminal Justice: Victims, Offenders and Community*, London: Sage.

Young, J. (1988) 'Risk of crime and fear of crime: a realist critique of survey-based assumptions', in M. Maguire and J. Pointing (eds) *Victims of Crime: A New Deal?*, Milton Keynes: Open University Press.

Zauberman, R. (1984) *Sources of Information about Victims and Methodological Problems in this Field*, Report for 16th Criminological Research Conference, Council of Europe, November, Strasbourg: Council of Europe.

Zehr, H. (1982) *Mediating the Victim/Offender Conflict*, Akron, PA: Mennonite Central Committee US, Office of Criminal Justice.

—— (1983) VORP *Volunteer Handbook*, rev. edn, Elkhart, Ind: Mennonite Central Committee US, Office of Criminal Justice.

—— (1985) *Retributive Justice, Restorative Justice*, Elkhart, Ind: Mennonite Central Committee US, Office of Criminal Justice.

—— (1990) *Changing Lenses: A New Focus for Criminal Justice*, Scottdale, Pa: Herald Press; London: Metanoia.

Zehr, H. and Umbreit, M. (1982) 'Victim/offender reconciliation: an incarceration substitute', *Federal Probation*, 46(4): 63–8.

Ziegenhagen, E.A. (1977) *Victims, Crime and Social Control*, New York: Praeger.

Zimring, F.E., and Hawkins, G. (1973) *Deterrence: The Legal Threat in Crime Control*, Chicago, Ill: Chicago University Press.

Statutes

Index